THE AES1

THE AESTHETICS OF ROCK

by Richard Meltzer

New Foreword by Richard Meltzer
New Introduction by Greil Marcus

DA CAPO PRESS

Library of Congress Cataloging in Publication Data

Meltzer, R. (Richard)
   The aesthetics of rock.

   (A Da Capo paperback)
   Reprint. Originally published: New York: Something
Else Press, 1970.
   Includes bibliographical references.
   1. Rock music – History and criticism. 2. Music – 20th
century – Philosophy and aesthetics. 3. Popular culture –
History – 20th century. I. Title.
[ML3877.M45   1987]   784.5′4′009   87-518
ISBN 0-306-80287-2 (pbk.)

This Da Capo Press paperback edition of *The Aesthetics of Rock*
is an unabriged republication of the edition published in New York
in 1970, here supplemented with corrections and a new foreword by the
author, and a new introduction by Greil Marcus. It is reprinted by
arrangement with Richard Meltzer.

Published by Da Capo Press
A Member of the Perseus Books Group
http://www.dacapopress.com

13 12 11 10 9 8 7

TO KENT
For the Records

Foreword to the Da Capo Edition

Aside from happening to be my own first book, this here what-sis was/is, without much question, the first "serious rock book" ever written (though hardly the first one published), an achievement which I must confess has yet to make me sick. In rereading it now, however, 16 years after it ultimately appeared, I can readily see why certain people might question my motives in sanctioning, at this point in my so-called career, its less-than-inevitable reappearance.

There are whole enormous sections of text that seem so subarticulate (inarticulate?) that it would take a guided tour (or a supplemental voice-over cassette) to clarify, or even hint at, what I might conceivably have been trying to "express" in the first place. I use the single word "art," for instance, to unassistedly denote/connote everything from "art history" to "the art experience" to "the art scene" to "artists and their ilk" to "works of art" to "the art-making process" to "artifice" to "the creative impulse" to I don't know, lots of this, that and the other. I overuse (misuse?) such terms as "trivial," "tragic," "repulsive," "chaos," "boredom," "authenticity," and "good/evil" 'til they just lie there dead and pasty like last week's pasta fazool.

Then, likewise, there are passages, paragraphs so druggardly opaque, arcane, abstruse that no authorly assistance – I know my limits! – is at this stage even hypothetically feasible.

It could be argued, furthermore, that my "scholarship" is

basically up my butt. As often as not I'll quote Schopenhauer or Heraclitus and then claim Dicky Lee did "Laurie," forget Hank Ballard did a version of "The Twist," and assert – with no probable cause – that Pete Antell's "Night Time" is about vehicular death.

But what *really* should embarrass me is all the misplaced idealism, all these gushing superlatives – "Rock is, after all, the first great in-context/out-of-context revealed religion other than the two-person love unit"; "Rock is the brute actualization where all earlier art is potential"; "Rock is the only possible future for philosophy and art" – for a form, a medium, which in the interim has given us little more than shitpissdooweewee w/ and w/out flies.

Lucky for me I don't embarrass e-z. In the course of my reread I've maybe occasionally *winced* a bit, but hey, I can take it. I can even take it when this jerk, Michael Corcoran, writes in the 8/15/86 issue of the *Austin Chronicle:* "Meltzer's book, *Aesthetics of Rock,* overshadows both the Hitler Diaries and Clifford Irving's Howard Hughes biography in the annals of literary hoaxes. It's been said that if you have an infinite number of monkeys pecking away at an infinite number of typewriters for an infinite amount of time, eventually one of them would write *Hamlet.* It would take about 50 monkeys a couple of years to write *Aesthetics of Rock."* As if he knows what it's like to be a monkey!

First of all, *A. of R.* is hardly a "book" at all – more like a box of very broken (and very greasy) automotive parts. At all stages of its construction I fancied myself as more a visual artist than either a scholar or writer, and insofar as the thing even *contains* writing, it's best viewed as simply a typeset *object* ("document") from BEFORE I LEARNED HOW TO WRITE. Now that I'm an international big cheese of the printed page, threading the language needle far, wide, and commanding in the process a whopping four figures (sometimes five!) in annual income, I am in fact *tickled* – you should be too – to face the evidence that I once upon a time mismatched subjects, predicates, *floundered* in the land of commas, and misspelled "cacophony" not once but twice in a single work. Mea culpa, mea culpa: I, monkey, can sure as hell dig it!

But as to the damn thing being a "hoax," geez, this fughead can't just be talking style, wordsmanly credential, degree of professionalism – he must be talking content. What the book "is." So what is it?

Well, as long as you're asking, *The Aesthetics of Rock* [get your felt-tip marker] is the nearly verbatim transcript of my first three years, 1965-68, of beating my head against various walls, personal and systematic, in an unguided, utterly ingenuous, unrestrainedly passionate attempt to make even *provisional* mega-sense out of something, far as I can tell even today, no one previous had particularly cared to "explore," verbally, much more than the frigging surface of: rock rock rock (and ROLL). Of which I was – gosh – a frigging, unwashed "disciple."

At each phase of my whacked-out journey I relied heavily, but not exclusively, on those tools, utensils, chalkboard paradigms proffered by the given moment's life-hand as dealt. In May of '65, for inst, a junior philosophy major (and art minor) at the State U. of New York at Stony Brook, I took an incomplete in something called Philosophy of Literary Form for the express purpose of taking my merry time with a term paper purportedly "about" rock and roll. While not my first stab at a "rock paper" – I'd already gotten A's for comparing Marcus Aurelius with the Beatles (two pages) and tossing off "The Concept of the Synonym in the Dave Clark Five" (three or four) – this one seemed like more than mere calisthenic, and I girded my loins accordingly. I huffed, puffed, read Nietzsche's *Birth of Tragedy,* saw the Beatles at Shea Stadium, revisited both sides of every scratchy 45 (and 78) I still possessed, and some months later turned in 156 pages enigmatically entitled "A Sequel: Tomorrow's Not Today." Topheavy with references to tragedy, comedy, and the proto-"performance art" shtick of my painting teacher, Allan Kaprow, the stack o' pulp got me not only an A + + + but the instructorly scribble – totally unexpected – "Should be published."

So I show it to this sociology prof who claims he'd gotten Grove Press to publish *City of Night,* he takes 'em a xerox, and six months later they say *thanks but no thanks.*

Meantime – fall '66 – I'm a grad student at Yale. To beat the draft, sure, but also to "extend the text of philosophy" by dosing it silly with rock and roll. I'm on this mission, see – my undergrad instructors have *perhaps* overencouraged me – so hellbent 'n' stoked I run full throttle, blind, into an ivy-covered wall. I do rock papers, *great* ones, better than last time, for courses with names like Laws of Nature, Being and Becoming in Greek Philosophy, and The Ethical Given in Kant's Second Critique, and for so doing I am KICKED OUT TOOT SWEET ON MY ROCK-ROLL CABOOSE. (A *sensitive* missionary, I cry a river.)

So now, lucky me, I'm out of academia, no way I'll ever be the McLuhan of Rock, and meanwhile a pair of fortuitous whatsems transpire to keep me merrily, zealously a-writin'. First, from out of the blue, there's this quasi-highbrow rock mag, *Crawdaddy!*, which while I was at Yale had already excerpted (and renamed "The Aesthetics of Rock") 20 or so pages from my original undergrad manuscript and which, more importantly, bore the earmarks of being an actual ongoing forum for the promulgation of a "rock consciousness." A far cry from *Song Hits, Hit Parader* and their pulp-teen hype-sheet ilk, *Crawdaddy!* was the first community of highfalutin "rock writers" per se, and through the spring of '68, when editor/publisher/zealot-in-chief Paul Williams and I had a terminal falling out over who can remember what, they printed virtually everything I gave them.

So I wrote a *lot.* I'd get up in the morning, smoke some dope, put on an LP, enter its, uh, *universe,* take profuse notes, play another album, jump from cut to cut, make the weirdest of plausible connections (no professors – wheeee! – to monitor the hidebound topicality of my thoughts anymore), more notes, more records, occasional meals and masturbation, more more, then hop in the car and drive to Boston for Jefferson Airplane – or Asbury Park for the Doors – and home to write it up on my sister's diet pills.

Still, continuing to regard myself as ostensibly a visualist (and confirming the i.d. by producing, at this nexus, such dandy *objets* as stillborn kittens in jello), I didn't particularly consider myself a "writer" at all: It was more like I simply had no choice but to get it all down. The far-as-the-eye-could-see (and -heart-could-feel) (and -mind-could-think) total gestalt of fortuitous whatsem #2, i.e., the emerging rock-correlated real-world *something* that by spring '67 had become one big fat undeniable Public Fact. Ten million new bands, a billion new tunes, a trillion nascent visions and revisions, a growing handful of viable drugs, a sense of *infinite* cultural possibility. When I'd started writing this crap there weren't even all-oldies stations, f'r chrissakes; now there were Jim Morrison, Arthur Lee, Jimi Hendrix.

With *articles* and *pieces* as my units of expression, I spent my time getting it down. For every *Crawdaddy!* piece ("Ah! Ontology," a treatise on "heaven rock"; the self-explanatory "What a Goddam Great Second Cream Album"; the first Hendrix feature in America, one which earned me the man himself's hearty handshake and a conspirational "You must've been stoned when you wrote that, man!") there were countless scribblings/typings intended "for no one." This was probably the only time in my writerly life where I kept anything tantamount to a notebook, and the constancy and fidelity of the exercise were, as I remember things, a continual source of general near-euphoria. (Of course, the continuing saga of my book – additional rejections by Macmillan, Dutton, Prentice-Hall, New American Library, and six-seven others – I recall with a twinge of utter grief, so recollections of work-related euphoria may just be so much wish-related b.s.)

Finally, in a pre-spring month of '68, I forget which, somebody went for more than the article, the piece. My old buddy and colleague (high school, college, *Crawdad*) Sandy Pearlman showed a xerox of you-know-what to artist/publisher Dick Higgins, out at Stony Brook for some sort of joint installation with Allan Kaprow and Nam June Paik, and after not too lengthy a self-conference he took it, bought it, agreed to have his Something Else Press publish the mutha. He gave me like six months to alter it, fatten it, do what I pretty much felt like, but the title – here he stood firm – had to be the arch-artso *Aesthetics of Rock.* Okay, fine, I can live with that. . . and I rose to the task of making the whole mess into a BOOK.

To the bitter end, I'm sure I continued churning out my daily quota of brand new text, tentatively adding it to the jumble of papers already covering the floor, but basically what I did was edit, truncate, order, reorder, mix 'n' match – composition, re-composition *ad infinitum.* Rereading the finished product, I notice very little *rewriting* was apparently done – bridges were built, footnotes added, but miles of original text were left untouched – and imagine my major editing cues must've come from *Bike Boy* and *Nude Restaurant*, Warhol films from that time frame which I *adored*...and in which footage used equaled total footage shot. Too much of my well-intentioned, yet subintelligible, undergrad hokum, for example, was run unaltered for me to guess that my gameplan could have been other than to let stand – for all bookspan eternity – pages I'd simply grown attached to. (How *else* to explain the retention of crude, earlier gropes at terminology – calling a vocal a "solo" or "lead," or a mono recording "single-tracked" – which had already been superseded by both conventional jargon and common cognizance?)

In addition to oh, I'd say 75 pages of unmessed-with college-boy mss., the *Aesthetics* which eventually saw the light of print contains huge chunks chipped from *Crawdaddy!* features, a review of Hendrix's second album rejected by the *New York Times*, a quasi-solicited "think piece" on jazz and rock rejected by *Down Beat*, scraps from the Yale fiasco, and even two pages (linking the Cowsills and the Rolling Stones) from *Soft Dull*, an attempted first novel I took pleasure in feeding to a Manhattan incinerator in 1972. As the operational rhyme/reason behind any given slamming together of textual readymades was often whimsical, ersatz, or just plain whuh?, it is hardly advised that the reader adhere strictly to the order to text through sequencings which appear governed by such long-forgotten expediency. In fact – heh heh – I've gained so much authorly compassion since initially throwing this slop together that on my recent read-through I couldn't help but jot down some prime alternate takeoff points for whenever you're bored, baffled, or backed into a swamp. Pages to jump to (you have my word they're *good'uns*): 204, 66, 148, 155, 222, 142 (paragraph 2), 156, 86 (footnote*), 318, 312, 146, 130, 256, 236, 220, 181, 173 (paragraph 2), 308 paragraph 3), 322, 261 (footnote*), 284.

---

*Generally speaking, footnotes were the last items of text added to the Something Else manuscript (there were probably fewer than ten in the original student version). I'm fairly certain that the final new shred of text was the reference to the Beatles' White Album added to preexistent footnote 136 (p. 152) some months

Anyway, I turned the thing in somewhere like mid-October, this is still '68, and it took them something like a year and a half to get it out. What took them so long was getting permission from all these music publishers to reprint lyrics; I'd quoted a ton. Something Else was this small artso company, they'd put out limited-edition concrete poetry anthologies and Claes Oldenburg, Merce Cunningham notebooks – no way could they afford to *pay* for reprint rights. So they had to bargain. For Beatle rights, they dispatched a signed copy of *Sweethearts,* by the Press's Emmett Williams, to Linda McCartney for Valentine's Day. (The Something Else-Beatle Connection – this is true! – had been established when John Cage, compiling an anthology of musical notations, assigned his former colleague Yoko Ono, in London for a gallery opening, the chore of obtaining a Beatle manuscript. She considered her options and finally chose JOHN as the Beatle to invite to the show . . .). How they got the Stones I'm not really sure. Dylan they couldn't get. Through hatchet man Albert Grossman he demanded $7500 per extended lyric; "Like a Rolling Stone," "Positively Fourth Street," et al – and virtually all text deriving from their quotation – had to be deleted from the book.

Also to go was the Appendix. Printing costs being what they were, a designated Epilogue was allowable, hey, but an Epilogue *and* an Appendix – don't be silly. So 30-40 pages went, including, if I remember correctly, treatises on Traffic, Pink Floyd, post-Monterey Otis Redding, and Quicksilver Messenger Service, a comparison of the second Vanilla Fudge album with, no kidding, John Coltrane's *A Love Supreme,* and a "sexual phenomenology"

---

after submission. Footnotes numbered with an *a* were in all cases inserted at stages when it seemed like too much bother to physically renumber all those others which in turn would be affected. While some footnotes, following from basic text in almost ventriloquist/dummy fashion (affording me as they did the luxury of second-guessing myself without further burdening the structurally overtaxed artificial bridgework), seem like the true heart & soul of the book – or at least its nervous system – others merely serve as convenient occasions for response to objections raised by Dick Higgins and/or Ned Polsky (and accordingly feel like dead meat).

(let's see, the boy-thing goes in the . . .) of "Norwegian Wood." I
kept no carbons, I never asked for the pages back, so let's
assume they're g-gone for g-good.

But the book – The Book!! – comes out, it's only 2-5 years out of
date, and on the basis of having authored it (though scant few
will in fact buy, read, or offer signs of "understanding" it) I'm
sort of a minor New York celebrity through the summer, fall,
winter of 1970. Lisa Robinson invites me to all her parties, at
one of which Lou Reed actually tells me I'm his *favorite writer*, I
get good tables at Max's Kansas City, and – happy days! – I'm at
last invited to join the front rank of gainfully employed rock-
writin' whores, an army of whom has been rising like scum since
Summer of Love '67, ready and willing to the last manjack to
shill shill SHILL for heinous corporate product in the papers,
mags, and press kits of Anglo-America. *Creem* and *Rolling
Stone*, post-*Crawdad* biggies whose combined lifetimes at this
point barely equal the time I've spent myself sussing out this
thing-called-rock (but to whom, until now, I've been an outsider,
an egghead, a bum), suddenly open their pages to me, their
checkbooks, as record companies galore second the motion by
sending me an unending stream of LPs, concert tix, trips to the
ends of the world . . .

All because I'd written the 15th or 18th book, see, on a subject
which was now their mega-livelihood. I looked like a shill, I probably smelled and tasted like a shill, I certainly (for the time being) accepted their "gifts" like a shill. Fortunately, in the couple
years that had elapsed since finishing *Aesthetics*, I'd somehow
acquired the wherewithal to occasionally string together
sentences that clearly, unequivocally *said something* – something even a simp could neither misread nor deny. And what I'd
say (about most bands, band members, albums, tunes, "trends")
was invariably a cross between *Screw this, screw that* and *Hey, it
all died in '68 (anyway)!* . . . it certainly wasn't very "alive" by '72,
'73.

By which time my pathetic insistence on keeping the (pre-
megabuck) rock-roll "faith" had pretty much rendered me per-
sona non grata with the mags, the record creeps, the promoters,
the publicists, whomever. Operating under the premise that
"high mischief" was the basic, irreducible nub of any "true" rock
experience, and that if *I* didn't commit it with ongoing frequency

no one else would (so, uh, BYE-BYE ROCK), I'd do things like jump in the fountain at a Rolling Stones press party, throw chicken bones at some annoying singer at the Bitter End, review (harshly) albums I'd obviously never listened to (or concerts I'd never attended), reverse the word sequence of a text to make it read backwards (or delete, for no particular reason, every fourth word)...so by '74 it was bye-bye me. And I've never looked back.

No, that's not true, I look back all the time. But further back, natch, than those wretched early '70s. Every time I come home drunk and weepy-eyed from some horrible party where kids half my age, and with triple my energy, sit around a room–there's *always* such a room–doing nothing (not even talk) but watch rock vids by who could care whom, I run for the headphones, pull out all these albs and singles from a time when the music was more concerned with *sound* than image, more about *risk* than fashion, more involved in the *dialectic* of profit than the 'fore-the-fact fact of it, more a touchstone of genuwine *liberation,* by gum, than a ring through your cultural nose awaiting the yanks 'n' tugs of the absolute forces of the status quo...I reach, as for a lifeline, for the records described in this book.

Hey, I didn't even *use* words like "culture" back then, concepts like "liberation." The goddam cup was so *massively* runnething over–what has elsewhere been referred to as "an embarrass-ment of riches"–that it hardly seemed NECESSARY to define its shape, measure its perimeter, scratch & sniff its biosphere, sociologize its tide patterns, or mop and save its spillage. What seemed like the chore at hand was to dive headlong into an ever-enlarging Sea of Possibility and micromap, between stroke and breath, the vast infrastructure of *all* that it was remotely possi-ble for the damn thing to *already be*...no fanciful speculation of "futures" on this swimtrip!

So when I slip out of my trunks, dry myself off, and declare (on p. 333) that "Hey Jude" exhibits a certain hefty quota of "osmotic tongue pressure," you'd better believe that not only am *I* on to something, but the something is shining–blazing!–in the cellular microblahblah of the rock-roll show & tell of I dunno, whatever month that was. That the osmotic tongue pressure of "Hey Jude" and related show'ems may have subsequently thrown in all possible towels is not the issue: Osmotic Tongue

Pressure *was*, and it was pretty all reet!–even if just as a lamebrain cellular pipedream. Actual futures have a way of disappointing, and the problem with rock is not so much that its future has always been NOW; it's just that its last viable now was pretty much THEN.

Food for thought...food for hope. Once upon a time you could be *nourished* by that shit: calories, nutrients, interest, surprise ...oral mammal urgency. What's there to hope for, to "imagine as possible," today? That Bruce Springsteen and Michael Jackson aren't *literally* the Monkees? That David Byrne isn't Stephen Sondheim? That "We Are the World" isn't "God Bless America" as sung by the DAR? That heavy metal, that last bastion of sonic integrity, is really more than "closet classical music," the digital-Mantovani replay of Wagner, Beethoven, Moussorgsky? Actually I don't mind heavy metal; I just never listen to it.

Except when I'm drunk and weepy-eyed, or at someone else's house, all I listen to anymore is jazz. (And a little dub music.) Rock, when it's totally, gloriously *on*, can go from A to Z–no sweat–*instantaneously*. Cock an ear to "Yes It Is" (Beatles), "Gotta Get Away" (Stones), "When the Music's Over" (Doors), "Here Comes the Night" (Them), "I See You" (Byrds), "The Red Telephone" (Love), "One of Us Must Know" (Dylan). Today, whatever I hear has trouble doing a credible A. Jazz can at least always be counted on for a good solid A, and usually B, C, D as well. (Dub: A, sometimes also B.)

Punk. Okay, yeah, I invested a lot of "hope" in punk. But only because I willingly disbelieved it had anything to "do" with rock, preferring to contend it in fact "wasn't" rock, it was "something else." Until '79-'80 maybe it was...

Anyway, fuggit, here's this book. A good book, maybe even a great book, in any event the most excruciatingly "inside IT" book (as opposed to an "on the bus with *purveyors* of IT" book) you will ever meet. Why, at this late date, would a writingperson choose to go even *halfway* inside the fugger anymore? They wouldn't. So this is it. I don't mind having written it, thanks for buying (or stealing) the reprint–thank you, thank you...now read everything *else* I've written (it's a whole lot better than this).

                                        –RICHARD B. MELTZER

Los Angeles, October '86

Introduction to the Da Capo Edition

Reading Richard Meltzer's *The Aesthetics of Rock* twenty years after first coming across excerpts from it in *Crawdaddy!* magazine, I'm most of all convinced that the book is not a joke. It was received as a joke, I think, both when those excerpts were published in 1966 and '67, and when the book itself came out in 1970: a timely ('66) or slightly dated ('70) parody of the then-new (or already-superannuated) form of rock criticism. In 1966 bedazzled college students like myself were helplessly dumping quotes from Plato on Beatle hits and Dylan albums, attempting to make sense of the emotions the music was provoking, trying to talk about the world the music seemed to be changing – changing forever, it seemed, and forever for the better. In the face of all that, Meltzer's book communicated not only as a joke – others might quote Plato; he'd simultaneously run rock 'n' roll through all of Western philosophy, and vice versa, not to mention turning the same trick on the better part of modern art, until you couldn't tell one from another – the book communicated as a pointedly cynical joke, out of tune with the mandated optimism of late '60s pop culture. That may be why a lot of people didn't like it, why it made them feel queasy, creepy. The tones of reverence, gratitude, or religious passivity present in so much of the rock criticism of the time were altogether missing in Meltzer's pages: he didn't appear to take anything seriously. He made fun of everything under the sun, collapsing all distinctions, standards, and categories, writing about Tommy James and the

Shondells as if they were as epistemologically significant as the
Beatles – and in the late '60s, to rock fans, that was a far more
heinous, heretical violation than talking about the Beatles as if
they were as interesting as Aristotle. Meltzer, it seemed, reduced everything to self-cancelling blather; the only question
was how, or why, he sustained the enterprise through 338 pages.
    Well, there are a number of things to add today, twenty years
after. Perhaps one should say first that, today, the book reads
less like a parody of "then" than an anticipation of "now": a
parody *avant la lettre* of the currently fashionable application of
semiology and deconstruction to popular culture. Semiology and
deconstruction are rooted in a disrespect for the object, the art
work, the socio-aesthetic event, in a refusal to take such things
on their own terms, an insistence that objects and events can be
deciphered, broken down, taken apart, and put back together in
new ways. In other words, it is now fashionable to refuse to take
one's putative subject matter "seriously." Meltzer did it all a long
time ago, and so, today, *The Aesthetics of Rock* does not read like
an artifact of some vanished time, but like an oddly energized
version of real cool academic discourse. And since semiology and
deconstruction at once call for the abolition of rules and
generate their own, and because Meltzer's book does the former
but not the latter, it will soon be, in certain circles, the coolest
book to be seen carrying. Be there or be square.
    Of course, all that means is that twenty years from now *The
Aesthetics of Rock* may be an item as dated as one might have
thought it would be already – and I don't think it will be. So we
have to go back to the question of actually reading the thing: to
the question of what it says, of what it's about (if it's about
anything – in '66 or '70, a lot of people were sure it wasn't). We
have to go back to the notion that the book is not a joke – even
though it is full of jokes, even though it's unfailingly funny,
sometimes manic, less a "discourse" than a stand-up comedy
routine or a bleary-eyed rant, built on puns, shaggy dog stories,
allusions that lead nowhere, elisions that only pull their own
slipknots, countless sentences meandering into dead-end streets
where the reader is forced to page back through the book in
search of a map that isn't there. "Rock 'n' roll," he says in *The
Aesthetics of Rock,* always contains and always implies "a

substratum of comedy.... All significant references to man's 'serious' nature are compiled on top of this joke." And that's how the book works, too.

* * *

Meltzer begins his philosophical account of rock 'n' roll, his rock 'n' roll account of philosophy, with the idea that rock 'n' roll is a "totality": as a "world in itself," rock 'n' roll can be considered as if it were "itself the world." Weighed down by a hundred pounds of philosophy books that he jokes about in order to keep them on his back as he walks, Meltzer talks about rock 'n' roll just like any obsessed fan: as if it were the only thing in the world worth talking about, the only thing that mattered, as if it can and does contain every variant of truth and lie, as if it's capable of generating versions of every experience and fantasy. Rock as a totality is the world in a grain of sand: in the Beatles' "I Am the Walrus," or Tommy James and the Shondells' "I Think We're Alone Now."

Starting with this premise (thrown away, like everything else in the book, like the best rock 'n' roll lines), Meltzer soon enough turns the premise back on itself, ties it into a slipknot that, for some reason, the reader can't pull: "Quine has noted, 'The unit of empirical significance is the whole of science.' The unit of rock significance is the whole of rock 'n' roll." This is a very complicated pun, too complicated to catch right away, given the reader's-impatience factor Meltzer plays upon as he rushes through the book; as a throwaway, it deserves a pause.

Quine is saying that science can be reduced to empiricism: the rational verification of hypotheses that hold still while experiments are performed on them. Science is facts, and that's all it is. But at the time Meltzer was writing, Thomas Kuhn, author of *The Structure of Scientific Revolutions,* had already proven that Quine's claim was nonsense, and Meltzer surely knew it. Kuhn's argument was that great scientific discoveries were powered by irrational impulses, and so was the acceptance or rejection of those discoveries. Science, Kuhn said, was sort of like real life: part predictable fact, and part poker. You couldn't turn a pair of deuces into a great speckled bird (unless you were very drunk), but a pair of deuces could beat three kings. Thus

Meltzer's reversal of Quine's reductionist formula through a simple play on words: if "the unit of rock significance is the whole of
rock 'n' roll," then any rock 'n' roll song, to be significant (and, in
The Aesthetics of Rock, all are), must contain and imply all of
rock 'n' roll. Rock is its own world, and it is the world: as "I Am
the Walrus" contains and implies the emotional and musical
poverty of "I Think We're Alone Now," "I Think We're Alone
Now" contains and implies the luxuria (the linguistic gluttony,
the aesthetic narcissism, the musical excess) of "I Am the
Walrus." What's going on is that, in Meltzer's book, rock 'n' roll
songs begin to talk to each other, to quarrel and argue, to fight
over the terrain they share – just like real people, in real life.
   The results of Meltzer's punning link up with another throwaway: "Rock is the brute actualization where all earlier art is
potential." That is, as one hears rock 'n' roll, as one responds to a
hit on the radio or a new lp in the living room, rock 'n' roll is "actually happening" – as opposed to previous aesthetic events,
representations or dramatizations of what did or didn't happen,
of what is or could be. Listening to "I Am the Walrus" or "I
Think We're Alone Now" (or the Searchers' "Ain't That Just Like
Me," B-side of their 1964 chart-topper "Needles and Pins," a
completely forgotten performance by 1965, and a crucial disc in
The Aesthetics of Rock), who hasn't felt this "brute actualization"
of what is, of what could be, at stake? Who hasn't felt this totality to be not simply represented, not simply dramatized (never
mind that rock 'n' roll is an "art form," trading in representation
and dramatization), but actually happening?
   Now, the question is, just what is actualized? Meltzer: "J. L.
Austin, in 'A Plea for Excuses,' advocates the reconstruction of
aesthetics by collecting all terms germane to the appreciation of
art. A selection for the rock vocabulary might proceed as
follows: incongruous, trivial, mediocre, banal, insipid, maudlin,
abominable, trite, redundant, repulsive, ugly, innocuous, crass,
incoherent, vulgar, tasteless, sour, boring. [Only] when it is seen
that such expressions have allowed for. . . a widening for form
and content" can more conventional "terms be brought near the
rock context vocabulary: poignant, sincere, beautiful, etc." Note
Meltzer's first word in the rock vocabulary: "incongruous." According to his picture, in rock 'n' roll ("trivial," "banal," "redun-

dant," "boring," etc. – and Meltzer means all of those words)
nothing should be possible, every attempt at significance should
be immediately contradicted by vapidity – and so, in rock 'n' roll,
for *anything* to be possible suggests that, in truth, anything *is*
possible. Anything can be said; anything can be done, especially
if rock 'n' roll as art is a "brute actualization," where to say is to
do. This is the totality: rock is the world.

If anything is possible, then all categories, which are false, empiricist restrictions on what one can say, on what one can do, collapse; then they reform in strange, new ways. "Why not judge
art by its sheer stubbornness, defiance of any and all objectification?" Meltzer writes. "The categories 'pony tail rock' (the group
the Poni-Tails; 'What Is Love?', which describes this emotion as
'five feet of heaven in a pony tail'; 'Chantilly Lace,' with its
reference to the hair piece as a criterion of socio-sexual adequacy), 'fear-of-loss-of-being rock' ('Going Out of My Head';
'Remember'; Dion and the Belmonts' absolutely obscure 'I Can't
Go on Rosalie') and 'march rock' (Little Peggy March; the beat of
'I'll Never Dance Again'; the tympani of 'Every Little Thing';
'Calendar Girl', which declares, 'March, I'm gonna march you
down the aisle') are as valid as such categories as 'folk-rock',
'Motown,' 'soul music'. . ."

Such a way of breaking down and recombining the totality of
rock 'n' roll, or the totality of life as it is or could be lived, is what
The Aesthetics of Rock is all about – and it is all, and exactly,
what rock criticism, through its attempts to decipher representations and dramatizations, to affirm them as brute actualiza-
tions of what is or could be, has struggled towards – and
avoided – since Meltzer wrote. This is why, and how, he found
the energy to follow his putative subject matter through 338
pages. The book is like a dense piece of music – re-reading it,
you're startled by how much you never noticed the first or second time through. What strikes you as remarkable is not how
long the book is (and it is still, I think, the longest book of rock
criticism ever published, one page longer than Dave Marsh's
Fortunate Son), but how short; not how much Meltzer got in (is
there another book on rock 'n' roll that mentions, let alone actually talks about, the Searchers' "Ain't That Just Like Me"?),
but how much he left out – how, and why, he ever stopped.

Meltzer confronts the confusion of rock 'n' roll, of real life, the refusal of both to speak in a manner than can be reduced to a unit of empirical significance: "Rock is the greatest intentionally organized junkyard multiplicity with possible recovery of anything as an element in the crud; and yet the whole thing itself is on the same level as anything hidden now or forever or a week or just gone or just there on top of wow on top of or almost visible through the dead goat's mouth.... Words out of step with phrasing, phrasing just sort of sorted out from the musical debris, no line-to-line consistency, no maintenance of the integrity of individual parts, words given on the album cover to only six out of nine songs, words clear enough only when on their own, and never when fulfilling their conglomerate function, pairs of transitionally indistinguishable songs clumped together as 'medleys', etc...."

Rock is a totality: it contains, or implies that it can contain, all varieties of experience. But because it refuses – or is, by some muse-given-or-taken-away impulse, unable – to talk straight, it collapses its own status as "art." Rock collapses into what Meltzer calls the "Quotidian." If rock 'n' roll is "art" in *The Aesthetics of Rock,* it is a marginal, impulsive version of art: a version of everyday life, which is what "Quotidian" means. Meltzer:

> Power is everywhere, it is to be found in orderings of experience which somehow are (merely) visible, and my silly objective labels, such as orgasmic monotony, are as applicable to that which is visible as are Nietzsche's silly objective labels, tragic, Apollonian, Dionysian. Nietzsche fears the nausea of confrontation with the Quotidian world: rock 'n' roll ignores it, inhabits it, spreads it, enhances it. But most definitely rock has expanded man's potential to experience this realm, where all objective analysis is equally applicable and equally wrong.

Paging back from this two-thirds-of-the-way-through-the-book passage, you realize that Meltzer's approach to the "Quotidian," his revelation of the centrality of everyday life to rock 'n' roll and vice versa, allows him, as a critic, to get at the significance of things other rock critics can still barely talk about – or to endow those things with significance when it seems obvious they have none. Everyday life is a realm of pettiness, of mindless habit, of repetition (of, as Meltzer counts down "the rock vocabulary," the "trivial, mediocre, banal, insipid...."). In Meltzer's book these qualities take on flesh, and they bleed – they come to life. The most "trivial, mediocre, banal, insipid" elements of art and life become interesting, and mysterious: a choice of one word over another, turns of phrase, lp covers (which are versions of TV commercials, billboards, of the coded social pictures to which we respond or from which we turn away), screams, silences, moments of inexplicable brilliance in a fog of stupidity, or vice versa. This is what Meltzer is looking for – the collapse of art into everyday life, and vice versa. And this may be why there is virtually no "music writing" in *The Aesthetics of Rock.* Meltzer almost never talks about what instruments do, about sound; it's all words, voicings (Meltzer calls them "tongues"), gestures ("moves"). The way you walk and the way you talk. Everyday life.

The Aesthetics of Rock is, along with whatever else it is, both the best and most obsessive book about the Beatles ever written; if rock is a totality, the Beatles, here, are the totality of the totality. ("'Beatles'," Meltzer says, "nearly became established as an official category rather than 'rock'.") Thus it makes perfect sense that Meltzer's whole, willfully disconnected argument comes to a verge with the release of the ultimate Beatle album, the 1967 *Sgt. Pepper's Lonely Hearts Club Band:*

> So, as expected, it had to be the Beatles themselves to do the job of (one-more-time) summing up the recent by summing up the whole thing

–rock 'n' roll; everyday life; the world –

> in a soft cataclysmic combination of death, sleep and multiplicity/ variety, as if they hadn't done it before (every album beginning with *Beatles '65, Beatles for Sale* in England, or maybe it was already going on album-wise with *A Hard Day's Night* or earlier), so this time it would have to be a *really* real end-of-culture/end-of-the-world thing. And that's precisely what *Sgt. Pepper's Lonely Hearts Club Band* was/is. Bringing with it the consequent death of art forever (until someone forgets) and subsequent everybody-influenced-by-everybody-but-particularly-the-Beatles-and-Sgt.

xxiv **The Aesthetics of Rock**

Pepper, eventually dispersing it everywhere and thus inevitably
devaluing the specific Sgt. Pepper focal point

What Meltzer means, I think, is that *Sgt. Pepper's* apotheosis
of rock-as-art, contradicted by rock's existence as no more than
a brute actualization of everyday life, produced an explosion.
The contradiction of "art" as superior to everyday life – when the
art work in question was only the apotheosis of a form that, as
"art," was merely a version of the "Quotidian," of everyday
life – was like nuclear fission. With *Sgt. Pepper*, art-was-dead
because it suddenly ceased to exist as a realm separate from
everyday life – as a unit of significance distant from it. The
record was so alive, so surprising, that people suddenly lived
their everyday lives with a new intensity. They walked down
their streets as if they had never seen them before. They didn't
necessarily connect that experience to the appearance of *Sgt.
Pepper*, just as they had not necessarily connected the dulling of
their streets to the presence of bad songs, or the vitalization of
those streets to the presence of good ones. Meltzer made the
connection, with "I Think We're Alone Now" and "Ain't That
Just Like Me" no less than with *Sgt. Pepper*. The death of art is
what rock 'n' roll, as the brute actualization, had aimed for from
the beginning; from the beginning, rock 'n' roll had meant to
change "art" into everyday speech. In *The Aesthetics of Rock*, you
can hear it happen. But then the triumph was forgotten; art
went back to "art"; everyday life went back to banality. Such is
the history, the prophecy, the thrill, and the tragedy summed up
in *The Aesthetics of Rock*.

* * *

Rock 'n' roll goes on; Richard Meltzer no longer writes about it.
He writes about architecture, the Navy, whatever interests him.
All I have presented here is a way of reading a book he wrote
long ago, which still speaks a language that has yet to be
recuperated: that has yet to be made well, made healthy,
brought back into the fold of what is socially and aesthetically
OK. Meltzer's insistence on leveling – his insistence, his proof,
that "I Think We're Alone Now" is as significant as "I Am the

Walrus" – remains subversive of what most of us think, do, want, settle for. We still live by means of the categories he wrote *Aesthetics of Rock* to destroy. The idea of "march rock" – the idea that a category as valid as "soul music" could be made out of "March," a singer's last name, a beat, an orchestration, "March," the month, and "march," the verb (a coded collapse and reformation of categories the likes of which the most extreme exponents of semiology and deconstruction have yet to fool with) – has yet to be recuperated.

If I've offered one way of reading *The Aesthetics of Rock,* there are many others. But there is one moment in the book I can't help but return to: another throwaway. In a paragraph beginning "Speaking of Foreshadowing," Meltzer writes: "Chuck Berry's 'Rock and Roll Music' predicts in 1957 the later outbreak of African nationalism, 'It's way too early for the *congo,/* So keep a-rockin' that piano'." Reading Meltzer, you listen back in your mind to the song; you realize Chuck Berry should have said (meant to say?) (did say?) "the *conga*" (in 1957, a popular dance – "too early" would refer to "too early in the evening"). But you know Chuck Berry didn't say "conga." He said "congo." Why? How? Richard Meltzer's book is the only book of rock criticism that makes such a question possible; that makes it obvious; that makes it real. And the question of why he stopped asking such questions becomes a challenge: rock 'n' roll goes on and, as you read *The Aesthetics of Rock,* you keep asking what it says.

– GREIL MARCUS
Berkeley, CA
November, 1986

A-well-a everybody's heard about the bird
Bird bird bird
The bird's the word
A-well-a bird bird bird
Well-a bird is the word
A-well-a bird bird bird
The bird's the word
A-well-a bird bird bird
Well-a bird is the word
A-well-a bird bird
The bird's the word
A-well-a bird bird bird
The bird's the word
A-well-a bird bird bird
Well the bird is the word
A-well-a bird bird
The bird the word
A-well-a don't you know about the bird?
Well everybody knows that the bird is the word
A-well-a bird bird
The bird's the bird
A-well-a . . . . .

1

A-well-a everybody's heard about the bird
Bird bird bird
The bird's the word
A-well-a bird bird bird
The bird's the word
A-well-a bird bird bird
The bird's the word
A-well-a bird bird
The bird's the word
A-well-a bird bird bird
The bird's the word
A-well-a bird bird bird
The bird's the word
A-well-a bird bird bird
The bird's the word
A-well-a bird bird bird
The bird's the word
A-well-a don't you know about the bird?
Well everybody's talking about the bird!
A-well-a bird bird
The bird the bird
Well-a bird
Surfer birrrrrrrrrrd *(prolonged sound of vomit-ing)* . . . . aaah

Pa-pa-pa-pa-pa-pa-pa-pa-pa-pa-pa-pa-pa-pa-pa-
   pa-pa-pa-pa-pa-pa-pa-pa-pa-pa-pa-pa-pa-pa-
   pa-pa-pa-pa-pa-pa-pa-ooma-mow-mow
Papa-oom-mow-ma-mow
Papa-ooma-mow-mow
Papa-oom-mow-ma-mow
Papa-ooma-mow-mow
Papa-oom-mow-ma-mow
Papa-ooma-mow-mow
Papa-oom-mow-ma-mow
Papa-ooma-mow-mow

Papa-oom-mow-ma-mow
Papa-ooma-mow-mow
Papa-oom-mow-ma-mow
Papa-ooma-ooma-ooma-ooma-ooma-mow-mow
Papa-oom-mow-ma-mow
Papa-ooma-ooma-ooma-ooma-ooma-mow-mow
Papa-oom-mow-ma-mow
Papa-ooma-mow-mow
Papa-oom-mow-ma-mow
Papa-ooma-mow-mow
Papa-oom-mow-ma-mow
Papa-ooma-mow-mow
Papa-oom-mow-ma-mow
Papa-ooma-mow-mow
Papa-oom-mow-ma-mow
Papa-ooma-ooma-ooma-ooma-ooma-mow-mow
Papa-ooma-ooma-ooma-ooma-ooma-mow-mow
Papa-oom-mow-ma-mow
Papa-oom-mow-ma-mow
Papa-ooma-mow-mow
Papa-oom-mow-ma-mow
Well-a don't you know about the bird
Well everybody knows that the bird is the word!
A-well-a bird bird
The bird's the word
A-papa-ooma-mow-mow
Papa-oom-mow-ma-mow
Papa-ooma-mow-mow
Papa-oom-mow-ma-mow
Papa-ooma-mow-mow
Papa-oom-mow-ma-mow
Papa-ooma-mow-mow
Papa-oom-mow-ma-mow . . . .

—"Surfin' Bird" by the Trashmen

Words and music by Al Frazier, Carl White, John Earl Harris and Turner Wilson.
Copyright © 1964 by Beechwood Music Corporation.

This is a sequel, not a formulation of prolegomena.[1]

I seek to view philosophical inquiry (and everything else too), already itself an effete notion, as afterthought. Historically, multitudes have wailed that all knowledge has already been stated. Plato's *Meno* reveals that man's reason can penetrate all reality by memory of his immortal soul; Plato proceeds to render all truth himself and thus virtually closes the door, allowing for minor revision by such men as Kant. Bob Dylan is not moaning when he says, almost quotingly, "All the great books have been written," realizing that man can no longer open his mouth without seeming to quote. Zooey Glass of J. D. Salinger's *Franny and Zooey* sees as frightening the possibility of man knowing everything of his predecessors. But man must strive to order aesthetically[2] the knowledge available to him, knowing always that the entire system can become "played out" and crumble. I must begin this

---

[1] Oh, you know, *prolegomena* (as in Kant's *Prolegomena to Any Future Metaphysics*)—sort of (clarification of) ground for future moves.

[2] Mere grocery list is order too, etc.

5

critique with the aesthetic notions presently compos-
ing the totality of my particular afterthought, realizing that they will quite likely be utterly different when
I finish. "Tomorrow's Not Today," written by Sandy
Fadin[3] of the obscure Tuckets, sets the tone for this
procedure. The bulk of my writing itself will have affected my contemplative state, possibly quite vastly
or minutely. In the course of my writing, objective
changes in the face of rock 'n' roll have themselves
taken place, and I began[4] dealing with "folk-rock" before the label ever achieved wide usage (and before
rock 'n' roll became known nearly universally as rock).
How I persist in my journey toward truth is inevitably dependent upon how bored I become before
completing it.

One intention early in the explorations necessary
for this work was the (athletic) struggle for neatly
articulate scholarly summation of a thing-system-
order-setup-stuff seemingly otherwise by itself; now
at the end I am a former scholar who doesn't give
much of a crap for any of that stuff,[5] and rock has
been infiltrated by scholarship as insipid internal
newly articulate reference to high art. It takes too
many words to sum it all up except merely metaphorically, so sentence and paragraph length have served
as inertial assurance of the elusiveness of the whole
obviously elusively obvious standard whole thing.
Part-whole articulateness has always been implicit in
everything: in rock it is (for the first time ever—if
that matters) the real-magical concrete-abstract ex-

---

[3] Man Ray's grandson or grand-nephew or something
like that.
[4] In early 1965 or so.
[5] And printed pages, black-on-white, are hot, stuffy
prisons.

plicit focal point of the explicitly explicit. Rock is the only possible future for philosophy and art (and finally philosophy and art are historically interchangeable). Warhol philosopherism and Warhol artiness have been the only major adjustments in terms of these fields proper, but rock is prior to (and more and less extensive than) Warhol, and Warhol has ended up within rock anyway. And *anyway* is a traditional final rock criterion. Etc. So. So. So *my* whole summation does whatever it does and does anyway too, but watch the anyway level. Preliminary Beatle reference: "Though she feels as though she's in a play, she is anyway." Summations of pretensions and a lot of things are pretentious anyway. Leaving only an inconsistent *present* finality.

John Dewey makes the mistake in *Experience and Nature* of tying a philosophy of art ultimately to experience without allowing for his own errors of observation of art itself, which precede any of his discussion of it, to be part of the system common to both the artist and himself. The aesthetician, the philosopher of art and the art critic can never be epistemologically capable of describing art by thinking *at* being, but must think *from* and *within* being. I have thus deemed it a necessity to describe rock 'n' roll by allowing my description to be itself a parallel artistic effort. In choosing rock 'n' roll as my original totality I have selected something just as eligible for decay as my work, and I will probably embody this work with as much incoherency, incongruity, and downright self-contradiction as rock 'n' roll itself, and this is good. Philosophers and artists alike have erred in describing chaos, for their moment of apparent fixity is a negation of the eternal state. Nothing is cognitively eternal, nor is it consistent, nor parallel, but that's just an empirical sidelight. Art must inevitably strive, and has striven during this century, to produce creations eligible for the same corruption and decay as they represent in form and content. Jean Tinguely's self-destroying machines have sometimes not worked and have thus failed to fail. Boehme's or Berdyaev's ordered suggestions of primary chaos (or yours and mine) can therefore be viewed in the same light, as positive inconsistency. John Lennon, once apparently working toward D. Gerber's[6] highest conception of art, that of senseless masochism,[7] seemed once prolifically endeavoring to build a tooth-pick pyramid that would blow away overnight.[8] "Who'd want to listen to an eighty-year-old Beatle?" he has asked.[9] So

---

[6] The great exhibitionistic Texan philosopher of science (1944–   ).

[7] You know, *senseless masochism*. But that of Frank Zappa of the Mothers (of Invention) surpasses Lennon's, because the former seems to have missed (perhaps by having become *too old* for a while!) the whole sequence of English rock explosions. Consequently Zappa thinks he has to bother with empty parodies of early rock emptiness without realizing that the Beatles and everybody else have coped with that work problem (that is, senseless masochism especially when there's nothing else left from before to bother with) and gotten it well out of the way and/or internalized it as second-nature roughage (and he never parodies much of England except Donovan). Too much dues to pay to archaeology and art-as-imitation, so Frank ends up back in high school. And that's nice too.

[8] Bob Dylan: "An evening's empire has re-turned into sand" ("Mr. Tambourine Man").

The Doors: "Try now we can only lose" ("Light My Fire").

The Beatles: "Love has a nasty habit of disappearing overnight" ("I'm Looking Through You").

[9] And the Rolling Stones: "Who wants yesterday's papers?"

far he too has failed to fail, and all the inherent personal inconsistencies of his system ambiguously relate to an ambiguous universe. My critique may be of value relevant to the positive garbage heap of philosophy and art which has preceded, or it may end up on a different, smaller garbage heap, eaten by worms and forgotten; either way I will deem it similarly futilely triumphant and triumphantly futile.

If all assumptions concerning the role of components of tragedy and comedy in the actualization of particular components of human emotion are placed aside for a while, one can still discover in any artistic event to be tested the range of components which will in some way relate to components in reacting man. Whatever it may fully entail, tragedy is at least (on first hack generalization) quite opposed to warmth and comfort, good fortune and unassailable yet impotent security; comedy, to a seriously considered mode of observing reality which emerges merely consistently boring. The combined antitragic-anticomic experience is thus blandly, numbly acceptable in its tedium. Tragedy and comedy are merely two escapes from this dulling state, in an aesthetic or ethical or metaphysical realm.

By and by a shift of emphasis thus can be labeled as the goal, as Milton Anderson (?) (!) has done. A high school teacher who, as *Life* has recounted, "had had his fill of the unmelodic grunts and groans from rock 'n' roll singing groups and decided to recruit a choral group composed of wholesome, handsome teenagers with conventional haircuts," he has formed a group known as "The Young Americans" and has insured that "not a note of rock 'n' roll would pass their lips." Disabled of "all" commercial drive, this group of fifty simulated eunuchs has been using its profits to embark on a good-will tour.

This is one such aesthetic, moral and metaphysical solution, aiming directly at some acceptable model of Aristotle's golden mean writ large. Rock 'n' roll has quite understandably avoided such a direction. The fused rock 'n' roll experience is an overt avoidance of this abyss (used negatively). Rock 'n' roll's abyss (used positively) represents a solution in a realm in which all solutions are basically equal in their applicability and inapplicability to human reality.

Conventionally, all artists must deal with such separable problems as the correlation of the final creation to reality, the authenticity of the creative experience, and the manipulation of human reactions, and concentrate throughout the artistic process on formal unification, while also focusing on the possibility of introducing what in historical context will somehow contain novelty. Whether reality is rendered through imitation or is introduced anew, if it is to be measured for its viability, art is reduced to a dry empiricist epistemology.

Similarly, any judgment placed upon the authenticity of artistic experience is as meaningless as any other use of this intentional epistemological label. Marcello Mastroianni has noted the need to maintain an ambiguous laxity in the application of a label so potentially desiccating: "I am looking for myself in my roles. There is this synthesis between the roles and the real me, as if I'm trying out in them. Who knows which is more authentic? Each one seems so at the time."[10] Memphis Sam Pearlman has sarcastically

---

[10] *Playboy*, July 1965, p. 49.

noted the inadequacy of evaluating artistic experience in so limited a context; his response to the wildly exhibitionistic performance of James Brown in the TAMI Show was, "He's authentic!" Moreover, the validity of a mode of artistic expression in the integration of the total personality of the artist is currently an important question to the otherwise ignorant or unconcerned. A frequent afterthought towards a work of art that is otherwise abhorrent is, "But it's fine if you enjoy it."

Trapped by the rigors of art, the theater of the absurd is merely one particular solution other than tragedy, comedy, melodrama. Nikolai Gogol's *The Overcoat* focuses upon one avoidance of a dulling type of boredom, which his character is not sensitive enough to appreciate. But the context of experience must be carefully examined. Rock 'n' roll is at first essentially the creation of an "out" group (systematically, non-sociologically), baffling to art as it exists prior to it. As the latest perversions of "out," it may be harmed by either the *Time* or *Life* explanations of its being or by its reductionistic connection[11] (by jazz

---

[11] Historical explanation is not necessarily "reductionist"—though it is, to be sure, when in the hands of boobs who think they can understand something merely by "placing" it in a "tradition." Historical reductionism is merely one facet of the general problem of analogy, which is a two-way relationship of both similarity and difference. The great filmmaker and rock lights man David Flooke has regarded the Rolling Stones' *Between the Buttons* in its entirety as hinting that the Stones are on the verge of sounding like Paul Revere and the Raiders. This can be twisted around rightfully if anyone feels like it to provide an analogy that would make Paul Revere and the boys feel pretty good to sound like what the Stones just might be on the verge of sounding like. Or *dis*similarity, pushed to total difference, can be emphasized.

critic Martin Williams or one-time folk singer John Hammond) to a crude developing form of the prior art. One seeking to analyze rock must realize that the context for experiencing it must be left intact. He must take the lesson of environment and happening, art forms which in their expanded use of spatio-temporality *contain the contexts for experiencing themselves.* All sorts of things are part of this context, as money, competition, survival, acceptance by adolescents, reaction by standard adults, peculiar reaction by the community of prior art. "In" and "out" are part of this broadened context of art in the world, both in its aesthetic and ethical toleration, not even in the camp sense of "in" and "out."

The sophistic objectification of evil out of context either weakens it directly, destroys it directly, or transforms it into something utterly benign. Profanity is never beheld for the exuberance of its direct experiential framework but is often reduced to a rather subdued quality of the (perverted) audience itself; one should cry "wow" to original profanity or it dies. Genet has slowly died through his literary acceptability, while Sonny Liston, as dealt with by Cassius Clay as "the big ugly bear," has flourished as a particularly (pseudo-) evil (hence lovable) figure.

The very possibility of judging a work of rock with no other response than "So what?" allows for its context to remain intact; "So what?" is thus a fine aesthetic judgment for two reasons, because it sums up a valid experience and leaves the work itself untarnished. Thus the tragic, comic, absurd are viewable as out-of-context considerations, while *The Overcoat* and rock 'n' roll in its uncontested uncontextualized uniqueness are still free.

In fact, why not judge art by its sheer stubbornness, defiance of any and all objectification? For art
to appear cognitively graspable, assumed is an *a priori*
willingness by the artist to follow a rationalizable
(even if not wholly rational) course of creation. To
rock 'n' roll any and all grids of objectification are
totally acceptable and thus wrong on one level, and
simultaneously significant and trivial on several levels.
J. L. Austin, in "A Plea for Excuses,"[12] advocates the
reconstruction of aesthetics by collecting all terms
germane to the appreciation of art. A selection for the
rock vocabulary might proceed as follows: incongruous, trivial, mediocre, banal, insipid, maudlin, abominable, trite, redundant, repulsive, ugly, innocuous,
crass, incoherent, vulgar, tasteless, sour, boring. When
it is seen that such expressions have allowed for such
a widening of form and content to be considered, only
then can the "in" terms (made out by their "alienation" from rock's "in") be brought near the rock context vocabulary: poignant, sincere, beautiful, etc.

Susan Sontag states in *Against Interpretation* that
art today is to be judged by its sheer appearance, by
how this appearance denies the critic ground for conventional analysis. Certainly a self-important lucid
surface is to be desired, but why not esteem those
elements in art which baffle the art critic, in other
words generate a totality of art and art criticism with
an internal chaos which serves as artistic self-nurture.
Surely rock 'n' roll has achieved the most in this direction. One of the clearest indications of intent to
cast asunder that previous structure which to Susan
Sontag would allow for direct castigation is a scene in

[12] Austin's Presidential Address to the Aristotelian
Society (1956), reprinted in *Classics of Analytic Philosophy*, McGraw-Hill, New York 1965, pp. 379–98.

A Hard Day's Night full of explicit Freudian overtones (if you want them that way). The Beatles are in a compartment of a real/symbolic[13] train, symbolically encased with a middle-aged gentleman who refuses to allow them to reduce their symbolic intimacy by opening a window. John Lennon introduces "homosexuality" by asking the man, "Give us a kiss?" and "pervertedly" placing a soda bottle to each of his nostrils. Later Ringo turns away from the advances of a beautiful woman with the explanation, "She'll just reject me and I'll be frustrated," adding that he therefore must "compensate with me drums." Such intentional and obvious psychological references are so blatant as to *be* the surface appearance itself, supplying an explanation itself with no further need to reach below; yet this new type of self-explanatory surface is such an overstatement that it baffles the analytical critic far more than ordinarily. The sheer overstatement[14] of rock 'n' roll presents a front which escapes all criticism, but which leads to an interestingly absurd body of this attempted criticism.

---

[13] Reality-fantasy-symbol. Reality may easily be regarded as the most fantastic category, as the most crudely symbolic category. Symbol may be the realest, most accessible, etc. Etc.

[14] That is, *systematic* (superstructural, meta-aesthetic) overstatement, as opposed to that involved in a mere content consideration, such as Ringo's overstatement, which is really mere protective device, but is, on a merely primary level, a *source* of paradigmatic multileveled overstatement. And source as genetic psychologism is here irrelevant (or mere additional accompanying data), it is the overstatement itself which is important. Cowboy "brag talk" is but one common old pop form of overstatement. And the Stones' "Jumpin' Jack Flash" is current overstatedly recontextualized brag talk.

One of the most frequent explanations back in its early days for the persistence of rock 'n' roll was that teen-agers, the original primary fans, have a tension/attention span not long enough to appreciate classical music; this attachment of value to the possession of that span which allows adults to appreciate "their" music is ludicrous. The explanation that rock fans would all be juvenile delinquents if it were not for the love with which they are imbued by the music is well worth noting. Just as noteworthy is Phil Spector's statement: "My job is to get that emotion into a record. We deal with the young generation, with people lacking identification, the disassociated, the kids who feel they don't belong, who are in the 'in between' period in their lives." The pseudo-hippy reliance on rock as folk is similarly sociological and (it happens) overly aware of explanation. Leonard Bernstein's comment that there is value in some rock, particularly that spark in the Beatles which in their "Love Me Do" is reminiscent of Hindu music, is an attempt to reduce rock to something other than itself in order to ascertain its validity. Frank Sinatra made his own reduction in the late 1950's in order to attack rock 'n' roll as being "dirty" and said that Elvis Presley might become a fair singer with the proper training.

Even those looking only at the commercial element at the surface and visible subsurface of rock have been both as futile and as artistically satisfying. You know, this kind of thing (just fill in the blanks): "While other groups were turning out carbon copies, each fighting the other for the same identical sound, the _____ decided to be different and daring. Then in August 1963 they cut their first record, _____. It was a sensation overnight, zooming straight

into the English music charts where it stayed right
on top for _____ consecutive weeks. The outcome
was the first ballad-style record by a group ever to hit
the top since the beat was beat."[15] Such analyses (of
the obscure), appearing in the hit song magazines,
are analyses by publications on the same level as rock
and not seeking a reduction, and hence they are justifiably wrong in their art-critical triumphs.

Statements about rock by rock artists themselves
are of the same character. Dave Clark's understanding of himself and his music was rendered through a
serious interview appearing in a song hit magazine in
which he was asked, among other things,[16] whether
he considered himself on the Beatle bandwagon or
considered his group a separate entity. His answer:
"Who are the Beatles?" And do they consider themselves mods or rockers? "Mods."[16] The Dave Clark
Five produces music which is most often rock-like,
but this misstatement of "truth" is beside the point.[17]
Whenever a rock artist speaks of his own art, he is
casually stating his observations, drenched in mere-
preferential value judgment, about his art; and significantly there is little aesthetic difference between the
casual snide remark and pure, coldly well-thought
objective analysis.

---

[15] Or _____ (anything written by a hack about
novelty).

[16] Lots more questions and answers, but the magazine
won't let us reprint them.

[17] And recent word from a random reliable English
freak indicates that early D. C. Five material had been
recorded by some defunct group well before the formation of the Five, with the boys just fronting it. Who
knows? Truth-functionality is here irrelevant.

The heterogeneity in the lists of the favorite performers of the Shangri-Las indicates, through their utter subjectivity (that is, prone to apparent inconsistency or whatever, which "subjectivity" used to imply in high-school English), the confusion[18] inherent in rock 'n' roll: "Betty's favorite singers are Dionne Warwick, Johnny Mathis, and Little Anthony and the Imperials. Mary Weiss likes Mary Wells, Jay and the Americans, and the Inkspots. Johnny Mathis, Dionne Warwick, and the Flamingos rate with Marge, and her sister Mary Ann digs Dusty Springfield, Johnny Mathis, and the Four Seasons."[19] Even without giving reasons couched in Freudian or Marxian (or even musical) terms, they have thereby implied an incoherency[20] to rock 'n' roll, of which they, bearing no direct relation to any of their favorites, are a distinct part.

Motown Marvin Gaye[21] has shown a similar lack of comprehension (and thus a higher instinctive comprehension) of the nature of rock in an interview with Don Paulsen:[22]

Don Paulsen: Who are some of your favorite singers?

[18] Well, confusability, possible confusion, potential for confusion, etc.

[19] *Rock and Roll Songs*, April 1965, p. 29.

[20] Or, that which can easily generate apparent incoherency, sort of close to (if you really want it to be) brittle, unrecognized easy confusion.

[21] A noted stylistic cripple who has *needed* (more than systematic choice) to enhance his own act (lots of self-perpetuation by self-feeding) by the addition of Broadway show material and, eventually, a nearly constant female partner, Tammi Terrell.

[22] *Rock and Roll Songs*, April 1965, p. 10.

Marvin Gaye: They all gas me.
Don Paulsen: Just name a couple.
Marvin Gaye: . . . Ray Charles, Frank Sinatra.
Don Paulsen: What do you think of the Beatles?
Marvin Gaye: I like them. I like their instru-
              mentation. Being something of a
              drummer myself, I think Ringo
              plays good drums.

Announcer Bruce (Cousin Brucie) Morrow of
WABC radio (New York) has displayed his similar
inadvertent disdain for the lucidity of the rock question by asking the Beatles during their 1965 American
tour such actually appropriate questions as how often
they washed their hair.

But perhaps the greatest source of public referential confusion is the attempt to objectify rock 'n' roll
as an evolving art form, complete with all the inevitable reductions to more articulate units of analysis.
The music of the Beatles has been compared to Carl
Orff's "Carmina Burana," the Credo of Gounod's "St.
Cecilia" Mass, as well as "Es fur ein pour gen holcz"
from the "Locheimer Liederbuch" of the fifteenth
century. George Harrison's reply to the suggestion
that these and others have influenced the Beatles'
style has been, "I don't know them." One really fine
description of rock 'n' roll "confusedly" describes Bo
Diddley as "the 26-year-old folk singer who is the
rage of the rhythm and blues field." Duane Eddy,
one of the founders of modern rock 'n' roll guitar
twang, is similarly described: "Duane, quite naturally, favors Rock-A-Billy and Blues."[23]

---

[23] In a program from a 1957 Alan Freed show.

To avoid the difficulty in using given terms to explain a rock phenomenon, Thomas Thompson created for *Life*[24] his own equally superficial terms, namely the Detroit (Motown) Sound, Nashville Sound, New York Sound, Chicago Sound, West Coast Sound, British Sound, and Phil Spector Sound. He has also contributed the finest interpretation/misinterpretation of the genesis of rock, in an illustrated chart (charts are always fun). It is too bad that the article did not appear a few months later, for new absurd connections of his branches became possible, with Ramsey Lewis demonstrating Thelonious Monk's direct influence[25] upon the mainstream of rock and Roger Miller doing the same by influencing the Fortunes. However I have never understood his exclusion of the Mormon Tabernacle Choir, for its impact on Jan and Dean is not too oblique, and this inclusion would have continued the influence of Thompson's religious branch.[26] A similar disappointment is his ex-

---

[24] May 21, 1965, p. 93–4.

[25] "Influence" contradicts anti-historicism. "Influence" presupposes "history." But for object-expansionist rock, history is *part of the object* and not (particularly) a ground for the significance of the object.

[26] Also, lots of real influence by pop Protestant music on some phases of rock and rhythm 'n' blues, as well as some direct appropriation (how about the Browns' "Three Bells" and that kind of stuff, or Wink Martindale's "A Deck of Cards"). Obviously some of the weakest gospel singing comes from non-sarcastic imitation of traditional respectable white church music, and (at least in rock) "weakness" is a groove. And there's Jew stuff too, with "Dance Everyone Dance" ("Hava Nagila") by Betty Somebody-or-other. And don't forget the Byrds' master-move into self-generating piety and generalized diffusely distinct sectarian non-sectarian religiosity. And, of course, the Cowsills are the wholesomely disguised

clusion of the Pacific Ocean's effect on surfin' music,
a connection which Trini Lopez has claimed to be
evident in surf guitar imitations of the rolling of the
surf.

Not so surprisingly, often rock 'n' roll content is
itself confusing, if not utterly baffling, to the expert
and unaided listener alike. In the earlier days of rock,
songs like "Get a Job" by the Silhouettes[27] and Huey
Smith and the Clowns' "Don't You Just Know It"
were virtually impossible to decipher. During the
same period appeared the Coasters' "Searchin'," replete with references to "Sergeant Friday, Sam Spade
and Boston Black-ie," particularly enigmatic although
more easily deciphered; one strange metaphor is
found in "I'm gonna walk right down that street like
. . . Bulldog Drummond." A song known as "Around
and Around"[28] (something like that) was mysterious-
ly just that, a dizzying repetition of that single phrase.
More recently, the Beach Boys' "Help Me Rhonda"
has proven itself a decoding problem. What D. Gerber
found it to say was, "Since she put me down, I but
I doin' in my pid," the last word of which I later
amended to "head" (or "bed"), just as meaningless.[29]
The Beatles' "Night Before" refers to several different periods of time with little coherency and consistency, if any; it may be merely an uninterpreted
deductive system, but the rhetoric of the rock song

---

familiar general religiosity move suffused with strong-as-
weak-as-hell religious music arrangements after-the-fact
and even some Jan and Dean ("Indian Lake").

[27] The "Shananana" was easy, it was the real words
that were hard to figure out.

[28] Not the Chuck Berry ditty.

[29] If you want it that way or if you want to call it that.

is predominant and logic isn't even allowed to be clear enough to be confusing. And in "The Name Game" Shirley Ellis presents confusion plus deep complexity, heightening that which accompanies the learning of any new game by sticking the instructions in a song that can't be slowly examined or immediately reread.

Vastly susceptible, the Dave Clark Five is just generally baffled as well as baffling, as exemplified by this captioned photograph:

Dave and Lenny look out on the city below as they contemplate their performanes on the Ed Sullivan Show. It was a big step, but they handled it with ease.

(From *Popular Annual*, September 1964, Vol. 1, No. 1, Tempest Publications, Inc., copyright reserved by Country Wide Publications, Inc.)

Often a rock 'n' roll song will contain an absolutely familiar motif but with an important transformation performed to alienate it from its original meaning. The Tokens' version of "The Lion Sleeps Tonight," by the addition of their own English to the South African song "Wimoweh," is excitingly meaningful/ meaningless in its truistic statement, "In the jungle, the mighty jungle, the lion sleeps tonight." But with this and other songs, rock 'n' roll is using contexts which are ethno-culturally external and are taken in their externality. Chubby Checker, in his multilingual recordings of "The Twist," had been doing this non-cognitively, as Connie Francis had been doing with her additions of Italian to English lyrics. The Beatles most definitely realize the vast possibilities of exploiting their own English accents for American sales, which necessitated American Bobby Rydell's recording of "World Without Love" (which, written by Lennon and McCartney, had become the first American hit for the English Peter and Gordon) with a British accent, the You Know Who's transformation of themselves into a British group (for one hit, "Roses Are Red My Love"), and the announcement by the New Beats of Nashville that they were English. Later the Beatles used a play on complete externality by recording "I Want to Hold Your Hand" in German, as "Komm Gib Mir Deine Hand";[30] John Lennon

---

[30] There was also a "She's a Woman" in Spanish, "Es una Mujer." Hey (merely), by the way, the original (Drifters) version of "Under the Boardwalk" prompted a Mexican version, but one just using the music and entitled (Spanish for) "Incident in a Cafe"; when the already old Rolling Stones joking remake (of the English-language original) was later released unaltered as a single in Mexico (it was never even noticed much in its

obviously has an understanding of when something can turn into a cliché and when and how to transform it if he wants to bother. The white Righteous Brothers have been using their variety of the "brown sound"[31] of Negro rock, calling it "blue-eyed soul."[32] Bob Dylan, originally a hard-core folk singer, took rock 'n' roll itself as full-fledged externality. The semiprofessional Tuckets of R. P. I. are toying with the strange externality of all art itself, inevitably most evident in rock 'n' roll.[33] Rock sees clearly the possibility of enthusiasm being generated by something given fully as a Buberesque "other," absolutely external even in a corrupt form, rather than as a lower, corrupt, or impure form of self. D. Gerber's term "traditional American darkie music" is thus positively intended, and inadvertent intolerance such as the discovery of "cuteness" in a Chinese baby or in a foreign accent is positively meaningful in this context. And Tiny Tim is exemplary of the palatable externality of unpalatable freakiness.

---

placement on the Stones' *12 × 5* album), its title remained the Spanish (equivalent of) "Incident in a Cafe" (externality in reversal of authenticity of origination).

[31] As Thomas Thompson has called it.

[32] Black-or-brown vs. white (-and-blue): not just (skin/eye) color as mere-other internal externality but visual as external metaphor for musical analysis. In "Red Telephone" Arthur Lee of Love uses more-than-mere-other color (more than mere other because he uses *all* conventional others together: *two*): "And if you think I'm happy paint me . . . ," then "white" and "yellow" uttered simultaneously (Arthur Lee is a musically non-racially-oriented black guy).

[33] A reference-to-obscurity externality move, since *everybody's* doing it, although Zappa may consider this his special domain.

I looked through an entire copy of Ripley's *Believe It or Not!* in an attempt to find something comparable in its topical (and topically eternal) incredibility/incredulity[34] to contemporary rock 'n' roll, not even the Beatles themselves or any of that. Francisco Maria Gropalde (1464-1515), who could simultaneously compose two Latin poems, one with each hand, is a striking case, just as the hen of Steve and Ben Skinner, who chased a cat and adopted her four kittens, is an instance of triviality.[35] But the mere content of rock 'n' roll is basically more incredible than the former. "Twistin' U. S. A." reveals the mysterious activities of several arbitrarily chosen American cities. Jimmy Jones reveals in "Handy Man": "Here is the main thing I want to say,/I'm busy twenty-four hours a day./(I fix broken hearts, I know I really can.)" The Drifters have notified man in "Saturday Night at the Movies" that "Movies are better than ever and just as dark as before." All these rock statements are a particular blend of the earth-shattering and the forgettably trivial. And earth-shatteringness is as trivial as an earth-shattering event may itself be/become. And the historical causally determined utterances of these words are every bit as trivially awesome.

Although no empirical comparison is possible, Nietzsche's Dionysiac revelry has been utterly surpassed

---

[34] Anything can be partially or temporarily externalized by being identified as beyond belief.

[35] Triviality is not, as it has been recently distorted to denote, comic nostalgia but rather forgettability. But you can still have it the other way.

by the rock 'n' roll frenzy. Such television programs as *Shindig* and *Hullabaloo* and especially *Hollywood à Go Go* feature a mechanical synthesis of the rock experience, with go-go dancers shaking it up erotically at various heights in the background as singers mouth the lyrics to their records. The night following the 1964 Presidential election, I attended an orgy of an election party partaking in the rock 'n' roll experience. As Barry Goldwater, great supposed foe of all implications of rock, lost, the Rolling Stones' first album was prominently played for everybody desiring its powers over chaos, triviality, and seduction. Songs such as "King Bee" ("Well I'm a king bee, baby, Buzzin' 'round your hive./I can make honey baby; Just let me come inside.") and "Can I Get a Witness" (with its grinding piano) precipitated, after drinking, such actions as couples disrobing in obscure attic bathrooms and the successful seduction of a university coed by a university professor, in addition to general rampant cavorting on the floors and couches. Justifiably the nominally transitory music of the one-night stand accompanied an actual multiplicity of facets of the actual one-night stand.

When the element of public idolatry is combined with the original orgiastic tendencies of the fused rock 'n' roll experience an amazing integration is achieved. As a helicopter circled above the upper deck of Shea Stadium in New York hours before the Beatles' August '65 concert there, everyone assumed that it contained the precious cargo of their "own sweet boys" and that it was about to descend upon the field. I myself gulped at such a prospect and stared at the moving object (actually carrying merely a television camera) while standing on my chair, motionless, until it finally departed instead. This shudder recalled Buber:

> Thenceforward if ever man shudders at the alienation, and the world strikes terror in his heart, he looks up (to the right or left, just as it may chance) and sees a picture. There he sees that the *I* is embedded in the world and that there is really no *I* at all—so the world can do nothing to the *I*, and he is put at ease; or he sees that the world is embedded in the *I*, and that there is really no world at all—so the world can do nothing to the *I*, and he is put at ease. Another time, if the man shudders at the alienation, and the *I* strikes terror in his heart, he looks up and sees a picture; which picture he sees does not matter, the empty *I* is stuffed full with the world or the stream of the world flows over it, and he is put at ease.
>
> But a moment comes, and it is near, when the shuddering man looks up and sees both pictures in a flash together. And a deeper shudder seizes him.[36]

What causes an additional shudder is the realization that all the implications of the world are to be found in the mere possibility (although even false) that four arrogant men might suddenly emerge from the heavens; what causes even more shudder is that the *I* is no more than the profaned perception of the preadolescent sublimating female. Thus can the awesome be experienced by the trivial and of the trivial. Certainly the rock 'n' roll experience must combine both the awesome and the trivial in order for either facet to be potent. I have discovered the following message, especially prepared to be thrown at John

---

[36] Martin Buber, *I and Thou* (second edition), Scribner's, New York 1958, pp. 71–2.

Lennon at Shea Stadium, although it never came within a hundred yards of him:

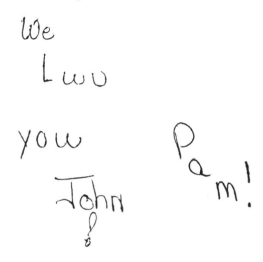

Cousin Brucie Morrow precipitated the climactic gasp of the evening by merely introducing the man who, everyone sensed, would eventually introduce the Beatles, Ed Sullivan, one who is not so much trivial as he is trivializing. His mere appearance, coupled with the flashing notation on the scoreboard, "THE BEATLES . . . THE BEATLES," created an uproar that was unending and in fact prevented all participating in the audience from hearing a single word actually sung by the Beatles. Only memory of past aural experience of the Beatles was needed to sustain this new outburst with the group now present.[37] Here

---

[37] Sure, the whole thing was *also* tactile and generally environmental and historical (cosmic). But those factors are everpresent concert (and private record listening) conditions: yet the words to songs (and even song iden-

is a mingling of *all* elements of space and time, all
levels of significance. Girls cried and girls pretended
to cry, and both responses were valid. Some men sat
in areas close enough to hear but remained absolutely
uninvolved, and they were also merged with the experience, since they had spent twenty-five bucks for
their seats and thus were at least fascinated by a
group which could so baffle them that their only response could be indifference.

The impact of Elvis Presley on his followers could
never amount to the chaotic frenzy of shudders that
the Beatles have achieved.[38] From music not only

---

tification) were never very palpable at Shea '65, and
their presence at all was an audience move (in tension
with its simultaneous aural interference move). The next
summer at Shea better acoustics precipitated an actual
lessening of audience aural interference, and the Beatles'
merely hypothetical awe-as-performed was supplanted
by a sometimes unwieldy *evident* awesome performance.

At Monterey in June '67, the mere rumored possibility
of the Beatles' appearance (in what would have been a
close followup to the American release of *Sgt. Pepper's
Lonely Hearts Club Band*) generated widespread presence assertion and experience-of-presence attempts
among the audience of the first major international rock
festival (no longer even populated by little girls). Etc.

[38] Well, you can easily say that response to Elvis
must've been as electric (qua mere electricity) as the
Beatle thing, adding that only nobody was as jaded then.
But this would call for a raunch epistemology of past
jadedness and jaded pastness, and the Beatles even *sing
about* this sort of thing ("Things We Said Today," "In
My Life," "When I'm 64," etc.) as a minutely manipulable focal point. And even if there is no greater awe in
the Beatle thing, there are far more things to feel awe
about, particularly with the clear/hazy notion of Elvis'
earlier generation of frenzy. Y'know like there was this

sexual in content but delivered with a nervously sexual style, he was able to elicit squeals from his fans,
then in their middle teens; he had no "secondary"
audience to speak of, to accompany his primary audi-

---

earlier Elvis scream thing and it disappeared and there
was no screaming for years and here it is *back again*
and not just reappearing but reappearing on the same
soil it had disappeared from by way of somewhere else:
two gaps, one temporal, one spatial, yet somehow a re-
surgence (spontaneity plus an already articulate notion
of it from Elvis), so readymade second-coming afterthought, operating the same whether within the sphere
of awareness or not. (In England, the first wave of
American rock, with Elvis and Little Richard and Bill
Haley, was mere fuel for England's already-in-progress
Teddy Boy scene; the Beatles signaled a wonderment
for England at the realization the *whole thing* could even
be generated there.) Where Elvis' charisma is brute raw
charisma, the initial (and continuing) Beatle charisma
is a superimposition upon raw charisma which is non-
political (no teen-ager-qua-teen-ager uprisings to worry
about anymore because that's old hat) and other than
directly sexual (Ringo as a sex idol is an *objet trouvé*
rather than an obvious unavoidable choice) while still
remaining brute raw charisma with political-sexual (-re-
ligious) import. And affinities of billions of charismatic
scenes that join up with the main rock one. Where Elvis
is the *big move*, the Beatles are the big *move move*. The
Monkees are a second *second coming*, but the gaps are
too small and the world too aware of everything for the
charisma to be any more than just one more instance of
second-time-around charisma (except to those young
enough to have not even yet formed any first-coming
conception, and this time they're so young they don't
even have any conception of rock mainstream and the
Monkees come off as children's music or television or
something like that). And the Doors' Jim Morrison (or
Jimi Hendrix or Janis Joplin) is but the superimposition
of the Elvis Presley archetypal singular power thing on
the Beatle transcendence-of-and-through-Elvis scene.

ence. The Beatles' music is often blatantly sexual in
its mere content, while their stage appearance is reduced in its sexual activity, but only a silly shuffle by
George Harrison is enough to prompt a reaction, as
it did in *Hard Day's Night* and at the Shea Stadium
concerts (and there George sang "Everybody's Trying to Be My Baby" and, although not too many
could hear him enough to know he was singing it,
sure enough everybody was trying to be his baby).
But importantly, the Beatles do not have to be seen
or heard to produce an audience reaction of awesome
magnitude. This represents the growth of true "inauthentic" experience. That this is a movement toward affirmation is exemplified by a cartoon I remember as picturing a bearded demonstrator bearing a
sign implying the nearness of the end of the world,
but followed by the inscription "Yeah, yeah, yeah!"
That the "yeah, yeah, yeah"[39] of the Beatles' early
lyrics can be seen by Beatle fanatics as being implicit
in the very grass the boys stepped on while running
along the stadium basepath is clearly awesome.

Before their 1965 *Ed Sullivan Show* appearance,
Paul McCartney remarked that he and the other
Beatles would like to make intentional mistakes and
watch the audience reaction they would have already
precipitated and look for variation in response. Having already stirred the audience to the heights of rock
experience, they would be able to experience themselves the frenzied creation of the audience. In its
fully developed form the rock experience thus sums

---

[39] "Yeah yeah" has already passed into French argot
as an alternate name for rock 'n' roll.

up the development of the artist-audience relationship as it has evolved this century through the works
of such men as Luigi Pirandello, Robert Rauschenberg, and Allan Kaprow. But in none of these men's
works is there such a mingling of the awesome and
the trivial, the divine and the irreverent as, illustrated
by this captioned photograph, the Beatles have rendered the rock experience.

*George sticks out his tongue at a performance, but
says, "I love my audience, I want them to
know me as I really am."*

(From *Popular Annual*, September 1964, Vol. 1, No. 1, Tempest
Publications Inc., copyright reserved by Country Wide Publications, Inc.)

After the completion of Allan Kaprow's *Calling*, a
happening culminating in the hanging of naked people upside down against trees in an uncomfortable
insect-infested forest, he commented ironically that
suffering had been involved, and thus artistic disci-
plinarians would esteem it highly. Obviously the burden of discipline and pain upon the artist in his
pursuance of a finished product (always ironic any-

way) has been seriously brought to question today.[40] Because Van Gogh and Jackson Pollock suffered as painters, and Dostoyevski's traumatic imprisonment spurred him on as a writer, a certain dignity is given to their works that is denied to Andy Warhol, who rarely touches paint or camera himself but is financially secure. All artists have been concerned with success in any of its manifestations and artistry thus is not fully separable from the realm of competition. The proprietor of Cousin's, a record store in the Bronx, commented to me that he judged the significance of rock 'n' roll by its ability to present continually a selling potential; he predicted the decline of Motown from its declining selling potential.

Often the validity of an aesthetic experience is limited by the ability or inability to sustain the experience. Thus, success, financial or otherwise, is significantly more inspiration to sustaining an experience than anything within the experience proper. This can easily be reduced to its opposite pole, but the direction of opacity remains the same; as Dylan has said, "there's no success like failure, and failure's no success at all." The Nashville Teens, originally labeled

---

[40] Paul Jones' stage performance in *Privilege*, complete with handcuffs, a cage and brutal cops, is a high point in later rock's relocation of suffering as (re)contextualized (ironic) mere content consideration. There is not only such rock suffering, but *easy, effortless* suffering as well, such as Jim Morrison's subjection of himself to the rigors of formal stage tedium and the Nice's use of ritualized soft sado-masochism. And the inescapable agony of Blue Cheer (instrumental volume well beyond the threshold of pain and painful as vibration as well as sound) is still initially effortlessly induced.

weak performers, but then strengthened by seeing
their first hit song, "Tobacco Road," on the top ten
charts, have said about artistic improvement through
success, "It is fantastic the confidence you get from
a chart disc."[41] Also frequently, creativity can be
eventually hampered by acceptance, so that the
method of salesmanship once it has been established
must become an integral part of the art so that it
will not corrupt it. Andy Warhol has in fact made
the theme of financial success through art consumption as important as any aspect of his work itself.
Rock 'n' roll has *always* been directly concerned with
the art of selling and has produced an aesthetic of the
hit. The Rolling Stones have had greater songs, taken
in a narrower sense, than "Time Is On My Side,"
"Satisfaction," "Nineteenth Nervous Breakdown,"
"Paint It Black" and "Ruby Tuesday," but only
these five have been *number one* songs on one or
another station in New York City. The feeling of
triumph in such an achievement is clearly part of the
rock 'n' roll experience.

Corot established a career with avowed masterpieces of warmth of tone before producing paintings
purely for public consumption. Elvis Presley created
rock masterpieces such as "Heartbreak Hotel,"
"Hound Dog" and "Don't Be Cruel" before getting
a movie contract and then being purged of his rock
drives by the army and ending up with an ambiguous

---

[41] (In *Rave*, some time in '65.) This type of line,
standard throughout the history of everything (and particularly big in the interview context), is finally at home
in-context inessential with the advent of rock (where
both essential/inessential and reduction-to-success/suc-
cess-reduction are big doings).

commercial drive somehow all-of-a-sudden alien to the rock 'n' roll market.[42]

When Andy Warhol's greatest (particular) commercial success is in the sale of commercially produced paintings dealing with such commercial subjects as soup cans and floral wallpaper designs, he is reaching for a high unity of artist, art collector, work(s) of art and act of art. Rock 'n' roll, however, has never even needed to manipulate its context so consciously, for intrinsic commerciality has never been as alien to rock as it could conceivably have been to painting. Rock as an art can be had wholesale on small plastic discs or free via radio waves; it can thus be felt immediately in ways Alexander Calder's mobiles can never be experienced in a museum staffed with guards who prevent direct contact.[43] Thus, there is possible a rugged empirical participation in artistic experience

---

[42] Elvis apparently was always more naive than his successors. Where they know (or have come to know through gradual education or sudden insight) what they're doing, he has only guessed and followed advice, ending engulfed by static wholesomeness as a traditional success-oriented pop end. And, in fact, his earliest success was not only out of context but inadvertently so, consisting *exclusively* of record sales to Negroes, who assumed him to be black (Big Boy Crudup was an early stated influence) and whose charisma system was so crowded that he had almost no recourse (if he wanted to make it big) other than to make it big elsewhere and just stumble upon the first rock throne.

[43] But the whole rock thing can itself, by making actual physical contact with an on-stage rock guy in the flesh (with cops all around) the focal point and desired end criterion of the experience, be forced to the point of confrontation with obstacles to direct contact too.

where "pure" art must be experienced obliquely. When it happens that the content of a rock song is as commercial as its style of production, it is thus most exemplary of Kenneth Burke's view of poetry as "symbolic action," that sort of stuff. It has been suggested that the Beatles' most passionate song is "Money": [44] "'The best things in life are free,/ But you can keep them for the birds and bees,/ I need some money." The Silhouettes' "Get a Job," the Miracles' "Got a Job," and the former's "Heading for the Poorhouse" are evidence of commercial groping and/or futility. Patti and the Blue Belles' "I Sold My Heart to the Junkman" commercially metaphorizes resignation of a profound sort; Dionne Warwick's greatest moment of early success was her introduction to a European audience by no less a metaphor than Marlene Dietrich. And of course there are the great albums of overstatement and over-unification, *The Who Sell Out*[45] and the Mothers' *We're Only In It For The Money*.

---

[44] A song that has provided less in royalties for them because they didn't write it. Ha. And underwriting the crucial/non-crucial nature of money is their "Baby You're a Rich Man": "You keep all your money in a big brown bag inside a zoo." When money isn't crucial it well may be crucially non-crucial or non-crucially crucially non-crucial, depending on what you think about zoos.

[45] The *live* Who have routinized the selling of a simulated destruction of (financially relevant) means of creation (and means of creation of a formerly regular means of selling). During their "My Generation" finale, Peter Townshend smashes his guitar, Keith Moon throws around drumsticks galore (sometimes even the rest of the time too) and his entire drum set, Roger Daltrey knocks his microphone into the cymbals, and smoke bombs are set off behind the amplifiers whose surfaces have been mutilated by the whole spectacle. The guitar

Just as the ownership of rock forms in their concrete manifestation is itself a monism in which an art
collection can degenerate into little more than a stack
of 45 r.p.m. "singles,"[46] Murray the K and lots of
others on the radio have developed a monism for rock
'n' roll with this same common denominator: every-

---

business takes place virtually every set, even when unexpected by the audience or irrelevant to it (as at the
'67 Murray the K show); the pseudo-destruction of
bigger (and more expensive) stuff than guitars even
costs extra (whatever smoke bombs cost) but that's just
minimal. (And the time lost to enforced stage silence
is slight, only a few seconds when just bassist John
Entwhistle is left playing, so the customers get a nearly
whole prior set of mere music anyway.) Speeding up of
the natural decline (generated by the making of music
itself) in material value of the sound-production ca-
pacity of musical instruments (particularly ironic when
everything is electric and machinelike, hence beyond
merely visual detection of flaws and working value) is
reduced mostly to brute physical means except for the
lighting of the smoke stuff (which doesn't even slightly
contribute to actual destruction but only to emphasis of
the objectified destruction display); Jimi Hendrix (occasionally) carries the fire bit onward to an even speedier
means for the guitar and as general burn-out metaphor
concretion. The Move, who destroy *extraneous* stuff like
television sets on stage, have additionally contributed to
the financial setback tradition by means of a law suit
incurred by their "Flowers in the Rain" ad which featured Harold Wilson as "disgusting depraved despicable"
(remarkable: absence of major law suits over copyrights,
etc.). (Oops, the Who got into legal difficulty too over
unsolicited references to extra-rock, to commercial prod-
ucts in *The Who Sell Out*.)
    [46] The eventual upswing in lack of concern for the
safety of albums too has occurred with the downfall of
relative significance for the single and the increase in
inclusion of the single as track on nearly contemporaneous album.

thing validly/invalidly judged to be rock is exactly equivalent; all is as trivial as the dust-catching membership of unit components in the pile of records.

The problem of the apparent absence of the explicitly tragic in contemporary art is often a problem germane to certain arts taken separately. For instance, contemporary drama may not be merely reflecting an absence of the classically tragic in modern man but reflecting a lack of novel means of expression; in effect, tragedy has somehow been "all played out."[47] This is closely akin, somehow, to the problem which confronted the Italian Futurist painters of the early part of this century when they saw conventional "humanistic" subject matter, such as the nude or the still life, similarly "all played out" by their predecessors in European painting. Tragedy, if it is a universally applicable focal point for viewing man, as Unamuno assumes, will always be implicit in man's creations. But explicit statement of this tragic element will often be inexpressible in art without emerging as blatant overstatement (with such consequent taste elements as the ugly). Its metaphysical view of man's tragedy notwithstanding, only rock 'n' roll of all contemporary arts is capable of dealing with overstatement in the necessary manner.[48]

---

[47] And hence the hack "contemporary" tragedian (like Arthur Miller) can easily be really embarrassing if he doesn't notice that tragedy is only a corpse and act on it (embarrassingly) accordingly.

[48] Even the banalization of actual prior objects of tragedy partakes of this level of overstatement. In so many ways that it would be boring to list them, Jim Morrison's Sophocles-referent "Father, yes son, I want to kill you; mother I want to arggghhh . . ." in the Doors' "The End" hurtles through this scene with a final fi-

Originally, rock 'n' roll dealt with tragedy as it is manifest most blatantly to the almost-present-day buyer of rock records, although this is seemingly a limited field, in death or through rejection by a loved one. In "Teen Angel" Mark Dinning sings of his girlfriend's death caused by her search for his high school ring in a car stalled on the railroad tracks. In "Night Time" Pete Antell cries of his love's death in another automobile accident. More recent but in this old class is "Last Kiss" by J. Frank Wilson and the Cavaliers; it follows the same pattern but not with as crushing a finality: "She's gone to heaven so I've got to be good/ So I can see my baby when I leave this world." In "Born Too Late" the Poni-Tails realize that one's very existential condition can be her tragic downfall: "Now my heart cries because your heart just wouldn't wait, why was I born too late?" "So Sad" is the Everly Brothers' description of the life of the rejected: "After all that we've been through/. . . How can you want us to be/Like sister and brother?" Not all of these examples are strictly in the Greek tradition, but they all conform to the highest standards of their art while expressing an assumedly inexpressible tragic view. Arthur Miller is never in the Greek tradition, but in addition his personal expression of tragedy is awkwardly at odds with his art.

As to the universality of tragedy implicit in man, rock is always ready to extend its successful tragic formula to other successful domains. "New York's a Lonely Town" is a surfer's tragedy, landlocked with his "woody outside, all covered with snow." "Wake

---

nality sufficient to render it beyond the present scope of further overstatement elaboration until somebody simply forgets about it.

Up Little Susie" is a provisional tragedy at the movies for a couple who have fallen asleep, suddenly shocked into the realization that "our goose is cooked, our reputation is shot." "Lonely Teenager" is the first-person story of one who is seemingly lost for eternity: "Now I'm seventeen, still alone." "Tragedy" is a tragedy identified as such: "You're gone from me/ O-o tragedy."

The wish for extension through all eternity is to Unamuno the source of the inevitability of tragedy. The wish for extension not quite so far is a source of rock's maudlin tragedy. Frankie Avalon bemoans the fate of "A Boy Without a Girl" and invokes a goddess in "Venus": ". . . goddess of love that you are /Surely the things I ask,/Can't be too great a task." The metaphor of the star is often symbolic of the distance one believes to exist between his wish and its fulfillment, leading to ready-made overstatement in rock. Such standard tunes have been employed here often: "I've Told Every Little Star" (Linda Scott), "When You Wish Upon A Star" (Dion and the Belmonts), "Swinging on a Star" (Big Dee Irwin).[49] One of the masterpieces of early rock is the Elegants' "Little Star," summarizing all the longing of man in one ecstatic section: "Oh-oh Go-o-od/Send me a luh-uh-

---

[49] Wishing a different metaphoric journey, that of actual spatial transition, the Rolling Stones, in "2000 Light Years from Home," avoid reference to stars as such and only hint at distance itself and celestial bodies in their specificity (Aldebaran). But the Byrds, long-time celestial voyagers, are also mere voyeur enough to experience starry-eyed limitation (in "Mr. Spaceman"), but limitation of novelty (a nice additional tragic over-statement of content): "Gettin' ready for to go/Out into the universe,/We don't care/Who's been there first."

uh-uh-ove/Oh there you a-a-are/Lighting uh-up in the sky/I need a luh-uh-uh-ove/Me-o me-o my-y-y-y! ! !" Brutally man has reached his goal ("There you are little star . . ."); thus his entire journey has been unbearably ecstatic rather than agonizing; ultimately rock 'n' roll is capable of evoking ecstasy through its unique potential to deal with the apparently tragic.

It is however a consideration of the comic aspect of rock 'n' roll which sheds greatest light on the true nature of rock and opens up the door to a consideration of rock as it is at precisely this moment. The very basis of the earliest rock 'n' roll, all the way back to Bill Haley and the Comets' "Rock Around The Clock," the first really significant work recognized as rock, and to great reusable stuff like "Crazy, Man, Crazy" and "Ham-Bone," has been the benign, the bathetic. Little Richard's "Tutti Frutti" and "Good Golly, Miss Molly" are pure monosyllabic, short-phrased bathos. Elvis Presley's "Blue Suede Shoes," written by Carl Perkins, is illustrative of this early, largely experimental blend of trivia, overstatement, and bathos: "You can burn my house,/Steal my car,/Drink my liquor/From an old fruit jar/. . . But uh-uh baby lay offa my shoes . . ."

Elvis' later hit, "All Shook Up," the last of his important songs, is loaded with similar visions, as its opening lines suggest.[50]

Larry Williams' categorizing of attractive women is particularly comic, from "Long Tall Sally" to "Short

---

[50] But which we couldn't get permission to show you.

Fat Fanny" to "Bony Moronie." Jimmy Soul's revival
of this tradition is seen explicitly in his (calypso revival) "If You Wanna Be Happy" with its spritely
refrain, "If you wanna be happy for the rest of your
life,/ Never make a pretty woman your wife./ And for
my personal point of view,/ Get an ugly girl to marry
you." Its dialogue ending is superb:

> Stranger's voice: Hey man, I saw your wife the
> other day and she's *ugly*!
> Jimmy Soul: Yeah baby, but she sure can cook.

Often this undercurrent of the comic has erupted to
produce what has come to be known as the "novelty"
record, in which the sense of mere irreverent fun becomes more clearly a part of the content. "Stranded
in the Jungle" is one of the earliest novelty songs, while
David Seville's "Witch Doctor" and his various chip-
munk songs, and Sheb Wooley's "Purple People
Eater" are representative of perhaps the period of
heaviest concentration of novelty songs, around the
spring of 1958. Many records, notably "Flying Saucer"
and "Santa and the Satellite" (a response to the first
Sputnik), worked with the theme of the humor inevitable in the sheer juxtaposition of fragments of
lyrics from rock songs and thus were basically frivolous in their comic intent.[51]

---

[51] Where Zappa (who goes for fragment juxtaposition
too) is only frivolous by way of being serious about
being comic. And his elements of mere frivolity are too
frivolous to be. And it doesn't even last (good). Originally Zappa was the (self-)definitive master of the
comedy-tedium continuum relocated in context. Also at
first there was a vital heterogeneity of (gropings for and
attainments of) audience response; then it became increasingly non-vital (or vitally non-vital, etc.) and more
merely natural. The only real change for Zappa has been

Rock 'n' roll has thus implicitly in its make-up a
substratum of comedy, and even a corrupt form of
that, combined with a generally irreverent outlook
towards what Aristotle (the famous Aristotle) would
label in his *Poetics* as "serious." All significant references to man's "serious" nature are compiled on top

the mass popularization of his machinery as clarified in
the simultaneity of new people considering him outasight
and others having become disenchanted and merely
bored. So: a (systematic and natural rock) degeneration
into the cycle of the almost comic and endless parody
chain no longer with any (first) ground safe from itself
(or memorable). Beating the "rap" of the initially comic
necessarily followed by the increments of decrease in
comic interest are Donovan ("The Observation": "*S.O.S.*,
S.O.S."), who has done it by happening to begin less
funny, and the Who, who have done it by pretending to
be naive while being only *sometimes* comic (or being
comedians with mostly "straight lines"). But Zappa,
whose humor is so all-pervading that it is capable of
becoming tedious to the point of extinction, is rarely
merely humorous enough at any one point to avoid being
susceptible to the conventional big laugh, which isn't
funny but merely meaningful. And Zappa has mocked
both the Doors (castrate the father, who enjoys it, get
sick after jumping on the mother, then jump on the
sister) and early-rock pathos, with only minimal gain via
conversion to bathos. Easy lazy avoidance of interest in
(pathos-bathos) dialectics mars his way, so he (here)
ends up an anthologist of past unqualified pathos-bathos.
And when Zappa aims for the cosmos, the Zappa cycle
of parody, even when self-referential with a vengeance,
is atemporal in the sense of being never a matter of up-
to-dateness or advancedness or avant garde, so equating
Zappa with the notion of innovation is essentially out of
the question. Associating Zappa with *Mad* comics, a past
and still lingering form of the pretense of innovation via
comedy/parody, is something else.

of this joke.[52] The current wave of rock ushers in this structure finally conscious of itself. Far earlier, Lead-belly compiled a musical universe on nothing but major chords.[53] Dr. Don Goodman sees in the Beatles' "I'll Cry Instead" this apparent ambivalence fully manifest with the proper overstatement proper to rock. The picture on page 31 illustrates the Beatles' twofold view. For an experience to be artistically viable it must be "cool," that is it must be serious enough to attract reflective interest and primary emotional response and yet contain a tinge of the comic or benign just great enough to prevent overindulgence in this seriousness. This is little more than Hume's theory of tragedy in which he speculates on the necessity for the tragic experience to be rendered through art with a limit to its scope so that it does not finally shatter the observer beyond his limits of direct engagement. The need simultaneously to emphasize the "cool" element is also in his tragic experience; it is merely a positive factor contributing to this limitation. Finality, in terms of ultimate effect on man, is in this judgment little more than an evaluation based on a classic aesthetic placed anew upon a human experience rendered viable through art. Experience, as viewed by rock 'n' roll, is no more tragically final or forgettably benign than the fleeting moment dictates; the core of humanity is as present in the Beatles' "I Saw Her Standing There" as it is in their utterly pessimistic (/optimistic) "Things We Said Today"

[52] Same for use of the phrase "the human side of _____" to mean "_____'s sense of humor."

[53] Well, not really, but he restricted himself to diatonic chords, usually used for punctuation, which results in monotony avoidance *plus* the intended whatever.

or their cosmically ambivalent "Day in the Life."
Anyway, the tragic label itself is a stultifying limitation, as painter Barnett Newman says of aesthetics
that it is to art as ornithology is to the birds.[54] Above
all, John Lennon, as a representative of this current
wave, obviously realizes that the emergence of any of
this as significant difficulty in the construction of a
"cool" aesthetics is nothing more than silly, even if it
correctly mirrors serious errors in rock's judgment.

In fact, tragedy can be viewed as melodrama in
which the expected system of rewards and punishments is shattered while in comedy this system merely
dissolves after prolonged unfolding of a context in
which it is ambivalent. What is meant here is that a
general conception of rewards and punishments is a
conditioned given always assumed present in the art
viewer's mind before confrontation with the art, even
if this conception is what George Harrison would call
"a drag, a well-known drag." After all, the standard
coincidental relation between art and ethics in classical tragedy, even in the particular subordination
Nietzsche prescribes, is just as much a drag. The effete
aspects of modern man's aesthetic personality (that
sort of cliché) are neither usable nor discardable, so
they remain and appear randomly. "You Like Me
Too Much," George Harrison's appearance on *Beatles
VI*, is the Beatles' exposition of a condition of existence worthy neither of full improvement nor complete
rejection. Man deserves neither immortality nor mor-
tality, and his aesthetic sensitivity merits neither
purification nor total degeneration of his artistic

---

[54] Kaprow has said he said it, and he calls the man
Barney.

forms. Additionally, the theater of the absurd's intention of leaving the ends of the human condition unresolved cannot fully suit the intentions of rock; the
ends of the human condition can be randomly selected
and made resolvable as necessary for necessity or
gratuitous satisfaction.

Early rock 'n' roll features a variety of Nietzschean
arrogance[55] that could conceivably be possessed by

---

[55] Arrogance is one particular intersection with tragedy; pain is another. There is a pain beyond tragedy,
beyond the systematic possibility for formulating it into
any art hunk at all. And there is a statement of pain
ironically yet evocative of such an experiential pain
status, and this sort of thing is systematically perfect
for rock when it is an overstatement in form and content
but not in sentiment (as opposed to the windup of
Wagner's "Tristan und Isolde"). So the traditional non-
connectedness of the art object and experience before
and after the fact casually comes into focus. "If I look
hard enough into the setting sun,/My love will laugh with
me before the morning comes" and "I see a line of cars
and they're all painted black,/With flowers and my love
both never to come back" were the most potently painful images to appear in rock or anything else when they
appeared in the Stones' "Paint It Black" in the spring
of '66. Soon thereafter, the Beatles' "For No One"
topped it for depth and richness of pain with really
poignant lines like "Your day breaks,/Your mind aches"
(this guy has to make his own day, there isn't even
such a thing as *the* day, bringing down the painfully
corny fury of the Sartrean make-your-own-meaning
hangup) and "A love that should have lasted years" (a
resigned double limitation, as if love is quantifiable in
terms of years first of all). Then the Stones' "Ruby
Tuesday" went even further with "Still I'm gonna miss
you," presenting a chick not dead or inaccessibly right
at hand but painfully remotely accessible. And the
Stones *mean* it without being Wagner or Willy Loman's

quasi-tragic man, virtually unaware of limitations. Dion's "Wanderer" appears during the end of this (empty/non-empty arrogance) stage but is a good example: "I go through life without a care,/And I'm happy as a clown,/With my two fists of iron,/And I'm going way, way on." "That'll Be The Day" by the late Buddy Holly and the Crickets appears prophetic of late rock in its arrogant implications, accepting jokingly the obstacle of death as the only possible limitation: "Well you say you're gonna leave but you know it's a lie/'Cause that'll be the day when I die." Today the Beatles exemplify the newer rock arrogance with "Any Time At All," which knows no limitations except in the implications of servitude to a merely mortal female. It and the Stones' "Heart of Stone" clearly exceed the arrogance of Prometheus while grounded in the comparatively mundane world, out of bondage and even outrageously successful. (The Bee Gees' "New York Mining Disaster—1941" is the "note of the normal struck in the heart of the tragic."[56]) The Beatles' "I'll Get You" contains absolute optimism, fully expounded: "It's not likely[57] to pretend,/ But I'll get you, I'll get you in the end!"

wife. Without *December's Children* as the wholesome nihilistic phase from which "true" sentiment could grow as the logical radical extension, the "Ruby Tuesday" sentiment would probably be dealt with (by esoteric connoisseur and moron alike) as sellout or camp. And since the novelty (or inadvertent novelty) pretense is necessary for such lines to have their sting, these rock guys will even grovel in the jagged mainstream of novelty and meaning qua pain.

[56] Struck in the heart of this explanation by Bob Somma, *Crawdaddy!* 15, p. 22.

[57] Maybe it is even "not like me."

"Whenever You're Ready" is an elucidation of the Zombies' comparative heart of jelly (introduced in "Leave Me Be"). It is replete with an invincibility the source of which is complete vulnerability and precariousness on the verge of annihilation.[58] Utter destruction can be cool, as the Stones' "The Last Time" implicitly states:

Well I told you once and I told you twice,
But you never listened to my advice.
You don't try very hard to please me,
With what you know it should be easy.
Well this could be the last time,
This could be the last time,
May be the last time, I don't know,
Oh no . . . . . oh no.

Well I'm sorry girl but I can't stay,
Feeling like I do today.
There's too much pain and too much sorrow,
Guess I'll feel the same tomorrow.

Well I told you once and I told you twice,
Someone'll have to pay the price.
Well here's the chance to change your mind,
'Cause *I'll* be gone a long, long time.

The most thunderous, ominous integration of music and lyrics in the realm of rock up to its time (and appropriately surpassed a million times since) culmi-

---

[58] Yeah, and that's the story with George Harrison's "I Need You" too.

nates in Mick Jagger's call, "Last time, baby!" which
generates a steady chorus of "May be the last time"
against his "No no mo'" repetition to the fadeout.
Notice that ominous is positively used in the rock
context.[59] The Moody Blues' "Go Now" would seem
to be beyond "The Last Time," presenting the actual
descent into the abyss. But to Heraclitus the way
down is equivalent to the way up; in rock's realm of
being, destruction is translatable into orgasmic coolness.[60] Allan Kaprow has noted to me that the explicit
tragic implications of "Go Now" are nullified by the
rock context, while the true tragic implications of
such a work are merely implicit; the tragic implications in any contemporary art are implicit therein;
the masking and revealing of nominal/real inner tragedy makes possible a whole set of nullification/nullifi-
cation-reversal moves on the level of form.

I see Lennon's conception of chaos as far exceeding
the cataclysmic chaos of mere (disorderly) destruction (of the orderly). His pagan revival in "Mr.
Moonlight," appropriately featuring George Harrison
on elderly African drum,[61] is a subtle example of this
vision. The limitations placed upon man are to him
much more subtle than those envisioned in a mortal-
immortal dichotomy. "Tell Me What You See" places
its emphasis on the mere existence of more than one
thinking, comprehending mind in the universe and

---

[59] But that's easy. So you could even add "ominous"
as "comfortable," and that's positive too, easy too.

[60] (Which may also be immediate transfer without the
mediation of translation.) Which is okay. Or as Pearlman sees in this song, "inertial sexuality," which doesn't
directly mean much, so okay.

[61] That's what the *Beatles For Sale* notes call it.

the given need to communicate with a carefully selected other such being:[62]

> Open up your eyes now,
> Tell me what you see;
> It is no surprise now,
> What you see is me.

In "Follow the Sun" pain dissolves into the practical,
which is itself capable of being cool: "Someday you'll
look to see I've gone, but tomorrow may rain so I'll
follow the sun." The pleasure principle itself is an
absurd principle to which man is enslaved. "I Should
Have Known Better" presents one who has totally
conquered and possessed a girl in the manner of what
D. Gerber sees as a vulgar German drinking song.
"Ticket to Ride" and "Can't Buy Me Love" deal with
the limitation by a materialism which can be readily
engaged in by the potentialities capable of being
brought into play. And "play" is just the word for it,
as the obviously blatant materialistic (?) frolics accompanying "Ticket to Ride" in the ski scene in *Help!*
and "Can't Buy Me Love" in a seemingly psychedelic
frenzy in a field in *Hard Day's Night* indicate. "Eight
Days a Week" can be used as an almost satiric reference to an Unamunoesque universal limitation, echoing the voice of doom; in it, even expansion beyond
all limits, as a multiplication of conventional time

---

[62] At about the same time (first half of '65) the Byrds'
"I Knew I'd Want You," by Gene Clark, handled the
same situation at the first stage of Beatle-Byrd parallel
world construction qua construction, and it came out
even *merer* (but not *more*) (the Byrds' later "I See
You" was more but not merer).

(existentially) by eight-sevenths, is the source of frustration, "is not enough to show I care." Obstacles impeding freedom and reactions thereto are far more random, however, as with "Baby's in Black":

> Oh dear what can I do
> Baby's in black and I'm feeling blue
> Tell me Oh what can I do?
> She thinks of him and so she dresses in black
> And though he'll never come back
> She's dressed in black.

Perhaps the most far-fetched of the interpretations of this song treats the girl as a nun waiting for Christ's second coming. And for the purposes of the song even the inevitability or impossibility of the second coming of Christ is no more awesome an imposition upon man than the longings of a metaphoric widow.

References to one who will answer the request "Tell me" are not suggestions of divine providence. The Zombies' "She's Not There" resolves this conceptual difficulty:

> Well no one told me about her—
> The way she lied.
> Well no one told me about her—
> How many people cried.
>
> But it's too late to say you're sorry,
> How would I know, why should I care?
> Please don't bother trying to find her—
> She's not there.
>
> Well let me tell you 'bout the way she looked,
> The way she acted, the color of her hair,

Her voice was soft and cool, her eyes were clear
and bright,
But she's not there.

All of God's (or anyone's) attributes can be enumer-
ated, even *a priori*, but this is of virtually no perma-
nent ontological significance. Only if God is dead, as
Nietzsche and all his insipid too-late pseudo-followers
state, can man, trivialized to the verge of dullness/
deadness, participate in this Being.

Thus the cry for an answer is directed at the controllable triviality of man himself. The call of "Can I
Get a Witness" is to "everybody, 'specially you girls,"
not much of an eternally reliable body of judges. The
implication therefore might be that rock is basically
existential (what a cliché, what a drag) in its outlook,
but this itself would be vastly limiting in its scope.
There is an entire school of rock which sporadically
produces "answer" records, which in turn answer previously released and popularly accepted records that
contain an anxiety seemingly in need of answer; this
answer consists of the same tune and plot with re-
assurance added by the alteration of a few key words
which might be mistaken for the original on a superficial listening. The Debs' reply to the McCoys' "Hang
On, Sloopy" is "Your girl Sloopy's gonna hang on,"
this being just about the most recent answer record
proper.[63] Whitehead has suggested that the history of

---

[63] That was a while back, wasn't it? So, the answer
record tradition has dissipated and been formally answered by such moves as the Royal Guardsmen's sequen-
tialization and sequelization of the "Snoopy vs. the
Red Baron" suspense show and the series of "trades"

philosophy has been a series of footnotes to Plato; others, such as Dr. Ben Nelson, have suggested that this should be amended to include Aristotle, Kant and Hegel, meaning that, although any number of changing answers could be sought and given, all questions asked by philosophers are variations of questions asked by these four. Thus proper questioning is stressed, and John Lennon has asked, within the domain of rock 'n' roll, in the Beatles' "No Reply," something which has seemingly not been asked before

---

between Love and the Stones ("Goin' Home" and "Revelation," "She Comes in Colors" and "She's a Rainbow," etc.) concerned with unwanted answers to non-questions. And Joshua Rifkin's *Baroque Beatles* is unwanted and unanswered except in kind, which is demolishing. And obviously this "dialogue" is, since *Sgt. Pepper* and *Revolver* and *Rubber Soul* and even *Meet the Beatles*, omnipresent in rock, but what're the questions? Well, the Byrds bother to *ask* (in response to "It's happening" and the equivalent mere "What's happening?") emphatically, "What's Happening?!?!" (And John Fred & the Playboys' "Judy in Disguise," "with glasses," in response to the Beatles' "Lucy in the Sky with Diamonds," is evidence of the ease of response and the easier ease of acceptable partial response.) And response to the maze inside the cover of the Stones' *Their Satanic Majesties Request*, a maze with one line extended into another to block the path, is (officially) restricted to partialness despite lucidity of vision into the form for total response. And Moby Grape's "Just Like Gene Autry; a Foxtrot" begins with Arthur Godfrey presenting the promise of a forthcoming question ("And now, emanating from the Secaucus Lounge of the fabulous Fandango Hotel in Weehawken, New Jersey, we proudly present the celestial melodies of Lou Waxman and his orchestra, who ask the age-old musical question . . ."), unfulfilled when followed non-interrogatively by a mere declarative sentence ("I would love to love you like I love to do . . .").

in the domain of rock.[64] He is urging response without really requesting anything like an answer and even offers a suggestion instead, in the conclusion:

If I were you I'd realize that I
Love you more than any other guy,
And I'll forgive the lies that I
Heard before when you gave me no reply, no reply, no reply.

Words and music by John Lennon and Paul McCartney. Copyright © 1964 by Northern Songs Limited. All rights reserved. Used by permission.

The Beatles have generally been unanswered within rock proper,[65] but they would readily admit that they

---

[64] Because what he asks is unknown and irrelevant yet easy to ponder, and *asking* doesn't have much to do with it, seemingly (that's a guess), it's reply to who-knows-what and "reply" as a whole grand catch-all cliché (truth/lie cliché associated with it too) meaningful in its lack of content as much as in its absence . . . otherwise it's old hat and thus it's in *old hat form*. What's new is the coincidence of nothing original (specifically detailed or alluded to) (including nothing), nothing initial (specifically detailed) alluded to ("This happened once before, I came to your door, no reply" . . . not even mention of a knock), nothing in response to it, no grounds for direct argument about it ("I tried to telephone, *they* said you were not home, that's a lie" . . . not even *your* lie, not considered a reply anyway), no continuance of future moves which aren't additional nothing moves unless the final offer ("If I were you . . ."), devoid of anything but the usual beseeching, gets a consideration and maybe even if it does (cliché content unavoidability too), etc. So: total exposure of the form/content of particularized response orientation.

[65] They have been, instead, the initiators of (merely massive) influence chains (sort of in line with the *form* of the "No Reply" conclusion). And, in "The Word,"

are answerable; the act of asking what is unanswerable in rock would be an assertion of false profundity, ultimately self-negating, considered positively. But they have indirectly received replies, as in the form of signs displayed by the audience at their first Shea Stadium concert: "We'll HELP you get your feet back on the ground ANY TIME AT ALL," "We wanna hold your hand," etc.

Perhaps the most interesting use of overstatement in contemporary rock has been the explication of actual philosophic viewpoints in the context of rock alone. Frequently the theme is Heidegger's fear of loss of being. Little Anthony and the Imperials' "Going Out of My Head" is a beautiful embodiment of this, beginning with droning strings accompanying an effeminately pained "Well I think I'm goin' out of my head," and later intensifying, "I see you each morning,/ But you just walk past me,/ You don't even know that I exist." The Rolling Stones' "Tell Me" follows the same pattern as other "tell me" songs but is additionally the culmination of their development, envisioning this same loss of connectedness with being: "I hear the knock on the door that never comes,/ I hear the telephone that hasn't rung."[66] The Shangri-

---

they even bother to set straight (for the hell of it) their own finality:

> Now that I know what I feel must be right
> I'm here to show everybody the light.

And its "challenges" to the Bible:

> In the beginning I misunderstood,
> But now I've got it, the word is good.

> Everywhere I go I hear it said
> In the good and the bad books that I have read.

Las' cries of agony in "Remember (Walking in the Sand)" signify even more of an existential need to order an ominously frightening experience into a total personal framework ordering past, present and future. Leslie Gore's "You Don't Own Me" is an existential statement of "to let be." The Beatles have embodied a multiplicity of unstrained particular (historical) philosophic notions in their works, most clearly in "There's a Place," which contains a perfect parallel to Marcus Aurelius' proposition that "all is but knowing so": "In my mind there's no sorrow, don't you know that it's so." (Quasi-Kantian) appearance/reality (at least in the guise of undercutting the surface appearance) is featured in "I'm a Loser" ("Although I laugh and I act like a clown, beneath this mask I am wearing a frown") and "I'm Looking Through You" ("You don't look different but you have changed"), which has hints of the flash of Plato's Divided Line ("You were above me, but not today; the only difference is you're down there, I'm looking through you, and you're nowhere"). In his short story, "The Fat Growth on Eric Hearble," John Lennon renders a modern interpretation of the Pythagorean conception of unity. Eric Hearble, with a newly formed speaking growth on his head (named Scab), must suddenly relinquish his job teaching spastics how to dance; the addition to his normal condition is just as harmful to him as would be any crippling defect, hence, " 'We're not having a cripple teaching our lads,' said Headmaster."[66a] Donald Goodman has seen their "She's a

---

[66] Even earlier than "No Reply," so it is conceivable that the latter's relevance is even as a topical reply.

[66a] In *In His Own Write*, in the combined *In His Own Write/A Spaniard in the Works*, Signet Books, New York 1965, p. 26.

Woman" as evocative of their every definition of philosophy:

> My love don't give me presents,
> I know that she's no peasant,
> Only ever has to give me love
>   forever and forever,
> My love don't give me presents.
> Turn me on when I get lonely,
> People tell me that she's only
> Foolin', I know she isn't.
> She's a woman who understands,
> She's a woman who loves her man.

Nietzsche has called truth a whore and said that
those relying upon classical "truth" do not understand
women; "She's a Woman" is in fact illustrative of so
many facets of rock, from the sexual motif to the
vulgar trivialization, that it may further elucidate the
rock-philosophical impact of the Beatles. For no matter how tragic a finality experience may impose, the
mere comprehension of it is as warm as a woman.
Therefore, the trite lust of "I Want to Hold Your
Hand" and the hackneyed passion of "My heart went
boom when I crossed that room and I held her hand
in mine" in "I Saw Her Standing There" are never
far removed from what Nietzsche would envisage as
the most powerful for man at the same time as they
maintain a non-entropic philosophic totality.

Surfin' and drag music in its fully developed form
is arrogantly illustrative of the primacy of the aesthetic over the ethical. Jan and Dean's "The Little
Old Lady from Pasadena" urges, "Go Granny, go
Granny, go Granny go," even though "She's gonna

get a ticket now sooner or later 'cause she can't keep her foot off the accelerator." Often its arrogance is grounded in a specified type of material power as shown in the Beach Boys' "409," Ronny and the Daytonas' "Little G.T.O." and the Rip Chords' "Hey Little Cobra." Norman Brown has remarked in his *Life Against Death* about such anality: "Defiance, mastery, will to power are attributes of human reason first developed in the symbolic manipulation of symbolic substitutes for excrement."[67] Arrogance is by this measure sufficiently purged of its religious pomposity in order to be placed in the proper perspective to be used in rock 'n' roll (where no such purgation is even necessary), which itself is similarly directed by its producers towards what Brown would consider anal ends (one mere Brown monism). But usually the Beach Boys soar to the heights of freedom through aloofness from the material basis of arrogance; "Fun, Fun, Fun" describes their freedom before, during and after the loss of possession.

Somehow, arrogant will to power and an amoral modesty have been blended together by the Beach Boys, as if it were hard, and that's the point. (Co-) leader Brian Wilson has said (in the introduction to a Beach Boys songbook), "Probably one word will always be akin to The Beach Boys, which is surfing, but, as time moves on, crazes change, the record industry concurs, and The Beach Boys try to fit into the pattern in their own little way. I would like to say on behalf of all The Beach Boys that we will always try to make two good sides on each recording issued by Capitol Records, and that we will never have any

---

[67] Norman O. Brown, *Life against Death: The Psychoanalytical Meaning of History*, Vintage Books, New York 1959, p. 192.

offensive material in same or on stage appearances.
We will always try to bring good wholesome songs to
the fans to whom we owe so much." Clearly this statement indicates an ethical ignorance which later came
to plague the Beach Boys.[68] At least Chuck Berry,
whose music was transcribed note-for-note in most
early surf music, understands his amorality; his only
real ethical stand appears in "Johnny B. Goode" as a
pun upon the ethical command which sounds the same
as the title.

With the recording of "When I Grow Up to Be a
Man" the Beach Boys abruptly cease to be boys, and
a true tragedy of rock transpires with the apparent
death of surf music which accompanies their apparent
demise. When the Beach Boys, arrogance gone, sourly
opine in "California Girls," "I wish they all could be
California girls," they are attempting to prolong their
dying musical virility with only the greatest struggle
(setting up a positive decadence program before that
of the late-middle Byrds). "California Girls" gives
the impression of attempting to extract the final ounce
of pleasure from a sexually worn body.[69] The product
of the vast orgasm of earlier creation is now an impotence which does not eternally continue by desire to
persist in its own being (and an actual orgasm-impo-
tence causality is functionally rare). After absolute
fulfillment the original sheer desire for ecstasy van-

---

[68] But the discovery that only Dennis Wilson was
much of a surfer assuages anything negative about it.

[69] Kant, in his "Analytic of the Beautiful" in *The
Critique of Judgment*, distinguishes aesthetics from
ethics, with the latter being concerned with *interested*
pleasure and the former with *disinterested* pleasure and
dissociation with the *need* for the object of pleasure.

ishes for a while (too) and the mind can be rational if one chooses.

Generally, flip sides of rock songs are calculatedly "weaker" than the hit sides; flip sides of Beach Boy records have always seemed strongly different from their hits, seemingly experiments in developing a warm and restful contemplative comfort. But "California Girls" is an attempt to use a flip side as a hit, and its warmth, comfort and bittersweet acceptance are made aggressively into the excessive symbolic masturbation of pity. The Beach Boys have in their new deadness created a masterpiece of old proportions by finding a Heraclitean tension in the juxtaposition of their anal qualities of an apparently insecure monetary drive (at about the same time they recorded a group of Christmas songs, their apparent most "adult-minded" commerciality to that point[70]) and

---

[70] Things were capable of seeming that way, with that set of terms/concepts, once upon a time. The only way such analysis might be utilized in the case of the more recent Beach Boys would be to talk of Brian Wilson's abandonment of the group on live tours, coupled with a conflict over commercial content relevance/irrelevance (whatever that can concretely mean anymore, particularly when the content-success formula has already been butchered) between Brian and the more definitively conservative Mike Love (leading to *Wild Honey* and *Friends*, which can be analyzed as sellout to the Beach Boys' own tradition and not even any new scene, like adults or creeps), coupled with the persistence of the great Beach Boy tour machine (they've even accompanied the Maharishi on tour), far removed from both the introspectiveness and (*de facto*) freakiness of *Pet Sounds* and *Smiley Smile* (and the never-released *Smile*). But the total Beach Boy picture is still aggressively wholesome: schizoid rather than eclectic.

their genital impotence in the face of actual sexual challenge, all bursting into a bright unfolding after a twenty-two second instrumental introduction.

But the mere attempt by the lads to grope for something dead and gone is revelatory of a necrophiliac trend that has been evident but not nearly as potent as repetition of the seemingly alive. Jan and Dean and assorted others have continually followed every footstep of the Beach Boys and have participated in burning out with this once brilliant movement, as Vlaminck, Derain, Van Dongen and others participated in the brilliant flash that was Fauvism at the turn of the century. Yet Jan and Dean, like Matisse, have survived to go on to other things; they have recorded a magnificent multitracked Coke commercial and a straight quasi-hard rock hit, "I Found a Girl."[71] The Everly Brothers, the true primitives of rock (in several senses of primitive: simple, naive, prophetic or at least first to foreshadow, etc.), have for years been attempting a comeback by reverting to their old style without the cognition that this style was what spawned all of modern rock. Ray Charles was rumored to have been absent from the recording scene because he was undergoing the cure for his heroin addiction, and when he returned (just as at almost all other points since he left Atlantic Records for ABC Paramount), rhythm & blues, blues and jazz fans (a standard mere grouping) clamored for him to return to his old blues style and content, since he is conceivably the largest influence on what has come to be known as "soul";[72] however, he has gone so far

---

[71] "Who cares for surfing now!" it says.
[72] Cannonball Adderley even credits the stylistically distant Ray Charles with being the spiritual father of mid-50's funky jazz.

afield from this that such a return would be necrophiliac retrogression.[73] To rock 'n' roll, renaissance is
merely necrophilia, and this notion has frequently
burst forth into the very content of rock song. Mark
Dinning's "Teen Angel" is such a song, as is nearly
everything recorded by Dicky Lee. The latter's
"Patches" ends with "It may not be right./ But I'll
join you tonight./ Patches I'm coming to you," spoken
to a departed love. His "Laurie" deals with a relationship with a girl dead an entire year.

The Beach Boys themselves have even used such a
theme in one of their flip sides, "The Warmth of the
Sun": "I'll dream of her arms/ And though they're not
real/ Just like she's still there/ The way that I feel/
Or else like the warmth of the sun/ It won't ever die."
Their "Here Today" focuses on the reiteration of
death rather than life,[74] as discussed by someone already previously death-trained and concerning someone who senses only the life-reiteration, with "today"/

---

[73] His only blues relapse occurs on *Crying Time* in the
form of dead-mother/lost-sight sadness. And maybe (occasionally) in his seemingly enforced isolation to the
problem of working his way out of other guys' songs
which deal in content with his general recent (past-per-
plexing) scene, "Yesterday" ("wait a minute!") and
"Eleanor Rigby" ("died in the church and was buried
along with her name, nobody came, all the lonely people
. . .") in particular.

[74] "Will the moon still hang in the sky, when I die"
("Ballad of You and Me and Pooneil" by Jefferson
Airplane) focuses standard rock necrophilial vision in
a conceptually imperceptible temporal modality. This
forced naive extension to the non-reiterative locates
functional necrophilia/renaissance (actually, suddenness
of vision of persistence/continuance after conceptual
gap of *a priori* inattention) in death/posthumousness
iteration.

"tomorrow" relational ambiguity in context musically reinforced: "Well ya know I hate to be a downer/ But I'm the guy she left before you found her/ Well I'm not saying you won't have a good love with her/ But I keep on rememberin' things like they were . . ." The temporal/epistemological split between the two males here with actual/theoretical involvement in the same mainstream is a formal parallel to the whole rock machinery in general.

If the classic tragic experience were actualizable it could still not, and should not, be sustained very long. Even if the universality of Unamuno's voice of doom were evident it is just as fleeting as the flippant telephone experience of the Big Bopper in "Chantilly Lace." That man cannot sustain even the "resigned despair" or "desperate resignation" which haunt the abyss of human futility, devoid of heaven, is realizable through listening to Dionne Warwick's "You'll Never Get to Heaven." Her major refrain is "You'll never get to heaven if you break my heart," but she importantly adds in her defense that "it would be so awful the angels would cry." Clearly she rejects the final sentence of Unamuno's *Tragic Sense of Life*, "And may God deny you peace, but give you glory!" Yet it seems that her experience of heaven is not transpersonal as tragic and orgiastic rock frequently can be. In fact, in order to perform her equally intimate "Walk On By," with its private yearnings, before an orgy-oriented audience at the winter 1964 Murray the K show in Brooklyn she had to discard its privateness and allow the audience to sing the title line when it arose. Man's most private experience is that of his heaven. For instance, in her deepest moments of despair at the acne she sees before her in the mirror a fourteen-year-old girl can feel ecstasy in the objectified chimera of the boyfriend she will eventually be assigned by Frankie Avalon's "Venus," and in her empathy with Dionne Warwick's longing for heaven she goes through a catharsis of paradise. Just as this momentary rejection of futility is itself doomed to collide with universal cosmic limitation and, specifically, no dates with any greasy adolescent male until she sees a dermatologist, all heaven rock can permanently transfix the listener; in fact people indulging in heaven rock reveries are quite often embarrassed at their discovery by other people, even rock fans. A fiftieth percentile teen-age girl (named Sheila) I interviewed told me that her private revery of involvement with the Seekers' heaven rock hit, "I'll Never Find Another You," seemed more valid to her with friends' admission that they too experienced the same privately: yet the group could not achieve any public, social appreciation of heaven rock.[75]

The playing of Dionne Warwick's "Here I Am" while Ursula Andress falls from the sky by parachute into Peter O'Toole's moving sportscar in *What's New Pussycat?* is evidence of the almost Dadaistic basis of heaven rock and perhaps tragic rock as well. Following the lecherous plot of the movie up to this point, the viewer is likely jarred by the sudden juxtaposition of a heaven rock context; but when I saw the movie for the first time, solidly drunk, I personally experienced the heaven rock in its own context al-

---

[75] The druggard public heaven still works if everybody closes his eyes.

though this could only produce a complete discontinuity in the plot of the movie. As Dylan says,

> i know there's some people terrified of the bomb. but there are other people terrified to be seen carrying a modern screen magazine.[76]

But the very creation of the Hollywood or heavenly experience is mechanically arrangeable and predictable. Possibly the private experience of heaven is most readily creatable through the cliché because of the nature of modern man—fine! Right now rock 'n' roll producers have a sufficient understanding of those bare elements of music and lyric which will mechanically produce a(ny) desired reaction in the listener, knowing full well that this will work at least now but inevitably will not work throughout historical time. The early Beatles have produced a number of mechanical tragedies, the most important of which is the nauseating "Anna": "Give back your ring to me, and I will set you free . . . go with him." "Misery" is a mechanical juxtaposition of the tragic and the bathetic, combining such lines as "The world is treating me bad . . . misery" with pseudo-classical piano fragments and a "la, la, la, la" ending; it is capable of producing a gamut of reactions and metaphysical positions.

Okay, now a concise sometimes nostalgic survey of the heaven rock scene (including reiteration):

I. *Prehistoric (but not preconceptual) heaven rock*
The greatest moment of in-context trans-contextual obviousness prior to the Morrison-Nico juxtaposition was the awesome Ursula Andress parachute scene in

---

[76] Notes to *Bringing It All Back Home.*

What's New Pussycat? Force-feeding an ultimately appropriate and relevant form-content goody, knowing it's easy, knowing it works: Dada qua Dada, finally, and it was about time too. At about the same time, some random chick revealed to a random me that she really was broken up by the Seekers when she listened herself; she told others about it and they told her similar stories about their own isolated corner antics with the song, but none of them could groove on it with spatio-temporal simultaneity. And who doesn't remember all the acne chicks neo-Platonically and pre-pubiclee bubbling along with "Venus"? And Dionne once had the audience do an audience-response boss-licks operation on "Walk On By" at that Murray the K show. Now on with the show.

II. *Dawn of history: Beatles, where've ya been, oh here you are, get off my Byrds Beatle-readymade with all yer bestness!*
Then, when being the Beatles or the Stones seemed to entail nothing more than formal hints at its rotten persistence somewhere near the Herman sector of St. John's Wood, the Beatles decided to capture the dusty heaven rock throne on Mt. Olympus, dust it off and establish the first quasi-natural across-the-board standard aristocracy ever, just about. "Tell Me What You See" + "Norwegian Wood" + "Here, There and Everywhere." Huh, huh, huh, huh, huh, thought some. But huh, huh, huh, huh, huh was obvious and that was the point. And "Here, There and Everywhere" was *under*statement, even. The Stones tried to follow the Beatles by the noncomplex-divinity route, sometimes getting opaque enough to qualify as heaven rock practitioners ("Back Street Girl" to at least a "Nowhere Man" extent, okay?), although that was of course an inessential aristocracy completion

for them. Needless to say, the Stones' famous piss
bust is never really too far away from the prettiest of
Brian Jones' miscellaneous instrumentation, however.
Now it's time to weed through some raunch epistemology.

III. *Vast generalizations, lots of empirical meat*
Paradigmatic explicitness is the case in heaven rock.
There are no candidates for heaven rock, it is merely
obviousness incarnate, straight proto-Marxian theology of theology made superficial enough to be significant. The copresence of nonheaven rock stuff on an
album, or in a random grouping with the true stuff, is
fully allowable, even as the mere waste track, ah the
infamous waste track. How else do you preserve "very
specialness"? Dionne Warwick averages eight to
eleven waste tracks per album; Tim Hardin (with
This Is Tim Hardin) has even masterfully produced
an entire waste album. Single-song heaven rock: D. C.
Five's "Because," Moby Grape's "8:05," Love's
"Orange Skies," Norma Tanega's "Walking My Cat
Named Dog," Buffalo Springfield's "Expecting to
Fly," the Fugs' "I Want to Know." The internal focal
relevance schemes of Herman's Hermits and the Byrds
cancel them out heavenrockwise: Herman's mere elaborate candy kitchen waste, the Byrds' church music-
Lefty Frizell disparity misses the specialness point by
less than one-fifth of "I See You."

The close proximity to trash-pop, Muzak and shit-
pretty poetry is crucial. So is the overstatement-under-
statement continuum, which the Beatles erased with
a rubber spoon only to show everybody that it still
remains, even if only fuzzily, on the spoon. Tim
Buckley is the new Paul Robeson and Alfred Drake,

but still makes it; Joan Baez is Kate Smith and "doesn't."

IV. *Tim Hardin*

A priori heaven rock dispersion, its only occurrence in fact. Tongue proficiency and tongue precision are just the thing in these clouds: unknown tongue field ("Don't Make Promises"), implicit meta-tongue pressure field ("Green Rocky Road"), constant tongue transition ("While You're on Your Way" once in a while), all as yet undefined. "If I Were a Carpenter" extends heaven rock beyond the preestablished but-had-you-gone-you-knew-in-time-we'd-meet-again-for-I-have-told-you line (Paul McCartney in "Got to Get You into My Life"). The saying-singing distinction in "Don't Make Promises"[77] is significant, super and even cute. The ending of "While You're on Your Way" ("While you're on your way,/ While you're on your way,/ How did the feeling feel to you?") is a merer mere addition than "I'd love to turn you on" was to "Day in the Life." Timmy could even have written "Love Letters in the Sand" if he had wanted to.

V. *Tim Buckley*

Beauty: out as all-encompassing aesthetic unifier, back in as nice and occasionally accompanying that which is nice and sometimes even categorically replaceable by all this nice trash unreflectively. This Tim is one of the few to demonstrate that poetry can embrace it all (both Arthur Lee and Jim Morrison are lucky colleagues) after the fact: one "Valentine Melody" is worth a whole bunch of darling-be-home-

---

[77] "Do you think I'm not aware of what you're sayin' or why you're singin'?"

soons once in a while, and that's nice. "Wings" and
"Morning Glory" go beyond the postorgasm of "California Girls." "Once I Was" is the intersection of so
many elusive flight-bound focal points. In "Song of
the Magician" and "I Never Asked to Be Your Mountain" he sings lyrics that couldn't possibly be merely
said, words that just gotta be really sung, whatever
that means, or they're just run-of-the-mill Eric Anderson, whatever that isn't. "Strange Street Affair
Under Blue" contains the only instance of Doorslike
intensity acceleration in heaven rock proper.

In fact Buckley's own self-irrelevance and very
specialness indicator involve recent Jim Morrison
affinity (he even performed *standing* at his Stony
Brook concert in September '67). Even though Morrison influence on an overt level is necessary, the old
Buckley position of merely ignoring and thus standing in a trans-influenced relationship to Morrison does
the trick too. Anyway, arrogance-vulnerability, inno-
cence-evil are probably the most basic temporal dialectics in rock (as opposed to *a priori* dualities or
duality-identities such as awesome-trivial). But
they're on the verge of becoming atemporal too.
Good as gold.

VI. *Nico*
She's standardly more than standardly beautiful
visually, so it wouldn't even matter whether or not
she could sing. She sings them all the same, with no
waste, although "excrement filters through the body
pores."

VII. *Jackson Browne*
Only the greatest poet of rhyme of all time, revealing all earlier masters to be hacks. Too authentic to

seem too authentic to be credible: quickest case of *ad hominem* pressure generation on record. Still a teen-ager these days, Jack used to surf with John Wiesenthal, who taught him some fundamentals of guitar. Played with Nico at the Dom in New York and dominated Nico's *Chelsea Girl* album (featuring the Jackson masterpieces "The Fairest of the Seasons," "These Days" and "Somewhere There's a Feather") by having his guitar lines drowned out by strings.

VIII. *Steve Noonan*
Champion of academic beauty, which some day soon we'll catch the full import of. "Leaning Back and Laughing": yum, yum. "Buy for Me the Rain" with its softly sinister "gravestones cheer the living, dear, they're no use for the dead": ah! I can say no more, so here are four blank lines to be filled in later (spaces can be used too) with good things:

IX. *Greg Copeland, lyricist*
A lyricist if there ever was one and capable of reviving the very concept of the (unmere) lyricist. Steve's lyrics are actually Greg's—and even Jackson's "Fairest of the Seasons" is a Copeland lyric.

X. *Donovan, recent Beach Boys, etc.*
In the great 1945 film classic, *Wonder Man*, Danny Kaye is shot by this guy who is dressed as a messenger claiming to be bringing him two dozen lilies. When Donovan hits the mere metaphor trail he sometimes ends up in the same vicinity. Once in a while he ends

up in heaven rock the same way, gropelessly groping,
producing "Celeste" or "Girl Child Linda," singing
"Come all ye starry starfish" instead of "Here I sit
the retired writer in the sun." Fairy tale . . . decadence . . . fairy tale . . . decadence: sometimes even
heaven rock.[78] The Beach Boys hit the heaven rock
trail with "Wouldn't It Be Nice," it was nice as hell
so they had to work out a whole super-program, during the *Smiley Smile* chapter of which they would
demonstrate that heaven rock could encompass even
the ethereal version of the Mothers as easily as Brian
Wilson's stomach can be the grateful digestive home
of his favorite vegetable ("With Me Tonight" + "Veg-
etables," absorbed via the tone of "Wind Chimes").

XI. *Hey what if you go back to the prehistoric and
preconceptual stuff like Bing Crosby or Stan Getz?*
Wow, that's next week and eschatologically just
about on schedule. Mantovani will be there, Perry
Como, Caterina Valente, Johnny Mathis himself, Bar-
bra Streisand of her first year, Ella Fitzgerald, Gary
McFarland.

---

[78] Donovan's "The Fat Angel," presumably about a
Hell's Angel ("He will bring happy-ness in the pipe,
Guela, right away, on his silver bike"), is nought but a
rough-and-ready dialectics project in this behalf, just as
is (Angel) Freewheelin Frank's (in *Freewheelin Frank*,
Grove Press) acid exercises in the articulation of the
(heaven and hell) angel theodicy (but *its* additional
cuteness qualifies it heavenrockwise). And an account
(by Hunter S. Thompson, *Hell's Angels*, Ballantine
Books, p. 151) of the super-applicability of the (very
same) Seekers' "A World of Our Own" (over the radio)
to an early morning Angels scene marked by joyful
meaning-cliché-resignation indicates the easy universality of heaven rock when articulate form is not at stake
and cognition of the total scheme is only epigrammatic
and mock-undialectic.

XII. *Likely soon-to-be-realized big move*
Pretty soon it's gonna be *all* Jackson Browne all over the place.[79] Being the only man in rock besides the Doors to do a Beatles-Stones isolated-content rock-introspection all-one summation, he's not far away at all from writing his "How High the Moon."

XIII. *Where's this "heaven rock" business get its name anyway?*
Oh, from Dionne Warwick's "You'll Never Get to Heaven," where heaven is actually just the indirect destination.

XIV. *Where's Roy Orbison, huh?*
Oops, forgot about him. Damn.

Bob Dylan's complete rejection of paradise in "Gates of Eden" is punctuated by "I try to harmonize with songs the lonesome sparrow sings." Paradise and tragic futility are to him categories just as mesmerizing, and hence equally detestable; either facet is improved if you can sing about it, of course, but the important aspect is the momentary punctuation of experience. The Rolling Stones' version of "Mercy Mercy" juxtaposes a punctuation to experience, "That's right," spoken masterfully after a drown threat. Ray Charles used the same phrase before in

---

[79] Hmm, already Earth Opera, Chrysalis, a few seconds of Morrison in the Doors' "The River Knows" ("I promised I would drown myself in mystic heated wine," even *sounding* like Jackson by way of Nico), and a hogshead of others, including the posthumously verified "Flying on the Ground Is Wrong" (Neil Young of the Buffalo Springfield, "City lights at a country fair/Never shine they always glare"), are evidence of the Jackson Browne spirit-at-large which has granted no direct recognition to him, but he's a cowboy not an aristocrat.

his quasi-tragic "Hit the Road Jack." The quasi-tragic is to the ends of rock more important than the tragic. "Sally Go 'Round the Roses" is a modern quasi-tragedy by the Jay-nets, juxtaposing "Saddest thing in the whole wide world . . . to see your baby with another girl" with the magnificent banality of "Roses they can't hurt you." "High Heel Sneakers," best recorded separately by Little Tommy Tucker and Little Stevie Wonder, hails the trap of mechanical preparation for any eventuality: "Put on your high heel sneakers,/ Wear your wig hat on your head./ I'm pretty sure now baby,/Girl you know you gonna knock 'em dead."[80] This is quite like George Harrison's remark in *Hard Day's Night*, "I'd be quite prepared for that eventuality."

There have been several songs about dying relationships revived in the memory by hit songs. "Those Oldies but Goodies remind me of you," sung in an opening verse by Little Caesar and the Romans, has this sentiment, as does "Our Favorite Melodies" (by someone I can neither remember nor discover through extensive research). WABC's 1965 summer policy of playing an old hit song after each present-day hit may have been an attempt to stir up the sentimentality of tender memories revived by the repetition of something familiar (and what's summertime anyway?). But now, when "solid gold" is anything out of the current hit survey for more than a second or two, this sentimentality is to be understood possibly as a craving for merely the repetition, increased in

---

[80] Dylan mocks this apparent total preparation in "I Shall Be Free #10" with an account of how the sneakers and wig hat prevented his entrance onto a tennis court.

frequency as rapidly as possible. Rock 'n' roll is now in the midst of a cataclysmic acceleration, both in this mode of repetition and in the cognition of its nature. And it always has been.

The Four Tops have masterfully demonstrated this intrinsic but usually only implicit factor in all rock music. In "It's the Same Old Song" they kinetically blast: "All you left was our favorite song,/ The one we danced to all night long./ It used to bring sweet memories/ Of a tender love that used to be . . ./ It's the same old song/ But with a different meaning since you've been gone." (The line "It used to bring . . ." sounds strongly like "The Supremes sing memories . . .," and the fact that the words *are* otherwise is irrelevant in light of their proximity within the Motown formula. The longing for the halcyon days of a relationship are thus secondary behind the sheer irritated recognition of the fact that the mere replay of anything by the Supremes, not to mention anybody else, can stir up such a memory, and that *anything* by the Supremes can bear a resemblance to a life situation.) If anything can unfailingly accomplish an end, why not repeat it again and again, both for its effect considered singly and then as part of a growing chain. The major release by the Four Tops was "I Can't Help Myself," an enormous hit using the thump of the Supremes' "Where Did Our Love Go?" with new words and minimally different arrangement; this can be regarded as an important creation of germplasm which will flow through rock 'n' roll for years (call it the Motown Germplasm). But with virtually everything by the Supremes sounding alike, particularly "Baby Love," "Back in My Arms Again," and "Nothing but Heartaches" (and everything else, with mar-

ginally variant similarity criteria), so does "It's the
Same Old Song" itself sound roughly the same as
most Motown hit stuff.

"La Bamba," a classic by the late great Richie
Valens, is a fairly incomprehensible rock song emo-
tionally uttered in Spanish and later revived by Trini
Lopez.[81] Yet its time and chord pattern appear in a
multitude of more comprehensibly worded and enunciated works, the most renowned of which is "Twist
and Shout" by the Isley Brothers, also noteworthy
for its internal duplication:

> Shake it up baby
> (Shake it up baby)
> Twist and shout
> (Twist and shout)
> Come on, come on, come on baby
> (Come on baby)
> Come on and work it on out
> (Work it on out).
>
> Well you twist so good
> (Twist so good)
> You know you twist so fine
> (Twist so fine)
> Come on and shake it up baby
> (Shake it up baby)
> Come on and show me that you're mine
> (Show me you're mine).

---

[81] José Marti's "Guantanamera," perhaps the very
origin of "La Bamba" itself, even became a hit itself (by
the Sandpipers, after Pete Seeger's revival) as a clearly
articulated version of a song too pretty for the long-time
rock fan archaeologist to notice.

Many Dave Clark Five songs released during the earliest stage of England's rock revolution are variations on "La Bamba," most prominently "Glad All Over" and "Bits and Pieces."

"El Paso" by Marty Robbins and "Come a Little Bit Closer" by Jay and the Americans are two "La Bamba" variations which additionally combine a Latin American motif with the tune. The latter group also followed their song with "Let's Lock the Door," quite La Bambaesque (so was their "Only in America"). "Down at the Club" by the Drifters, while not overtly a product of the same germplasm, contains an instrumental rendition of "La Bamba" as a break between two sections of lyrics.

"Louie Louie" by the Kingsmen has been heard over and over again through such hard rock works as "Game of Love" by Wayne Fontana and the Mindbenders, "Hang On Sloopy" by the McCoys, and "All the Day and All the Night" by the Kinks, whose early distinct resemblance to the Kingsmen is echoed in the likeness of their names. And "Louie Louie" is almost "La Bamba."

"Going to the Chapel" by the Dixie Cups and "Whenever a Teenager Cries" by Reparata and the Delrons are equivalent, as are many sections of "People Say" by the former group and the Supremes' "Nothing but Heartaches." Chubby Checker's great pace setter, "The Twist," exactly duplicated the tune of "Finger Popping Time" by Hank Ballard and the Midnighters, released only days before it. Chubby Checker's "Pony Time" and "Let's Twist Again," as well as his later multilingual "Twist" recordings are all of this same family.

"Needles and Pins," the Searchers' first masterpiece, the two (possible) renditions of "Since You Broke My Heart" (Searchers and maybe Everly Brothers), and "I'll Feel a Whole Lot Better," as sung by the Byrds, are virtually identical.

The trumpet solo in Barbara George's "I Know (You Don't Love Me No More)" is taken note-for-note by the Shirelles for their version of Doris Day's "Everybody Loves a Lover." The ending of "A Hard Day's Night" by the Beatles is used by We Five in "You Were on My Mind" and as a formalized rhythmic addition near the end of the Stones' "Goin' Home." Very significantly, the George Harrison lead guitar break in the Beatles' "Any Time at All" is veritably copied by him in their "Every Little Thing." The latter being the "Thou" counterpart of the "I" of the former (any time at all for you, any time at all for me) seems to indicate that the Beatles' later work has been the construction of the "other" to accompany the self they originally developed. The use of a similar musical passage in each indicates the extent to which both I and Thou can metaphorize each other in the Beatles' (or anybody's) unity.

Even classic hits can be carbon copies. After all, the story of Phaedra was used frequently by the Greek tragedians. Thus, "Do You Want to Dance" and "Do You Love Me?" both sterling examples of rock masterpieces, are audibly the same (sometimes).

And themes from classical music itself have been employed by rock 'n' rollers, as "Asia Minor" by

Kokomo (something by Grieg), "Somewhere" by the Tymes (Mozart's Sonata I in C Major), something or other by Jackie Wilson (Tchaikowsky's First Piano Concerto in B Minor). Sam Cooke's "Bring It On Home to Me" contains a bass line echoing Berlioz, emphasized in its remake by the Animals. Pearlman's "ground" theory, relating rock 'n' roll most closely to European music, is most clearly embodied in Martha and the Vandellas' "Nowhere to Run, Nowhere to Hide" (Rachmaninoff's Third Piano Concerto). The Toys' "Lover's Concerto" (Bach) and "Attack" (something ambiguous but classical) and the Supremes' "I Hear a Symphony" (nothing) represent the brief but briefly noticed classic-rock move; Procol Harum's "A Whiter Shade of Pale" (Bach cantata "Sleepers Awake") is the specific disguised as general (and past mainstream avoided by distant-past relative obscurity) classic rock-classic move. The Duprees' "My Own True Love" is the addition of words to movie music, "Tara's Theme," utterly familiar as the theme of New York television's *Million Dollar Movie*. "I'll Never Dance Again" by Bobby Rydell is rumored to be taken from a Nazi march, as "I Will Follow Him" is rumored to be the linguistic objectification of will taken from an Italian march and recorded by a girl appropriately named Little Peggy March. The Tokens' "The Lion Sleeps Tonight" is, of course, the latest development of the South African folk song "Wimoweh," while Miriam Makeba's "Pata Pata" is both the rejuvenation of this scene and the rejuvenation of mere musical authenticity. The incorporation of anything originally alien into a rock 'n' roll germplasm lessens the actual discrepancy between one's conception of the actual likeness of straightforward classical music to familiar old-fashioned pop and their actual historical, musical similarities. The Beatles' soundtrack album from *Help!* features one track described thusly:

> 6. IN THE TYROL (BMI—2:21) Introducing Wagner's Overture to Act II of LOHENGRIN, Beatles' Style.

No attempt is made to alter Wagner's original composition, for the "Beatles' Style" version is played by Ken Thorne's Orchestra in exact duplication of some traditional manner, changed at all only by its context in a rock 'n' roll movie.

The Rolling Stones' "Spider and the Fly" is a more/less sophisticated, more/less articulate addition of new words to Jimmy Reed's "Baby, What You Want Me to Do." "True Love" is Clyde McPhatter's replica of the Royal Teens' "Believe Me," or maybe it's the other way around. Virtually *every* Bo Diddley song is identical, and a whole batch of them use only one chord.

But of all schools of musical repetition, none has been as prolific as Chuck Berry. His "Maybelline" is nothing but his "Nadine." "Nadine, baby is that you?" becomes "Maybelline, why can't you be true?" "Up in the mornin' and out to school" from his "School Day" later evolves into "Drivin' along in my automobile" in his "No Particular Place to Go." In short order, all Chuck Berry songs sound exactly alike to both the skilled and unskilled listeners. Many have been attracted to this and the result has been numerous remakes of his standards. The Beatles have recorded his "Rock and Roll Music," whose decree, "It's got a back beat, you can't lose it," indicates Berry's deep understanding of exactly the orgasmic monotony he is mechanically producing. The Dave Clark Five has done his "Reeling and Rocking," being

honest about the song's point of origination to place
their own remake in its reverberation field. The Rolling Stones have remade "Around and Around," "You
Can't Catch Me" (the Blues Project's done this one
too), and "Carol." And Johnny Rivers, Sandy Bull,
and John Hammond have all been inspired to work
with his masterpiece, "Memphis":

> Long distance information get me Memphis, Ten-
>   nessee,
> Help me find the party trying to get in touch with
>   me.
> She could not leave her number
> But I know who placed the call
> 'Cause my uncle took the message
> And he wrote it on the wall.
> Help me information get in touch with my Marie,
> She's the only one who'd call me here from Mem-
>   phis, Tennessee.
> Her home is on the south side, high up on a ridge,
> Just about a mile from the Mississippi Bridge.
> Last time I saw Marie she was waving me good-
>   bye
> With hurry home drops on her cheek
> That trickled from her eye,
> But we were pulled apart because
> Her mom did not agree
> And tore apart our happy home in Memphis,
>   Tennessee.
> Help me information, more than that I cannot
>   add,
> Only that I miss her and all the fun we had.
> Marie is only six years old, information please
> Try to put me through to her in Memphis, Ten-
>   nessee.

Unamuno describes the man behind the philosopher,

> And thus, in a philosopher, what must needs most
> concern us is the man.
> Take Kant, the man Immanuel Kant, who was born
> and lived at Königsberg, in the latter part of the eigh-
> teenth century and the beginning of the nineteenth. In
> the philosophy of this man Kant, a man of heart and
> head—that is to say, a man—there is a significant som-
> ersault, as Kierkegaard, another man—and what a man!
> —would have said, the somersault from the *Critique of
> Pure Reason* to the *Critique of Practical Reason.*[82]

Just consider the man Chuck Berry (whose "Brown
Eyed Handsome Man" could be an indication of what
he might think of what-a-man particularized human-
ism) and his song "Memphis"! Today, variations of
its chord pattern (as well as carbon copies *per se*)
can be found in new releases every week. "Can I Get
a Witness," recorded by Marvin Gaye and later the
Rolling Stones, is "Memphis." "High Heel Sneakers,"
sung by Little Tommie Tucker, the Searchers, and
Little Stevie Wonder, is "Memphis." "3/5 of a Mile
in Ten Seconds" by the Jefferson Airplane is "Memphis." It has become simple for a rock producer to
create something with immediate hit potential by
simply applying words to a slight rhythmic/harmonic
variation of "Memphis." Somehow the cryptically aph-
rodisiac-or-whatever-the-hell pulsation of its rhythm,
as best exemplified in its interpretation by the Stones
in their "Can I Get a Witness," and its equivalent
"Now I've Got a Witness," has struck upon a passage
which has naked immediacy and eroticism, even after
numerous repetitions, even after the very concept is

---

[82] Miguel de Unamuno, *Tragic Sense of Life*, translated
by J. E. Crawford Flitch, Dover Publications, Inc., New
York 1954, p. 3. Reprinted through permission of the
publisher.

boring. Petula Clark's "I Know a Place" bristles with this pulsation, regardless of the insipidness of its content (it's the "Memphis" equivalent of "Down at the Club," the geographicalization of "La Bamba"). The Ad Libs' "Boy from New York City" has it, as does Ian Whitcomb's otherwise insipid "You Turn Me On." Jimmy Reed's "Shame, Shame, Shame" is also "Memphis," as is the Shangri-Las' hard rock song "Bull Dog." Quite appropriately Herman's Hermits have incorporated it in a deceptively naive and innocent "Little Bit Better," while the Beatles have relied on a similar, although not identical, pulsation in their Freudian flight dream, "You Like Me Too Much." Dylan, both unmoved by marginal variety considerations and anxious to rigidify mere repetition (and particularly, in this case, repetitive reference to traditional rock hidden-reference-or-non-referential mere repetition), has filled an entire album *(Bringing It All Back Home)* with lots of super-obvious "Memphis," notable to the point of distraction on "Outlaw Blues."

The entire body of surfin' music is lifted directly from the compositions of Chuck Berry. "Surfin' U.S.A." is a collaboration between Berry's writing and the Beach Boys' vocal magnificence and plagiaristic imagination, all a transposition of the former's "Sweet Little Sixteen." The opening of his "Brown Eyed Handsome Man" is duplicated in the opening of the same surf opus. "Surf City," "Drag City," "Hey Little Cobra," "Three Window Coupe," "Little Honda," "Hot Rod U.S.A." (which extends geographic consideration to North Cincinnati), "Honolulu Lulu," "Amusement Parks U.S.A." and many others, too numerous to list, are direct repetitious outgrowths of this original investment in mere surf music possibilities by Berry ('s genius, as it might be identified in days of yore).

Having sat in as drummer with the Tuckets, I have come to discover that virtually all Dave Clark Five songs use the same drum pattern of maintaining a beat with one stick while doubling its beat with the other (and a roll once in a while). They have also successfully used for their rhythm section in "Glad All Over" and "Bits and Pieces" the foot-stomping motif, originally (which means "earlier") employed in such works as "Hootchie-Kootchie Man" and "Foot Stomping" itself.

Hand clapping appears similarly in Reparata and the Delrons' "Whenever a Teenager Cries," Herman's Hermits' "Can't You Hear My Heart Beat," and the Beatles' "Eight Days a Week" among innumerable others—similarly in that they appear all to participate in the same universal bank of trivial rock hand clapping.[83]

---

[83] So hand clapping gets to be a staple, then repetition is minor mainstream instantiation, hardly noticeable in its unnoticeability. Lots of guys have hits and follow up with immediately recognizable similarity; a second repetition and it's *style* rather than point-to-point repetition (and *style* is itself an echo from the critical reference scene of yesteryear). After a gap of a while with no major repetition/style hit series, the Union Gap has struck with "Woman, Woman," "Young Girl" and "Lady Will Power" (right on the heels of the Beatles' "Lady Madonna"), each resembling the next with such a high level of theme/form isomorphism that replacement on the charts over the air comes off like one continued never-diminishing (except *a priori*) hit. Len Barry's first hit away from the Dell-Vikings and the Dovells, the Pythagorean "1–2–3" ("Come on let's fall in love, it's easy, like taking candy from a baby"), was reiterated in "Like a Baby" and there never was a hit #3.

Stylistically, Conway Twitty resembles closely Elvis Presley, who is echoed by Terry Stafford, who
sounds (just) like Del Shannon. Marianne Faithfull
can be thought of as an anemic Joan Baez; Adam
Faith is essentially the same as Jimmy Soul both
stylistically and nominally. Dee Dee Sharp has resembled the Orlons, who in turn (can) resemble the
Marvelettes. (Adam Wade never sounds different
from Johnny Mathis, although Mel Carter does—
when he sounds like Sam Cooke.) The instrumental
sounds of the Tornadoes and of Johnny and the Hurricanes display no distinct difference. The late great
Buddy Holly (Sam Cooke's late great too) has been
posthumously heard in the singing of Tommy Roe
and Bobby Vee, who has even used Buddy Holly's
Crickets. Donovan's almost initial move was to resemble Bob Dylan in sound and dress. Some vocals
and harmonica solos by Dylan and by John Lennon
have sounded so related that one rock 'n' roll magazine has said that they might be the same person
in different (dis)guises. Jay and the Americans sound
like the Fortunes, who sound like the We Five, who
sound like the Ivy League, who sound like the Beatles,
who sound like the Zombies, who sound like the
Searchers, who sound like the Everly Brothers, who
sound like a multitude of white country blues singers,
who sound like black country blues singers, who can
sometimes sound like urban black blues singers, who
sound like the Rolling Stones, who sound like the
Nashville Teens, who do not even look like Jay and
the Americans.

In ordinary works of fiction, direct quotation in the
form of acknowledgment of an earlier work would be
difficult and would quite likely jar the particular
image-reality context of the work; in creating some-

thing intentionally fictional, where would the mention
of antecedent similar creations fit? Only with the
(almost) recently more intensified ambiguity in art
between art proper and life is the direct quotation
possible. Matisse, in his "Blue Room," quotes a Cé-
zanne painting, in which a tree appears juxtaposed
behind a chimney, by placing smokelike foliage behind a kerosene lamp. By the time of Genet's "The
Blacks" the ambiguity is quite heightened, with men
posing in multileveled disguises and even integrating
themselves with the audience; in a similar context,
Jasper Johns has produced a painted sculpture of a
pair of ale cans, heavier than the real ones but seemingly just as real (and what's a real Ballantine can
anyway and does it depend on who makes it and all
that). Rock 'n' roll realizes that its songs function
within life itself more than any previous art historically ever has and that this secondary level also
functions in the primary context, while all levels are
involved in the art-life problem; to rock this all resolves into a perfectly acceptable *reductio ad ab-
surdum*. That form of repetition which exists in relationships between these levels often takes the form
of quotation. Billy and Lillie's "La Dee Dah" refers
to "Bee Bop Baby," "Special Angel," "Little Bitty
Pretty One," "Lot of Lovin'," "Lips of Wine" (if there
is such a song, otherwise it's "Kisses Sweeter than
Wine"), and "Silhouettes." Bobby Darin's "Splish
Splash," written in less than twenty minutes, quotes
from "Lollipop," "Peggy Sue," and "Good Golly, Miss
Molly." An instrumental, "Stick Shift," quotes Ray
Charles' "What'd I Say," as the San Remo Golden
Strings' "Hungry for Love" quotes a Motown frag-
ment. Little Richard, returning to rock 'n' roll (after

spending years as an evangelist) with a remake of "Whole Lot of Shakin' Going On," opens by screeching, "I been over there in England, and they got a whole lotta shakin' goin' on," in reverence for all that the Beatles, etc., diametrically opposed to his earlier style, have done for rock, enough in fact to coax him back from organized religion. Sonny Bono mentions his conspicuously absent partner, Cher, in the dedication of "Laugh at Me," itself important in the way it transforms actual mere protest within life into art.[84] Bob Dylan plays upon this entire mode of creation with his particularly overstated references, as to the aforementioned "High Heel Sneakers" and Cassius Clay's poetry in "I Shall Be Free #10" and to "What'd I Say" in "Talking World War III Blues." Similarly, both the Beatles and the Stones refer to the Four Seasons' falsetto in their work, the former in "Tell Me Why" (and "Paperback Writer") and the latter in "Mercy, Mercy" (and "Dandelion" and "Take It or Leave It"). Most subtly of all, the Beatles refer to themselves, without discontinuity of context, when in "If I Fell" John Lennon summons the memory of their most representative early work, "I Want to Hold Your Hand," by opening, "If I fell in love with you,/ Would you promise to be true/ And help me understand,/ 'Cause I've been in love before/ And I found that love was more . . . than just holding hands." And their "All You Need Is Love" contains, at the end where everything sounds like the emergence of audibility for weak stations nearby on the radio dial, "We love you, yeah, yeah, yeah."

---

[84] A hick laughed at Sonny's hair, Sonny wrote about it, and it was recorded, all in a day or so. Released, played, and of influence all in the same bundle too.

Internally rock 'n' roll is in appearance the same as it is in the relation of all its members, of course; actually early rock contained within itself the repetition that was to become manifest in external repetition. "Surfin' Bird" is perhaps the most repetitious of all rock works ever, but today cognitive rock has seemingly developed more subtle repetitions (a great fun paradox, understated overstatement) as the opening line of the We Five's "You Were on My Mind" attests, "When I woke up this morning,/ You were on my mind,/ And you were on my mind." This brings to mind Kierkegaard's comment on the relevance of memory in logic: the law of identity is the signification of a familiarity of association.[84a] Rock's

---

[84a] Van Dyke Parks' "The All Golden" reaches its high point with "You will know why hayseeds go back to the country," which suggests that the whole thing up to that point must've been an elusive step-by-step argument for just this hayseed bit. Then, play it over again from the beginning and the initial elusiveness of the words in their syrupy opulence suggests that following the argument would require a real struggle, particularly with its lengthiness recollected from before. And that therefore additional pertinent memory chains would be, at this stage, out of the question. And that only by memory is the original supposed logical consequence interesting enough anymore and that only its contextual visibility is (by memory) what suggests even bothering the step-by-step follow-through. And that even if the consequence (as consequence) and its presumed antecedents (as antecedents) could be embraced together, the connectedness by means of continuity of syrup would be made irrelevant since moment-to-moment memory assertions would negate the ability of syrup to be homogeneous (and hence irrelevant to empirical memory). So it's nice that the hayseed bit turns out to be something you can know only empirically, with the song only yielding hints which you know already.

internal and external familiarity with itself appears almost as a Democritean collection of atoms, just happening to have posited its special loose solidity.

The standard argument people offer against pop art is surprisingly valid. They suggest that once a familiar article such as a soda bottle has been used by art it is left fully devoid of its artistic usefulness; I would only turn this argument backwards toward all art and suggest that once virtually any article of experience, such as a tree, a bowl of fruit, a crotch, or a crucifixion scene, has been portrayed, it is equally played out (and, of course, fully usable as something played out). Influence is a glorified reference to imitation, duplication, plagiarism, forgery. Kurt Schwitters, aiming for artistic negation (and deglorification) at the height of his Merz movement, ended with compositions inevitably close to the compositions of his predecessors Picasso and Kandinski;[85] Robert Rauschenberg, vastly increasing the very palette of the artist, cannot escape bumping compositionally into Mondrian. Aristotle's view of art as imitation at no time really compensates for the common material of both reality and the image of reality. Zeno's paradox of motion viewed as succession of points infinitesimally different and, ultimately, vastly the same, cannot be resolved by the artist either. Rock has, however, formulated a useable poetics of sameness. In "A Symposium on Pop Art"[86] Dore Ashton says,

> The artist who believes that he can maintain the "original status" of an object deludes himself. The character

---

[85] And his *Merz* is second generation Dada. And Merz *equals* Dada, but equals doesn't always equal equals (except always, sometimes, and never).

[86] *Art News*, some time in '64 or '65.

of the human imagination is expansive and allegorical. You cannot "think" an object for more than an instant without the mind's shifting. Objects have always been no more than cues to the vagabond imagination. Not an overcoat, not a bottle dryer, not a Coca-Cola bottle can resist the onslaught of the imagination. Metaphor is as natural to the imagination as saliva to the tongue.

René Magritte's surrealism is evocative of the cliché that is the inevitable eruption of poetry, which itself can erupt. Andy Warhol's placement of repetitions of things side to side in unhampered quality/equality is still an increase in poetic meaning. If an eruption of traditional "quality" is what is here desired; it need not be, but if you want it, it'll erupt for you.

The concept of orgasmic monotony can readily cope with repetition which results in monotony, which in turn can result in boredom. Kenneth Burke has said, "It is the style of men and women whose occupations have become dissociated from the bodily, and whose expression accordingly does not arise from a physical act as the rhythms of a Negro work song arise from the rhythms of Negroes at work."[87] Monotony can serve as a rhythm of all life. Although a moment of insignificance can readily be forgotten, somehow the progression of moments throughout an experience felt as boring can be orgasmic.

Nietzsche's relation of tragedy to archetypal myth cannot itself escape being viewed as repetition. John Lennon's version of Chuck Berry's earlier "Rock and

---

[87] Kenneth Burke, *Philosophy of Literary Form*, Vintage Books, New York 1961, p. 15.

Roll Music" is in this same class of affirmation of validly acceptable archetypes. Affirmation is validation, seemingly suggesting the necessity of this repetition, for how can one affirm without echoing? The Dada manifesto of negation and affirmation as equivalent is here interesting in its implications. In one sense duplication is ridiculous, nonsense in a context of creation, and yet it is the most perfect common affirmation of life, art, and artist. John Lennon has in his work always considered the impossibility of committing an act which predecessors did not also in some way commit, of creating art without a multitude of precedent. After having written *In His Own Write* and *Spaniard in the Works*, Lennon has been, of course, utterly delighted to learn that James Joyce had much earlier written in the same style, since the starting point of a tradition extending into the past is the present (duplication of the tradition of duplication).

The distinction between the traditional and the traditionalistic has often been applied to contemporary painting to designate the difference between simple influence derived from the classically solid past and a *use* of the past (as in the way of punning). To rock, the distinction, while implying an everpresent duality, clearly collapses as a conscious conceptualization of the process of what is basically a case of repetitiveness. Pearlman has considered unconscious "traditionalisticism" to be just traditionalism, but what really is operating here is merely the former made easier. For the traditional to be a pun, and for the traditionalistic to be a more mechanical method of certification of the old, is a great advance.

Even if repetition in the mainstream of rock were to take on overtones of farce, it would merely be a question of analyzing the poetic implications of farce itself. In four years at Stony Brook I watched the same maneuvers attempted by upperclassmen in the seduction of freshman girls and laughed at (and participated in) this *farce*. When the brazen commercialism of rock is what leads to the repetitiveness of rock, since such a pattern would be the easiest and often most assured of success, this could be labeled by both the knowing and unknowing as farce. But farce is itself a quite valid aesthetic judgment, quite expendable as a positive one. And there's the business of repetition in sex, which is part of the source of the erotic impact of rock and which Luther acknowledges as farcical and which Zappa drools over the refusal to drool over.

An article in *Hit Parader* or one of them about Del Shannon states that Del rocketed to fame with "Runaway,""Hats Off to Larry"and "Little Town Flirt" —all tunes he'd written himself and, says the writer, introduced a new sound to the musical scene. "But every once in a while you have to change your material to keep the interest of your fans," the article quotes Del as saying. Although his earliest creations, while ontological and metaphysical masterpieces, contained standard rock 'n' roll repetition, Del Shannon's decision to record remakes of "Handy Man" and "Do You Want to Dance" has given the totality of his work a song-to-song relationship of repetition which has allowed some older roots of rock 'n' roll to become reborn. Rebirth is merely repetition of that which has not had the psychic energy to prolong itself temporally; a renaissance may be a euphemism for kicking a dead horse. The image of "change" as an essential periodic retreat is an implication that sought-after novelty is only to be found in a rejuvenation of the past.

The cover design of the Beatles' *Something New* album contains a visual echo of the title:

Clearly implied is the same relationship of novelty and repetition, focused slightly differently. And *Rubber Soul* is the brazenly multiply-punful erudition of all this.

Both Del Shannon's earliest and latest releases of prominence reveal his notion that isolation may be the end of all metaphysical search. In his first hit, "Runaway," "I'm a-walking in the rain,/ Tears are fallin' and I feel the pain,/ Wishing you were here by me/ To end this misery . . ." While reliving a prolonged past agony, he has seen the inevitability of the mingling of isolation with the entire community of rock. So many groups have recorded works about the rain that his privacy in this weather condition is limited; the Everly Brothers, the Cascades, and Lee Andrews and the Hearts are also there moaning. So Del Shannon continues his properly futile although valuable search, best recounted in a later hit, "Keep Searchin'": "We gotta keep searchin', searchin',/ Find a place to hide,/ Searchin', searchin',/ She'll be by my side . . ."

In *Semantics, Science and Poetry* Richard McKeon cites three possible philosophic approaches stemming from three distinct semantic positions, circumstantial, dialectic, and operational. Rock 'n' roll offers a fourth, often necessarily scorned, merely a loose dialectic, circumstantial, and operational strategy for all three turned upon themselves as many times as desired: the eclectic.

In a world of such things as random values, metaphysical inconsistency, and the constant unavoidable interruption of pure aesthetic perception by random events from within and without, eclecticism is the only valid position (as far as the eclectic choice of the validity grid goes); and other stances may be measured by virtue of their distance from the eclectic. Andy Warhol has devised one of the simplest of all schemes, the selection of a popular motif, from Troy Donahue to floral prints to Campbell's Soup, followed by mechanical multiple reproduction of this motif, with the consistency and inconsistency being a function of the mechanism of creation. Rock 'n' roll, however, cannot rely upon the selling power of random circumlocution of the originally acceptable motif, but turns toward the utter compression of popularly acceptable, yet eclectically arranged, images. "A Little Bit Better" by Herman's Hermits begins with the instrumental introduction from the Four Seasons' Coca-Cola commercial, proceeds with the sinister spirit of the Rolling Stones' "Play with Fire," sung with the vocal style of the Zombies, to the tune of Chuck Berry's "Memphis," and in possession of a title clearly reminiscent of the recent hit by Wayne Fontana and the Mindbenders, "A Little Bit Too Late." Wayne Fontana himself sounded like a clear version of the Kingsmen in his first hit, like the Searchers in his next (and the eventual Mindbenders by themselves sounded like the Beach Boys in "Groovy Kind of Love"). The Beatles have taken from visceral John Coltrane in "Love Me Do," the Four Seasons in "Tell Me Why," Larry Williams in "I'm Down," Bob Dylan and Scottish marching bands in "You've Got to Hide Your Love Away," Bob Dylan in "I'm a Loser," Jefferson Airplane in "A Little Help from My Friends," etc. They have used elderly African drum in "Mr. Moonlight," violins in "Yesterday" and "She's Leaving Home," tympani in "What You're Doing" and "Every Little Thing," packing case in "Words of Love," unusual amplification maneuvers in "I Feel Fine" and "Yes It Is," sitar in "Norwegian Wood," the whole electronic bandwagon in "Tomorrow Never Knows," horn in "For No One," etc. They have used multiple tracking on several records, sometimes so obviously that it can be easily noticed, even as apparent discrepancy (in *Hard Day's Night*, John Lennon's mouth harp line can be heard while he is shown singing lead vocal in "I Should Have Known Better." It does not matter if part of the Beatles' formula is visible; after all, even Lennon's bathing suit is clearly visible in a bathtub scene).

Teilhard de Chardin's philosophy (of education) as expounded in *The Phenomenon of Man* is readily visible in the eclecticism of rock. Just as branches of life strive for continuation, sometimes to succeed and sometimes to reach a dead end, with nature always using a multiplicity of interrelated strivings in its drive toward the "Omega Point," rock 'n' roll is clearly viewable in terms of crude persistence. As long as a fixture "works," it remains in the forefront and shouts its presence; when it ceases to work it is relegated to relative obscurity[87a] until a new context presents itself and allows for favorable reacceptance. No branch can ever really become extinct if it continues

---

[87a] One nice rock move is to transfer prominence of some sort to obscurity of another sort. Sometimes this is due to security in new location, as with the Doors' "Crystal Ship," where the "One Last Kiss" of *Bye Bye Birdie* becomes the inovert, contextually functional and non-sensational, safe-as-milk "Before you slip into unconsciousness, I'd like to have another kiss, another flashing chance at bliss, another kiss." Another publicly unmissible show biz item, "Together," seems so unlikely as the source of the Zombies' "Friends of Mine" that it is taken as merely a reference in passing; and its location in a near-waste track is further assurance of obscurity, with an outside chance of indiscoverability. Like Duchampian hidden undisclosed objects without any material obstacles helping out. At the point when it seemed least likely, Indian classical music became safe for just about forever via George Harrison's "Within You Without You," which turned out to be sitars plus violins in the form of exotic movie music. And it's further safe because it's still absent and unlikely to return as anything but pure external pertinence, which would be a great handicap for its being defamed any further, since the initial superficialization of it has already occurred and requires no repetition except in the form of repetition.

to function in the memory, even dormantly, and if old but undiscovered branches from both the "within" and "without" of things past, as Chardin uses these terms, can always appear in active functions in contemporary rock. The almost forgotten minor 1957 hit by Kathy Linden, "Billy," features an expectation of obscenity in its final passage: "And when I sleep .../ And when I sleep .../ I always dream of Bill." This anxiety of waiting for the impossible use of "sleep" in the last line is not too overtly common in the rock of any period, but suddenly in the summer of 1965 it arose in Tom Jones' "What's New Pussycat?" "Pussycat lips," "pussycat eyes" and other "pussycat" features are mentioned until, with the final verse, the singer is hesitatingly approaching something more openly sexual and finishes, "You and your pussycat . . . nose."

Here is the appearance of a branch of rock with now at least two evolutionary members, a branch which can be called the "pussycat school." Rock has had its "rain school" ("Raindrops," "Teardrops," "Rhythm of the Rain," "Crying in the Rain," "Rain," etc.), a fine eclectic grouping which is ambiguously between the inner and outer world of artistic evolution. Cousin Brucie has used even flimsier branches over the radio, as the branch of all songs with "tell" in their titles ("I'm Telling You Now," "Tell Me," etc.) and that composed of "animal" titles. Rock has implicitly operated on this infinitude of random, eclectic evolutionary pathways, something merely suggested by Thomas Pynchon in *V.* and *The Crying of Lot 49*. The categories "pony tail rock" (the group the Poni-Tails; "What Is Love?" which describes this emotion as "five feet of heaven in a pony tail"; "Chantilly Lace," with its reference to the hair piece as a criterion of socio-sexual adequacy), "fear-of-loss-of-being rock" ("Going Out of My Head"; "Remember"; Dion and the Belmonts' absolutely obscure "I Can't Go On Rosalie") and "march rock" (Little Peggy March; the beat of "I'll Never Dance Again"; the tympani of "Every Little Thing"; "Calendar Girl," which declares, "March, I'm gonna march you down the aisle") are as valid as such categories as "folk-rock," "Motown," "soul music," or even "rock-which-legitimately-renders-human-experience" or "that-which-consist-ently-conforms-to-the-standards-of-classical-music-and-art rock." The San Francisco rock scene grouping (Jefferson Airplane, Grateful Dead, Big Brother and the Holding Company, Quicksilver Messenger Service, Charlatans, late Great Society, Country Joe and the Fish,[88] Moby Grape, some more) was a move to make major significance out of the intersection of the geographical and the geographically nominal in amplification of some actual affinities. This gimmick was used in the case of Boston to generate the merely nominal Boss-Town Sound, which began with many more far more minor groups (hmm, groupings, groups: mere nominality as the identification mark of the more-than-merely-nominal, it's at least a bunch of guys) with irrelevant affinities (Beacon Street Union, Bagatelle, Apple Pie Motherhood, formerly C. C. and the Chasers, Ultimate Spinach, the rest).

At the same time rock has transcended any difficulties encountered in the sociology of knowledge. Because it is so wantonly eclectic, any moment's

[88] Actually from Berkeley.

linear connections can bear contradictory relationships to those of the next without difficulty. "I Can't
Stop Loving You" has succeeded "I've Had It,"
"Tequila" has led to "Too Much Tequila," and "Eve
of Destruction" and "Dawn of Correction" have appeared almost concurrently. William James has seen
the impossibility of viewing philosophical constructs
separate from the temperament which has led to
them; rock has never for a second viewed the con-
struct and temperament as anything but the same
phenomenon, or noumenon, for that matter. Quine has
noted, "The unit of empirical significance is the
whole of science."[89] The unit of rock significance is
the whole of rock 'n' roll, and this is not merely the
result of the failure of reduction, as Hegel's unit of
historical significance as all of history seems to be.
Just as permissible, anyway, is the Jamies' position
in "Summertime, Summertime," which resembles
Hegel's end of history, "No more studyin' history."

The possibility of artistic evolution presupposes
questions of evolving legitimacy and illegitimacy.
Once a new approach has been legitimatized through
acceptance it may be repeated; in the case of rock 'n'
roll the very process of legitimatization itself can per-
tain to rock 'n' roll's total picture, and this repetition
of course is driven through the ground, just as I have
obliterated the concept of repetition by overuse so far
in this very book. But when the mere juxtaposition of
a still extraneous element can lead to either friction
within an art or between it and the audience (which

---

[89] Willard Van Ormond Quine, "Two Dogmas of Empiricism," reprinted from "From a Logical Point of View"
in *Classics of Analytic Philosophy*, McGraw-Hill, New
York 1965, p. 211.

to rock is equally internal), more than simple vulgarity and tastefulness are in question. Moreover, rock
has dealt with legitimacy and illegitimacy in a manner which frequently annihilates the distinction.
Often something is capable of being observed as both
at home in a rock context and utterly alien. When
Elvis Presley followed his early hard core rock hits
with a ballad, "Love Me Tender," the music of which
had been taken from Stephen Foster, several questions arose. Could Elvis now be considered a popular
musician in the "adult," Muzak-oriented sense? Was
rock 'n' roll, not yet too many years old as an identifi-
able movement, on the verge of fusion with this popular mainstream? Or was Elvis about to lose his
designation as a rock 'n' roll singer by flaunting
"legitimate" popular music? Pat Boone built his entire early career on music ambiguously legitimate to
both rock and pop, with titles like "Love Letters in
the Sand," "Anastasia," "There's a Gold Mine in the
Sky," "April Love," "When the Swallows Come Back
to Capistrano," and the Quaker "Friendly Persuasion."
Perhaps he was interested mainly in attaining pop
legitimacy for his own songs, imbued already with a
pseudo-rock energy, without concentrating upon how
that energy itself might enhance what he conserva-
tively judged to be legitimate. The Platters, perhaps
the biggest *group* during the early days of rock 'n'
roll, strained to sound so "legitimate" that they have
completely vanished (until they reemerged for a few
minutes sounding like anonymous Motown, the ra-
cially merely legitimate successor to the legitimate
merely). As rock developed, a significant change took
place: ballads became illegitimate. That is, they were
no longer ambiguous "good" music but were now
eligible for use by rock 'n' rollers. Beauty could now

reenter rock 'n' roll with full "badness" to it; there was no longer a need to equate beauty with the sub-mundanely pretty, as Muzak sort of necessitates: beauty was now free and ontologically energized. "Soul" encounters a similar problem, resolved completely by Ray Charles. His early blues and gospel (which followed his Nat King Cole period) contained an intense, lyrical poignancy that seemed unbreachably removed from rock's trivial sentimentality. Charles' "What'd I Say" and "Swanee River Rock" alienated his work from its earlier more conservative legitimacy and introduced to rock a variety of soul far more "righteous" than that of standard rhythm and blues. One of the first great ballads of this new era of rock was Conway Twitty's "It's Only Make Believe," perhaps an indicator of the self-cognition necessary for such a transition beyond limitation by dubious distinction: "People see us everywhere,/ They think you really care,/ But myself I can't deceive . . . / I know it's only make believe." The problem of delegitimatization has sometimes reduced to a problem of trivialization. The Righteous Brothers' "Unchained Melody" is a song recorded scores of times in a "legitimate" context, but only they (actually only one Brother sings on the record, a dubious trivialization itself) could make it completely renderable through a rock context. The trick was to slur the phrase "your love" in the final "God speed your love to me" so that it is not clearly audible on a faulty transistor radio. Bob Dylan brought his harsh folk songs of protest into rock 'n' roll by following the latter's pleasure principle, recording for single releases (separate from his albums) those songs which were the most aurally pleasing, as "Like a Rolling Stone" and "Positively Fourth Street."

The Beatles have been variously rejected, accepted, and rejected anew, and have seemingly offered a capsule summary of varieties of rock legitimacy.[90] They were castigated as both mods and rockers, praised by Butterfield[91] for being musically superior to the Rolling Stones, rejected by Jean Shepherd for taking themselves overly seriously. Their haircuts were viewed both positively and negatively as either turn-of-the-century Lord Fauntleroy or contemporary Beatnik (in the days before the hippie). Then there was their psychedelic appearance-reality ambivalence. The most far reaching of all the hypothetical considerations of their legitimacy appears in "Fads Undermine Faith" in the Jehovah's Witnesses periodical *Awake!*:[91a]

> This terrifying, hysterical reaction is so typical of the fad in rock 'n' roll singers that the fans are sometimes called "scream-agers." The fans scream also for Britain's other noted groups of entertainers, the Rolling Stones, the Pretty Things and the Animals. When the Animals played in New York City, a news report in the New York *Times* said: "They make the more sedate Beatles look paralyzed." The frantic fans were a volcano erupting with screams, hysterics and objects hurled up onto the stage.
> Is this hysterical screaming and swooning something to which Christian parents want their children to succumb? Not if they want to please God as parents under

---

[90] The Stones are the objectified version of this, with a strengthening of artist-audience dissonance and dissonance dissolution and an intensification of the epistemological confusion pose. There's no way of telling whether Ed Sullivan forced the Stones to sing "Let's Spend the Night Together" as "Let's Spend Some Time Together" or if they set it up themselves or lied about it. Good.

[91] (So) strange as it now seems (that it becomes "supposedly").

[91a] December 8, 1964, p. 6.

divine obligation to bring their children up "in the discipline and authoritative advice of Jehovah." (Eph. 6:4)
Wisely they help their children to learn to manifest the
fruitage of God's holy spirit, which includes "mildness,
self-control." (Gal. 5:22, 23) They firmly steer them
away from fads that undermine those traits.

Localisms out of season. But above all the Beatles
have established the necessity of at least watching the
action. When the Dave Clark Five produced its revival of the Contours' "Do You Love Me?" they
strongly emphasized the phrase "Watch me now!"
What to the Contours meant the observation of the
lamenter's dancing, "now that I can dance," is to the
D. C. Five a metaphor of universal nascent consciousness.

The Beatles have in their own work mirrored the
entire development of rock 'n' roll. They began with
primitive emotional music ("Love Me Do"), went on
to hard core affirmative kineticism ("She Loves You")
and triviality (Ringo's wail, "Okay, George," during
"Boys"), progressed to highly sophisticated arrogance ("I Should Have Known Better") and straightforward profundity ("I'll Be Back"), pessimism
("Things We Said Today"), modern overstated tragedy ("No Reply") and artiness in general ("Day in
the Life"), with Eastern instrumentation ("Norwegian Wood") and the Eastern freakout ("Within
You Without You") and the mere freakout ("Tomorrow Never Knows," "Yellow Submarine") in
there too, while at all stages relating themselves to
the roots with revivals ("Dizzy, Miss Lizzie") and/or
retrogressions to early non-cognitiveness, written by
them ("I'm Down"). The nearly hard sound of "Hard
Day's Night" happened to be a narrow precursor of
harder Stones hits (and the Nashville Teens and
Them and even the Chocolate Watch Band), "Yes-

terday" led to a repository of general sweetness (even good-time music like "Day Dream" by the Spoonful), "Rain" foreshadowed the Association, *Sgt. Pepper* (which ended art forever until somebody forgot) set up an overly wholesome meaningfulness freakout and the Stones' *Satanic Majesties* which set it straight (and ended it forever until somebody forgot) by making an obvious case for the opposite (the bummer and the sloppy bummer). They have noted the evolution of the multitracked recording, with "Help!," a single-tracked recording, at its pinnacle. In this work juxtaposed Greek drama-like lead and chorus seem separate in echoing each other, suggesting that the Beatles' self-restraint in limiting the song to a single track divided between George and Paul, and John, is a self-conscious comprehension of the effect of one being fully capable of echoing himself and yet refusing, a queer addendum to a movement continuously felt throughout rock 'n' roll history.[92] Representing the evolution of rock made conscious of itself (just as Chardin asserts man to be the crown of the natural evolution of the universe, made conscious of itself), the Beatles have made ontologically important the concept of anachronism. (And the concept of mereness of mere evolution and mere consciousness.) Just as the Parmenidean One "at all times . . . both is and is becoming older and younger than itself," Beatlistic unity implies anachronism in its novelty, not just infinite extension of nostalgia. And so on for all of rock.

---

[92] In "Yellow Submarine" John Lennon's disguised sea captain voice answers itself "Aye aye sir," breaking some ice. The Velvet Underground's "Lady Godiva's Operation" carries it the other way by means of splitting up the single voice, sending new voices at random for a word or few into John Cale's lead.

"Keep On Dancing," the nth variation of "Twist and Shout," became[93] a huge anachronistic success, a sudden eruption of a facet of the human eclectic sentiment which can never be fully denied or forgotten. Just as Parmenidean unity can imply inevitable effeteness, it suggests corequisite continuity of functionality, even if as an object of the effete. Amazingly rock is ontological evidence of the unity of the eternal and the utterly transitory. Superfluous evidence. Better.

The uncontested vulgarity of "Surfin' Bird" by the Trashmen is a sign of the growing consciousness within rock 'n' roll itself of its potentially base and vulgar nature. Elvis Presley's "Hound Dog" only implicitly combined relentless beat with vulgar context: "You ain't nothin' but a hound dog,/ Cryin' all the time./ You ain't never caught a rabbit/And you ain't no friend o' mine."[94] Often vulgarity has been a function

---

[93] Fall '65.

[94] Earlier, a more articulate vulgarity is there but one which misses the vulgarity of structural violation. The mid-30's "Ugly Child," as sung by Teagarden or Brunis, is nice as a pack of words.

> You some ugly, you some ugly, you some ugly chile
> You're knock-kneed, crosseyed, bowlegged too
> There's a curse on your family and it fell on you
> Oh your hair is nappy
> Who's your pappy
> You some ugly chile,

but still the full extent of its vulgarity rests upon stylistic givens which only hamper the full comprehension of these words. For Elvis and "Hound Dog," the whole thing is too crudely simple for either the words or the vocal delivery to do anything but enhance each other. And the fact that Mama Mae Thornton recorded it first adds some additional bogus vulgarity understatement.

of the presentation of the context in such a way that the lyrics cannot be comprehended. "Get a Job" by the Silhouettes is an example of such an approach; little or no comprehension is possible at normal speed. This is a problem of intentional carelessness of presentation, practiced extremely often by uninhibited rock performers. But later the very content of rock music is increasingly vulgar, hence more unified.

The Rolling Stones' "Satisfaction" is on first hearing utterly baffling, beyond interpretation with words intentionally elusive (they sound like "flagellation" and words of that ilk) and music loud enough to further obscure them. This first "Satisfaction" experience is one of ambiguous defiance. Eventually the words become audible and understandable, yielding a second-level (lewd) "Satisfaction" (where the word turns out to be " 'magination"). Finally, hearing the song with stereophonic earphones and attending to each (erotic) nuance is the third-level "Satisfaction" encounter. From ambiguous vulgarity embodiment to lewdness to eroticism.

Similarly, rock music has always been basically erotic,[95] while its content has only slowly moved in an increasingly sexual[95] direction. Early rock contains hidden and disguised obscenity.[95] The Elchords' "Pep-

---

[95] "Erotic," "sexual," "obscene" are distinct yet easy to collapse terms under a rock raunch epistemology. The physical and the purely valuational, when conjoined non-cognitively, present a first-class large area of decipherable confusion with lots of conventional self-polarization of both desirability and cold valuation internally and structurally. Equating sex and vulgarity may have

permint Stick" has a chorus creating sound sufficient to cover their culminating verse, "Peppermint stick, will you eat my dick?" which in written form might appear as "Will you be my chick?" Gary U.S. Bonds, using multiple tracks of his own voice, camouflages his spoken introduction to "A Quarter to Three," "Spread your legs baby, here I come." In "Louie, Louie" the Kingsmen produce a relentless vulgar camouflage for such messages as "She's got a rag on" and "I'm never gonna lay her again" appropriately deleted or changed whenever written in the rock mags. A recent release, although part of this older tradition, "Wooly Bully" by Sam the Sham and the Pharaohs contains the vocal cry of "Hand job, hand job" to accompany its other merely suggestive lyrics.

Rock 'n' roll of the last few years, however, has dealt with overt obscenities, sometimes subtle but never hidden (obviousness is becoming more intrinsic and lucid in all facets of rock anyway), at the same

gone out with spats and the Pierce-Arrow (or at least more recently with Cadillac tits), so reintroduction of it or pretending that it still lives without being corny leads, again, to conceptual necrophilia, another term to conjoin to the whole easy uneasy pack. And for the vulgarity to be itself non-sexual yet inseparable from the sexual is additional mere nominal meat with experiential crossover possibilities. (Eric Burdon's "overly" vulgar version of "Rock Me Baby" is good test borderline material.) Sexual smut and scatology can be intersected too . . . (and smut and public profanity) . . . and borderline smut-at-all (maybe between smut and bad-boy nastiness and straight neutrality), with Love being nasty and really forcing the issue (in "Live and Let Live"): "Oh the *snot* has caked against my pants, it has turned into crystal. . . ."

time as *roll* has gone from *rock* in general usage.[96] In "I Get Around" the Beach Boys talk about the sexual prowess of the North American surfer, "We ain't missed yet with the girls we meet," as well as "None of the guys go steady 'cause it wouldn't be right/ To leave the best girls home on a Saturday night." Their rallying cry, "Shut 'em down," has changed from a reference purely to drag racing and has taken on sexual overtones (and become too corny even for the primary context). The Drifters discuss the primary public fornication place in "Under the Boardwalk":

> On a blanket with my baby, that's where I'll be . . .
> Under the boardwalk, people walking above,
> Under the boardwalk, we'll be falling in love.

"I Should Have Known Better" is for the Beatles a song of sexual conquest, as D. Gerber has noted. Paul McCartney's smile in *Hard Day's Night* as the line "If this is love you gotta give me more" is sung gives further relevance to this interpretation. The reference of "I'll get you, I'll get you in the end" is obviously sexual on several levels in the Beatles' "I'll Get You." The Rolling Stones' "King Bee," already mentioned, is a Slim Harpo song not blatant in its original blues context because of copresent blatancy everywhere

---

[96] So what, since this sort of stuff runs through the whole history of jazz lyrics; even the word *jazz*—in the Fanti dialect of West Africa, from whence it came, and in early jazz lyrics (such as "Jazz Me Blues")—sexual intercourse. A good so what, making it all gratuitous at the start, rather than urgent, and in the long run urgently gratuitous and gratuitously urgent.

else in it; but rock offers it a chance to be lewd over-statement. The Stones' "The Last Time" has Mick Jagger singing, "You don't try very hard to please me;/ With what you know it should be easy." Their "Satisfaction" is drenched in a multi-faceted obscen-ity, and most blatant is "I'm trying to make some girl."[97] The McCoys, who record for Bang Records, sing in "Hang on Sloopy" the blatant (pubic) pas-sage, "Sloopy let your hair down, let it hang down on me." Herman's Hermits create a *de facto* obscenifica-tion in their recording of a formerly female song, "I'm into Something Good," as does Cilla Black in her recording of a formerly male song, "You've Lost That Lovin' Feeling," with her fellatio reference, "Baby, baby, I'll get down on my knees for you."[98] And in the Stones' "My Obsession" there's someone so aged "I could almost be your son" and the acknowledg-ment "I blew it now, confession," legitimately smutty in its contextual stubbornness.

Sexuality of a deviant[99] variety has been the unify-ing force in most of the work of the Four Seasons (but

[97] That's if you don't know all the words. When you get to know them and all the written interpretations you find out there's something menstrual in it, so even its apparent hiddenness keeps abreast with the blatant hiddenness of menstruation in general.

[98] Big Brother and the Holding Company's "Down on Me" is the use of traditional material (which could have been obscenified any time a female sang it) undeniably obscenified by Janis Joplin, who can and does do the job for any and all material worded any way at all.

[99] Deviant in a topical sense only and only as an illu-sion (or an illusion of an illusion): rock as a setting for readily destructible and eternally quaintly dull mere fan-tasies of official smut designation, since smut considera-

only as a hint in the Batman-Robin sense), some of whom have been Asbury Park, New Jersey, hairdressers in their thirties. All their songs are sung with an intent to sound female, transcending the need for

---

tion is only irrelevant fun and specific-content smut embodiment (like vulgarity embodiment) is resoundingly absurd and obnoxious enough to be equally irrelevant fun. When the Beatles sing (in "Penny Lane"), "Penny Lane is in my ears and in my eyes" and "In his pocket is a portrait of the queen," and when the Velvet Underground sing (in "Sister Ray"), "Too busy suckin' on the ding dong," that's just irrepressible after-the-fact (-of-overstatement-to-the-point-of-the-obliteration-of-any-fun-in-blatancy-anymore) smut. Which is, after all, what the Stones have always been concerned with even if the general rock public maintenance-of-interest level has acted up peculiarly out of phase with what the Stones have done.

And, might as well mention the Doors just to finish up the footnote. With the Doors it's either sex/smut as objectified smut, or neutral poetry ("weird scenes inside the gold mine") or functional completion (cycle of the orgasm: "Still one place to go, still one place to go, let me sleep all night in your soul kitchen . . ."). And their total seriousness in performance heightens the irrelevant fun and its irrelevance.

And the Velvets' "Lady Godiva's Operation" (a hysterectomy?) is medicinality cooling off (ha) straight porno.

And the Stones' transvestite move (jacket of "Have You Seen Your Mother Baby, Standing in the Shadows?") is the intersection of their mere calculated ostentation (like Mick stuffing an erectile handkerchief in his pants before performances) with the artists-alto-gether-in-the-studio photo tradition of the old days (The Stones're dressed to look old too). And then along comes Zappa (*We're Only in It for the Money*) with his own transvestite parody on the *Sgt. Pepper* cover with the addition of pillow-stuffing pregnancy. (Transvestism as the easiest uncommitted "deviance": all you need is falsetto. In many of their songs, sexual identity is pushed into primary thematic importance, as in "Walk like a Man," "Big Girls Don't Cry" and "Big Man in Town." "Dawn" deals with (self-inflicted) sexual rejection, and "Bye Bye Baby" deals with adultery (particularly heinous to the Catholic Four Seasons). In the sexual tradition of the Four Seasons are the Majors and Lou Christie, whose "Two Faces Have I" masterfully portrays a schizophrenic bisexuality.

But the very core of all true rock 'n' roll reeks obscenity. Legs Forbes has stumbled upon a method of analysis which reveals underlying obscenity in any work of rock, "underlying" only in the sense of not completely voiced. While listening to a New York Giants-Washington Redskins pro football game during the 1962 season, Forbes and I heard announcer Chris Schenkel describe a deceptive move by a player, "He faked him out of his jock . . . (oops!) . . . and his football shoes . . . and his . . ." Later in the game he slipped again: "And he faked him out of his . . . shoes!" The Forbes theory of replacement, in its first interpretive operation, centered about the second blunder. Forbes noticed a similar hesitation in Ringo Starr's vocal from the Beatles' version of "Matchbox": "I been sittin' here wond'rin',/ Matchbox holdin' my . . . clothes." Seeing this awkward expression, Forbes substituted "cock" for "clothes" and stumbled upon a universal receptacle symbol. D. Gerber has applied the Forbes system to "Love Potion Number Nine."

---

costumes, mere specific costumes with mere specific connotations; sexually ambiguous costumes, like Donovan gowns, are readymade connotative ambiguity of satiric/ nonsatiric commitment as well.)

"I told her that I was a flop with chicks,/ I've been
that way since nineteen-fifty-six" becomes an early
reference to narcotics (in fact to dope qua narcotics,
narcotics was once real heinous), "I've been this way
since I got my last fix,"[100] much more appropriate
since a temporal reference restricts interpretation
(and adds to the datedness of its replacement). (Incidentally, dope references were for a while a clue to
the new direction in rock unmentionables,[101] for Bob
Dylan was then mentioning marijuana in such compositions as "Subterranean Homesick Blues.") The
Four Seasons' "Big Man in Town," with its refrain
"I'll be a big man in town,/ Just you wait and see,"
is so patently obscene to begin with that its transformation into "I'll be a big hairy wong" (or "I'll eat the
big hairy wong") conveys to Forbes only a higher
unity.

(The Forbes Law of Replacement is the first formulation of what has generally been understood by
the tacit lawlike assumption that "under the covers"
can be consistently added to the titles of any rock 'n'
roll song, that sort of archaic scene; that is, rock
is obscene, but laughably universally obscene. By
Forbes' method, for any rock 'n' roll context A, including *the* rock context, containing element x, there
exists a far more obscene element x', which, when

---

[100] And Chris Curtis, formerly of the Searchers, who
did a remake of "Love Potion Number Nine," went on
to form a group called the Fix.

[101] Sure as hell was prophetic once upon a time, but
even better now 'cause it's just truistic. And it's nice for
mere time to have affected the substitution for mere time
in "Love Potion #9."

substituted for x, will not radically alter the original context A. Amplification with non-alteration.)

Moreover, "Ain't That Just Like Me" by the Searchers can be examined for its affinities to Marcel Duchamp's sex machine metaphor. The liner notes on the cover of the album on which it appears (sinisterly) beckon: "If you've been looking for an introduction to a brand new musical experience—Meet the Searchers." With this in mind, one can then penetrate the aptly supplied (vaginal) center hole with an erect steel spindle protruding from the revolving turntable. Once the spindle has fully penetrated, the record is in contact with the turntable and they both move with the same precise rhythm. While in such intimate contact, in a perfectly consistent repetitive circle (Aristotle's symbol for perfect motion), the sex machine now produces aural manifestations of the game in which it is indulging. One song is "Cherry Stones," another proclaims, "I know the chicks back home gonna jump and shout,/ When they hear old Tricky Dicky busted out." The tour de force is "Ain't That Just Like Me," which begins in the guise of Mother Goose rhyme. The sexual ambiguity of "put you down" directs the song to its logical symbolic orgasm. There is a long moment of ghastly silence (the moment of intromission), a scream, and then a progression of moaned suggestions, "Take it easy," "Come on, come on now," "Shake it up now," finally "Wooooo!" and "Don't you wanna love me tooooo."

"However, there are two kinds of 'unutterables,' the unutterably good as well as the unutterably bad, with an ambiguous area containing both."[103] Here Kenneth Burke elucidates[104] the ambivalence of that which is labeled obscene; religion is replete with examples of unmentionable divinity, such as the spelling "G-d." Shirley and Lee's "Let the Good Times Roll" suggests a (mere boy-girl) orgy as if it could be nothing other than good, as the title describes, but still it is basically unmentionable, as the line "Come on baby, let's lock the door" suggests, so it's still other than truistic. Just as the rock understatement is so alien that in effect it becomes itself the most extreme form of overstatement, ordinary double entendre concealed offenses burst into blatancy in the realm of rock. The Impressions' "Amen" slides from an explication of the life of Christ to a final "Keep on pushing now, hallelujah now," a quotation from their traditionally obscene "Keep On Pushing," showing the intrinsic common origin of religion and common sexuality, a ubiquitous readymade. Bob Dylan is quite cognizant of this inevitability and often reveals his outright puns, quite like Cassius Clay yelling, "Get up, you bum," to a fallen Sonny Liston.

Truth may be unutterable in the sense of far beyond communication or in the sense of too blatantly immediate to be formulated into communicational rudiments. The paradoxical use of this as the implicit mode of communication has been a definitive quality of music in general and, even more (as pop paradoxicality), of rock 'n' roll. Someplace between the incap-

---

[103] "Dear Miss Morse" by Pearls Before Swine is double unutterability of another sort. Their coded spelling of F-U-C-K is both commentary on conventional public censorship and shy seduction of a chick.

[104] *Philosophy of Literary Form*, p. 46.

turably transitory and the imperceptibly infinite is the stage upon which something is acted out between the ungraspably holy and the forgettably profane. This is Cannibal and the Headhunters' "Land of a Thousand Dances"; this is the realm of the unknown tongue.

In September 1963 Memphis Sam Pearlman and I came across a *Time* review of a Ray Charles concert. Lauding his amazing ability to communicate to any audience and through any type of material with his awesome depth of emotionality, the article mentioned, "Southern gospel experts have said that he speaks the unknown tongue." Trying to isolate the "unknown tongue" in his work, we decided that his introduction to "I Got a Woman," as recorded at Newport in 1958, best fulfilled the standards of what an unknown tongue should be able to accomplish. He says: "Well sometimes, sometimes I get a little worried,/ But I just wanna tell you it's all right/ Be . . . cause I got a woman 'way over town . . ." The transition from the static body of the introduction to the pulsating kineticism of what follows is carried out by the particular syllabication of "Because": (the definitive primal unknown tongue).[105]

Hence the material cause of the unknown tongue consists of at least various musical-verbal maneuvers for transition. In "Talking 'Bout You," Ray Charles uses one unsustained note (in early circumstances similar to "I Got a Woman") to convey the dynamics of the confrontation of forces similar to those of his primal tongue song.

---

[105] Elvis Presley's version of "I Got a Woman" handles it similarly: "*Well-l* . . . I got a woman . . ."

In "If I Fell" the Beatles use a drum tap by Ringo[106] to connect Lennon's solo with the vocal and instrumental entrance of the others (as well as early with later early Beatles via the hand-holding cognition just preceding Ringo). The harmonies achieved by the Beatles together in this song around the later word "love" produce a fine verbal unknown tongue, sounding (suddenly) absolutely intense without physical straining for intensity.

An unknown tongue played on the lead guitar on the Byrds' "Eight Miles High" is reinforced verbally by the metaphoric distance of the opening phrase, "Eight miles high . . . and when you touch down," producing a masterful dual (musical/verbal) tongue. Along the same lines, but with an evocative silence in between, the Stones stop playing and return with Mick Jagger's vocal reentry in "Can I Get a Witness" thusly: "Let me hear you say 'yeah, yeah' . . . Up early in the morning . . ." One of the finest Motown tongues is found in the Four Tops' "I Can't Help Myself" rather diffusely during the growing tension of one passage going into "Sugar pie honey bun." In the Yardbirds' "For Your Love," unknown tongues are produced by the juxtaposition of three incongruous sections of major length. The unknown tongue of the Zombies' "She's Not There" is a gasp. That of the Ivy League's "Tossing and Turning" is felt as part of a crescendo toward the end of a group of grammatically separable (but contextually unified) lines sung with increasing speed and increasingly rich harmonies: "What ya gonna do tonight/ Nobody to hold you

---

[106] Love uses Michael Stuart for the same kind of drum stuff (the really spiffy roll) in "Red Telephone."

tight/ Are you lonely . . ." The very first note of "All My Loving" is made into a tongue by Paul McCartney, expressing overtly the abruptness of a confrontation with being, interrupting a revery over non-being, which later becomes apparent with the unfolding of the song, with the context of meaning of the entire song making the use of an opening note (which in *all songs* is an abrupt break with silence[107]) as an unknown tongue:

> *Close* your eyes and I'll kiss you,
> Tomorrow I'll miss you,
> Remember I'll always be true,
> And then while I'm away
> I'll write home every day
> And I'll send all my loving to you.

Like the last reverberation of an orgasm, which the song connotes, the very last note of the Searchers' "Ain't That Just Like Me" is tonguelike. The final dissonant "yeah" of the Beatles' "She Loves You" is a staggering moment of stasis at the end of an otherwise rhythmically aggressive song and before the si-

---

[107] Always conscious of this sort of entry problem, the Beatles use a really long drawn out (quiet-the-audience/ get-the-band-started) entrance into the initial "Sgt. Pepper" cut and, hence, into *Sgt. Pepper* proper. The "space entry" by the Stones into "2000 Light Years from Home" from "Gomper" is the metaphor spatialization of this move. The Buffalo Springfield's sloppy discontinuous merely musical equivalent move from "Everydays" to "Expecting to Fly" becomes airily tonguelike spatialized by the content of the latter and its timbre distance from the mere airiness of the former.

lence which follows (both as a single recording and on the American album in which it appears last[108]).

The perception of particular change or movement within a continuous flow involves the perception of specific points at separated moments of attention, plus the apprehension of difference (*that* there has been change or movement). Music (of any degree of regularity), by fragmentizing change and motion as felt sequences of moments attended to into units of sound and silence in audible vacillation, controls, more strongly than a mere continuum, an observer's attention, and thus the perception of the particular change and movement. In music there are, additionally and necessarily, momentary successions of non-configurations in alternation with successions of formal configurations.

An unknown tongue is an element of transition which compels, structurally and spiritually, (Heraclitean) forces or principles of opposition. The best visual representation of this conception of the tongue occurs in the films *Hard Day's Night* and *Help!* during chase sequences. In the former film, John, Paul, George and Ringo rush from a crowd of pursuers into a dead end, whereupon they merely turn around 180 degrees and escape by running headlong into the crowd. Meanwhile, their manager, by contrast, struggles in a futile attempt to open a mere container of milk. In the same film they sit in a railroad car playing cards and are suddenly engaged in singing "I Should Have Known Better," and just as suddenly they are back again playing cards. In *Help!*, they

---

[108] Last note of "Day in the Life" is the easily automatic full distention of this.

slide down a slope and then almost immediately re-appear as uniformed musicians in an orchestra.

But music, even if only empirically so because of historical conditioning, is more capable of polarities essential for abrupt change than visual arts because of its fragmentized (but tight) structure, the rapidity of succession of these fragments possible before a per-ceiver, and the immediacy of the relationship of the perceiver to the art object, additionally allowing the greater persistence of parts through a totality (in memory). Compared with the visual arts, music's components are simply located and diffusely located, and quantitatively denser. Once music has become regular and change can be felt against a patterned background, all its Heraclitean flux of Democritean atoms can be intensified in contrast to this regular background. But musicians like John Cage and Or-nette Coleman have abandoned an explicit regularity for one merely implicit and relative within a chaos of irregularity, anti-regularity, a-regularity, and random regularity. But the most radical form of chaos is order, in fact a permanently contingent order. At any time in history music is such an Anaxagorean crystalliza-tion from the haze of psychological temporality; but today, after a music of paradigmatic "disorder" has become historically prominent, a music with a high degree of regularity, particularly one whose regularity becomes ultimately monotonous repetition, is even more radical. It has changed into even more a vehicle in which *change* is so vital. Here is where rock 'n' roll enters. All music is overstatement of a sort, any music after Cage and company is overstated overstatement, and rock 'n' roll is overstated overstatement taken as subtlety (as well as itself).

Rock 'n' roll using the unknown tongue is music on all the ordered levels that music may attain. Possessing an invincible relentlessness, it assumes an original ground from which one is to move to secondary and n-ary grounds, objectifiedly undaunted by the displacement and often either more powerful ("turned on") or satisfied, that is objectifiedly experientially enriched. The confrontation (/resolution) of opposing forces is akin to that in tragedy, except tragic man's transition leaves him affected differently from the rock 'n' roller's transition by way of the unknown tongue. Prometheus' confrontation with an opposing force leaves him merely himself, writhing on the rock, placed there in "too unsubtle" a manner; only the daily reappearance of his liver and the eagle is tonguelike.

Tragedy originates in musical polarities; rock finds instant Heraclitean opposition to be conveniently "just there" after the fact. The metaphysics of opposition offered by the Beatles' "Rain" exemplifies rock's attitude toward essential experiential prerequisites used as a manipulable grid of analysis after the fact which has such experiential cash value after the fact:

> If the rain comes, they run and hide their heads,
> They might as well be dead;
> If the rain comes, if the rain comes.
> When the sun shines they slip into the shade,
> And sip their lemonade;
> When the sun shines, when the sun shines.
> Rain, I don't mind.
> Shine, the weather's fine.

Schematized, the unknown tongue experience has precisely four components: 1) Change, abrupt movement, sudden transition structurally and experientially; 2) Musical awe; 3) Objectified awe, mere awe, "awe," awe at awe itself; 4) Taxonomic urgency;[109] 3) and 4) might be grouped as linking the fusion and confusion of the structural and the valuational with objectivity variations in these elements. Classical music most assuredly possesses the unknown tongue (when heard by a contemporary rock ear) and undoubtedly has also classified it and schematized its emergence. Jazz pianist Thelonious Monk's "Ruby My Dear" contains several manifest tongues which result, consciously "creatively," or mechanically or inadvertently, as he meanders around the keyboard. Even the final portion of "The Star-Spangled Banner" has been played with an unknown tongue. But only in rock 'n' roll is the unknown tongue the natural, logical outcome of development. And only in rock does the tongue define its own importance self-referentially (as by criteria 3 and 4). Thus, although schematizable, tongue manipulation is not fully reducible mechanically to classical simples; this "concreteness" must contain with it an aura of "concrete mystery," almost a pop "purposiveness without purpose"[110] by mere designation.

(That which is "unknown" about the unknown tongue is the manner in which it trespasses across the realm of separation between primary and secondary state. Here is where the obscene, erotic face of rock 'n' roll is united with a truly sexual structure. The

---

[109] Taxonomic urgency: you know, you just gotta label it *tongue*, as in *"There's a tongue."*
[110] Kantian aesthetic jargon.

greatest and most familiar analogue to the unknown
tongue (anyway) in mere human experience is the
(mere) orgasm. An orgasm, as we all know, arises
slowly as it builds up and suddenly strikes, leaving
one back on earth but perceptively richer. The compression of neural experience in an orgasm is mirrored
in rock's compression of eclectically selected elements
into juxtapositions which yield unknown tongues.)

In various musical contexts, the unknown tongue
plays numerous roles by itself and in conjunction
with an eclectic selective attention in structuring
musical experience with a supply of focal points. In
the context of repetition, novelty is a surprise. Given
novelty and structural variety, repetition is surprising. Within a framework of mixed novelty and repetition, surprise is of mixed variety and expected surprise emerges, as well as frustration of such expectation. By a relevance criterion of a selective attention
it may be that nothing is a surprise or that, if it is,
surprise is not relevant to the musical experience. Or,
similarly, everything may be relevantly felt as change
which is excitingly abrupt and surprising even if not
intended by the musicians involved to evoke such a
response. And a song drenched in tongues may be ignored. This is all part of a selective rock consciousness.

It might seem that an awesome section of a work
could be regarded as only an awesome non-tongue;
but rock systematization allows for salvaging anything, even if by rationalization.[111] It would be easy

---

[111] Rock is the best-worst suited for being verbally dis-
sected because it doesn't matter, and at the same time
rock analysis can be validly insipid and harmless-harm-
ful enough to be irrelevant to rock as music.

to accept the category of awesome non-tongue or to claim (admissibly) a new category, erroneous tongue. Yet even more circuitously is full legitimate extension of creative taxonomy carried out. Gabriel Marcel speaks of historical past and personal psychological past as an essential part of musical reference. "And it can be shown that anytime musical creation consists first of all in conjuring up in us a *certain past*."[112] "In this instance, the past is not any particular section of an historical becoming more or less explicitly assimilated to a movement in space, such as a film sequence. It is rather the inner depths of oneself, inexplicable with respect to what the present not only arranges, but again, and most particularly, qualifies. These multiple pasts are really sequential perspectives according to which life can be relived, not as a series of events, but to the extent that it is an indivisible unity which can only be apprehended as such through art—art, or perhaps love."[113] Hence the switch from involvement in the "now" of a song to a past personal modality is a transition capable of being called an unknown tongue. "Quotation tongues" are eruptions of reference, as to parts of other songs. The final segment of the piano introduction to the Stones' "Flight 505" refers to their earlier familiar "Satisfaction." A middle passage of the Beach Boys' "Wouldn't It Be Nice" echoes a small portion of their slightly less familiar "Help Me Rhonda" (this is a tongue designation historically conditioned).

---

[112] Gabriel Marcel, "Bergsonism in Music," in *Reflections on Art*, ed. by Suzanne K. Langer, Oxford University Press, New York 1961, p. 147.

[113] Marcel, *op cit.*, p. 149.

In the case of any awesome non-tongue, the reference, if there is reference, is to abstract awe or formal awe; this requires a collapse of form and content. Although such a roundabout quotation tongue is, by classical standards, just a confusion of levels, it is experienceable as such in this very form-content fusion/confusion context, a convenient tool of analysis after the fact anyway. Similarly, form can be taken as field, and an entire song can be treated as a "tongue field," packed with inevitability and real movement, but no concrete moments of eruption, a Heraclitean One with no instances of concrete realization. The Kinks are practitioners of the tongue field, as in "Something Better Beginning," and the quotation tongue field, as in "Where Have All the Good Times Gone?"

Metaphorically, or merely metaphorically, as well as concretely, the rock tongue presents simultaneous prerequisite and corequisite twin infinities; the reliance upon such a short temporal span itself as a focal point of order in the song points towards the linking of the infinitesimal with the finite and infinite. After all, the movement of (once again) orgasm is more or less diffusely instantaneous, a definite *now* abruptly following a plunge toward a future, yet one desires to expand it as to infinity. Thus is the Beatles' "I'll Be Back" a masterpiece (okay) of this genre:

> You know
> If you break my heart I'll go
> But I'll be back again
> 'Cause I
> Told you once before goodbye
> But I came back again.

I love you so—oh,
I'm the one who wants you
Yes I'm the one who wants you
Oh-oh-oh-ho oh-oh-oh-ho

Oh you
Could find better things to do
Than to break my heart again
This time
I will try to show that I'm
Not trying to pretend.

I thought that you would realize
That if I ran away from you
That you would want me to (o)
But I got a big surprise
Oh-oh-oh-ho oh-oh-oh-ho

Oh you
Could find better things to do
Than to break my heart again
This time
I will try to show that I'm
Not trying to pretend.

Oh
I wanna go
But I hate to leave you
You know I hate to leave you
Oh-oh-oh-ho oh-oh-oh-ho

Oh you
If you break my heart I'll go
But I'll be back again . . . .

There is return e(x) ternally, hence constant instantaneous transition via unknown tongue; one leaves, but must return. Pseudo-syllogistically, the song suggests, in a convenient form-content unity, the disappearance of *a priori-a posteriori* distinctions in the confrontation with this mystical force. Words cannot even fully describe the situation, nor can music alone sum up its force, hence the song is both fully expressive and fully expressive of its inability to be so; one is in control and yet subservient, arrogant and yet absolutely vulnerable. The song seems to extend to infinity in both directions in its alternating disturbance and peace. (The very process of describing this has left me strangely enervated.)

Often an unknown tongue is *felt* as merely implicit in a song but excluded explicitly, creating the tension of the meta-unknown tongue. In such a case the tongue is no longer unknown but even expected, and its exclusion is one of the high points of metaphysical overstated understatement. Different level surprise if at all. The Beatles' "If I Fell" judged as a whole is in this category, as are "The Tracks of My Tears" by the Miracles and a segment of the Beach Boys' "Surfin' Safari," "Let's go surfin' now/ Everybody's learning how/ Come on a safari with me." The greatest paradigm masterpiece of this school is the Beatles' "You Like Me Too Much" (George):

> Though you've gone away this morning
> You'll be back again tonight
> Telling me there'll be no next time
> If I just don't treat you right
> You'll never leave me and you know it's true
> 'Cause you like me too much and I like you.

You've tried before to leave me
But you haven't got the nerve
To walk out and make me lonely
Which is all that I deserve
You'll never leave me and you know it's true
'Cause you like me too much and I like you.

I really do
And it's nice when you believe me
If you leave me
I will follow you and bring you back where you
   belong
'Cause I couldn't really stand it
I'd admit that I was wrong
I wouldn't let you leave me 'cause it's true
'Cause you like me too much and I like you.

In the transition from "And it's nice when you believe me" to "If you leave me" the listener feels the mounting pressure and anticipates an unknown tongue. It does not arise from Ringo's drumming, for he actually reduces his brushwork over the passage. And the connection between the line ending with "believe me" and that ending with "leave me" dematerializes when the latter connects to "I will follow you . . ." Quite a spiritual gap has been traversed without an overt tongue. There is no rest from the business at hand and the pressure incredibly continues. Like a Freudian flight dream, the song sustains a constantly growing, pulsating erection.

"The hidden harmony is better than the obvious"[114] proclaims Heraclitus. Modified, this is a basic criterion

[114] Heraclitus, fragment 116, in Philip Wheelwright, *Heraclitus*, New York 1964, p. 102.

for evaluation of particular instances of the unknown
tongue, which is both hidden and obvious; that is,
merely hidden and obvious to a tongue-aware musical
scrutiny, in fact obviously hidden (as well as exclusively obvious). The employment of an absurd
taxonomic jargon insures that the unknown tongue
experience be unhindered by the experience's taxonomic character. Often the specific label bears a "cute"
and/or banal relationship to the material of the song,
for it to be both fully relevant and fully harmless in
application. For instance, the Beatles' "Yellow Submarine" contains (wave-bobbing) "aquatic unknown
tongues." Similarly, the tongue type may be a "philosophical" label, hence as bizarre as most philo-
sophically derived labels (such as "ontological" or
even "authentic") when used in ordinary (that is,
common and "unphilosophical") language contexts;
one such tongue is the aforementioned meta-unknown
tongue (or simply the meta-tongue), a quite structurally important tongue, thus using borrowed philosophical jargon also as an elevating factor, making
use of the objectified heights of the out-of-context
connotation of "philosophy."[115] The brevity and
quickness of the average rock recording also makes
taxonomic abstraction too rapid an experiential accompaniment to alter the unaccompanied immediacy
of mere tongue exposure. I have found in trying to
reveal a particular unknown tongue to casual listen-

---

[115] The United States of America's "American Metaphysical Circus" is a typical overuse of philosophical
jargon as spookiness, but at least its semantic misuse
here makes it doubly irrelevant. (And the very term
metaphysics is merely a bibliographic composite for next-
to-(Aristotle's-)*Physics*, so a nude syntactical use of
metaphysical as mere adjective is appropriate.)

ers that a "That's it" is not enough; this brevity hence even makes the experimental data of a tongue epistemological analysis immediately *repeatable*.

The analysis which Aristotle uses in application to dramatic forms, which are sufficiently long enough for difficulty to arise, contains a jargon which, once familiar, actually molds (even too regularly, which might be judged negatively) the experience of movement and change in viewing actual instances of tragedy. "These should each of them arise out of the structure of the plot itself, so as to be the consequence, necessary or probable, of the antecedents. There is a great difference between a thing happening *propter hoc* and *post hoc*."[116] Such a systematic understanding of plot rigidifies audience anticipation and leads to such (perhaps destructive) alterations of the art object, as into one which transforms discovery into merely discovery of a new taxonomic opacity, or one whose interest is now the particularization of such taxonomic opacity. Robert Brumbaugh, in describing the University of Chicago project in the 1930's to apply an "all-inclusive" grid of analysis to art, specifically that of Aristotle's four causes, states, "One might, for example, concentrate on *expression*, the author as efficient cause; on *style*, the medium, the material cause; on *idea*, a Platonic notion of truth or message as a disembodied formal cause; or on *audience effect*, a rhetorical reduction of the work of fine art to a remote final cause."[117] But what becomes of the work of art when it is grasped for its *style*,

---

[116] Aristotle, *Poetics*, 1425a–17.
[117] Robert S. Brumbaugh, *The Philosophers of Greece*, Thomas Y. Crowell, New York 1966, p. 202.

128 The Aesthetics of Rock

medium, material cause or *audience effect taken as rhetorical reduction of fine art to a remote final cause?* Its aesthetic opacity is now a philosophical opacity, or a mixed aesthetic-philosophical opacity. This is trivially true for the object of any philosophical analysis. But in the field of temporal art experienced in time, an *Oedipus Rex* upon which can be superimposed a convenient grid of analysis such as Aristotle's becomes *Oedipus Rex, tragedy* or *Oedipus Rex, tragedy each part of which can be taxonomically labeled promptly.*

The whole analysis-of-music bit sort of calls for the use of a pack of words to tack onto a pack of sounds juxtaposed with another pack of words. Every creep who has ever bothered with that has to groove on how silly, in the good sense, the whole operation has to be. How do you *talk* about music, anyway, particularly when. . . . It's also a matter of temporality and analysis, that scene. Aristotle, the original pumper, gives you a hunk of quasi-decent explicit categories that make it so that you alter the way you see drama forever, like you see it as Aristotelian sculpture drama, which is a groove but it drags too. So you take the concept of the rock track: it's short,[118] it's not a long tedious grinding thing-in-front-of-you that you not only have to pay attention to to keep up with but where labels sort of imprison your whole

---

[118] Part of the original basic rock move is the short track. It's easier to take a short track and pack it pumice-full with goodies than a long one; and then the long one takes on too much of the temporal ordeal drama aura. But some rock guys, notably the Doors and the Who, have been able to carry the move into that.

temporal thing with the expectation bummer because they're so easy to stick on legitimately. But you can urinate on Sophocles anyway (the Doors do).

The superimposition of explanatory labels is, how-ever, spiritually acceptable in rock,[119] just as is the hair length and color of a rock performer grasped in conjunction with his musical performance. It has been suggested that no work on aesthetics, beginning with the *Poetics*, has ever done justice to the total work of art, including those elements which are not artistic. Perhaps a consideration of adventitious causes would improve the situation. But, in opposition to Aristotle's implicit criterion of comparative relevance whereby adventitious causes would have to remain essentially irrelevant in order for the truly relevant causes to be prominent and retain their relevance, in rock the ad-ventitious may be the prominent, although still irrel-evant. Thus such coloring devices as unknown tongue designation become relevantly irrelevant, while the aspects formally important in terms of Aristotelian analysis become correspondingly irrelevantly relevant. Consequently, rock may utilize the tools of a non-musical art such as drama to interpret the music. Drama being historically and structurally derivative from music, its grid of analysis as used after the fact of derivation and even in ignorance of this origination is structurally analogous to rock's relevance reversals.

---

[119] The single-word commands, "break" and "blow," in the Stones' "Complicated" and "Cool, Calm, Col-lected," respectively, bolster transitions to instrumental breaks which would ordinarily be just the same old thing but which are now the same old thing labeled at the point of impact.

The rock label procedure thus produces a multi-leveled object for discovery, extended beyond the temporally fragmented to the taxonomically fragmented. Selective attention (in any form) to a moment of a temporal organic whole (even one quite short in duration) must obviously alter the whole as experienced. Bergson observes: "Might it not be said that, even if these notes succeed one another, yet we *perceive* them into one another and that their totality may be compared to a living being whose parts, although distinct, permeate one another just because they are so closely connected? The proof is that, if we interrupt the rhythm by dwelling longer than is right on one note of the tune, it is not its exaggerated length, as length, which will warn us of our mistake, but the qualitative change thereby caused in the whole of the musical phrase."[120] However, the destruction of musical primarity has given way to a new level of Schopenhauerian potency. When "destroyed," rock is legitimately destructible. Musical continuum consciousness becomes tongue plot consciousness, with field now becoming form. One may say *so what* to the loss of merely musical integrity as readily as he says *so what* to the intrusion of intellectualization. Indeed, such a listener's relevance criterion is at least permissible, considering the rock content's dominance over systematic form (when convenient).

Yet there are occasions in which rock presents itself as vulnerable to Aristotelian analysis, yeah sure. Aristotle points out, "Even tragedy itself is in part Complication and in part Dénouement: the incidents

---

[120] Henri Bergson, *Time and Free Will*, London 1910, p. 100.

before the opening scene, and often also of those within the play, forming the Complication; and the rest of the Dénouement. By Complication I mean all from the beginning of the story to the point just before the change in the hero's fortunes; by Dénouement, all from the beginning of the change to the end."[121] Such a form superimposed upon experiential expectation entails struggle and serious (perhaps irrelevantly serious) tension. The rock audience's general rejection of cumbersome structural resolution is akin to not bothering to resolve tricky dialectics in philosophy because it would be inevitable and thus not worth the bother. Uncomfortable musical resolution contexts are therefore the occasion for the "anti-tongue." The most prominent anti-tongue song is the Association's "Along Comes Mary," whose words have been confusedly obscure enough to prevent semantic resolution; sheet music accounts of the words are just irrelevant to the song as *heard*. Paul Revere and the Raiders are another big anti-tongue (or you could say anti-unknown tongue) group. With their anti-tongue there's slick tension as to how that which obviously must be inevitably resolved musically will actually be resolved; it's like sticking overly obvious tongue indicators in your face so the multilevel thing can't be more than merely structural. But then again, tongue as mere structure is sort of the whole pre-rock musical scene anyway.

The anti-tongue extended to the meta-musical, interpretive level may manifest "tongue pressure," which establishes complication-resolution interplays between levels of tongues themselves; the only ex-

---

[121] *Poetics*, 1455b–23.

ample of full tongue pressure is the Beatles' "Doctor Robert," although the break in Donovan's "Epistle to Dippy" contains some degenerate tongue pressure, the perfect thing to be degenerate. The Association, by cleaning up semantic obscurity inside a tongue pressure structure, and thus reintroducing semantic obscurity (on the level of form-content interaction this time), have produced anti-tongue pressure in "Pandora's Golden Heebie Jeebies."

Parallel is the use of complication neutralized to the level of mere repetition or background drone as a basis for objectified inevitability, after which any abrupt resolution is miraculous in its *actual* appearance, both as relief and as relief plus other peripheral tongue qualities fortunately accompanying it. Success-in-itself is given up to gain access to teleological success by comparison. The single-note repetition at the beginning of the Beatles' "Good Day Sunshine" gives way to an entry by Paul McCartney which can be said to *burst* into being. The Association has contributed elaboration of even this ground, with their great "irrelevance tongue," aptly demonstrated in its transitions through tedium and insipidness in "Looking Glass" and "Another Time, Another Place."

Also inherent in the notion of the unknown tongue is the possibility of a whole attaining valuational significance through the possession of merely one fragment of "formal" excitement. For instance, the movie *Seven Year Itch* is without much value except for the appearance of a minor character whose wondrous name, Krahulik, gives to the movie vast significance. A woman on *I've Got a Secret* once proclaimed that

she had seen *Alexander's Ragtime Band* thirty-five
times merely to see Don Ameche (who to her must
have manifest the unknown tongue throughout something otherwise quite dreary). One of the Beatles'
worst performances is their remake of Carl Perkins'
"Everybody's Trying to Be My Baby," but, however,
it possesses a nice enigmatic guitar ending which by
its position at the end of the work insures anxious
listening. On the other hand, "Chains," also one of
their worst efforts, possesses an even nicer beginning
and is thus "worthwhile" although greatly anticli-
mactic. The Beach Boys have truly taken seriously
the need for tongue replacement in lieu of tongue
inclusion.[122] Virtually all their works contain short
moments of greatness. Their "Dance, Dance, Dance"
contains a dandy "alright" shout, "When I Grow Up
to Be a Man" features a fine summation of pessimism
at the end, and "Fun, Fun, Fun" ends with that ecstatic "woo-woo" repetition. One of the most frequent
manifestations of this system of general intensification (plus out-of-context particular intensification)
is the sale of albums where *one* selection or even the
cover or liner notes is the basis of sale and even
enjoyment.

Just for the sake of historical reductionism, all
varieties of the tongue can be found in the work of
the Beatles. Several groups have set up mutual quotation tongue fields between each other, and the Beatles
have been the earliest to be successful with any sort

[122] With the Beach Boys in *Pet Sounds* and *Smiley
Smile* you've got the mere fact of a specific *other* music,
Beach Boys rock classical form, unavoidably tongue-
laden just for the sake of tongue-subservient structure.

of self-quotation tongue field on the merely musical level.[123] "Yellow Submarine," with its aquatic tongues rising and falling as an object bobbing about on the ocean, hints that their future course may be a new emergence or final or provisional sinking, introducing the additional temporal sense of prophecy. As the unofficial masters of the tongue as a conceptual totality, covering the whole spectrum, the Beatles even use tongues where other groups have attempted to show the impossibility of tongue interest. Take "2000 Light Years from Home," it's "Baby You're a Rich Man" without tongues and not far enough afield from the tongue universe to be beyond the tongue. Now if they did it as a move out of the tongue universe along with all other universes, getting progressively further away . . . but it's nice and homey that they don't and ironic as a chair to see the Stones homey.

The Stones have always been different from a standard tongue orthodoxy, and that's swell. But they regularly use stuff like the Jagger Crescendo, exemplified by the "You know I'm smiling baby" which carries from a static falsetto passage to the group's full reentry in "Let's Spend the Night Together." A single subtly intensified word, "from," produces a moment of forced concentration in "Ruby Tuesday." With this instead of the strict tongue, they get into second-orifice tongues by hitting you with tongues which appear such that their appearance itself is tonguelike, right? So the big change in "I Am

---

[123] The Stones, by mere repetition-longevity have done it since. And everybody does it on the mere (non-musical) overall quotation level (like the Mamas and the Papas with "Creeque Alley": "Cass was a sophomore, planned to go to Swarthmore . . .").

Waiting" is a big big big change, utterly brutal in such a sweet song. In melodically and verbally referring to the Kinks, who are the big boys in the quotation tongue field field, and in being plagiaristic in general, any use of the quotation tongue is such on top of being brutally plagiaristic as well: "Take It or Leave It" from "Ring the Bells," "Connection" from "Party Line." At the end of "Something Happened to Me Yesterday" Mick's reference to the fact of straight spoken reference is erroneous ("Our producer, Reg Thorpe") at the same time that it is very much like "a funny lookin' dog with a big black nose" (in "Snoopy vs. the Red Baron") and certainly not that at all. But the Stones aren't post-tongue as much as they're pre-tongue in a post-tongue world.

And who's post-tongue? The Doors, Love, stuff like that. With Morrison, you've got verbal and vocal freakouts and explosions working at an intensity so different from the moves in the tongue structure of the instrumental thing that it hits too thick to be just a tongue, the tongue is overshadowed. But sometimes there's this overshadowing hitting in fusion with the traditional internal tongue motif anyway. Love uses tongues which are irrelevant merely as tongues because they have series of entire tongue universes standing around too big for the detail to matter in kind; Arthur Lee's tongues are not straight reference tongues but actually tongues by reference, reference to specifics, reference to the very fact of music as absurd.

The San Francisco rock scene is sort of an attempt of tongue avoidance if anything; it's sort of an attempt to work out a rock with a pre-tongue structure but without a tongue acceptance principle, like check out "Morning Dew" by the Dead, the tongues don't hit as hard as the hardest part of a song would imply by rock implication. That's sort of the opposite of what the Byrds do with Dylan stuff. But Moby Grape has as wide a tongue move in operation as the Beatles and they even compress about three or four albums worth of tongue maneuvers into one, their first (but then their tongue pertinence diminished slightly when they did the same thing all over again, compressing the same whole bunch into their second, *Wow*). And the Grape of course understands the short track as a move.

Anyway there's a whole bunch of tongue transcendence and tongue playedoutness too of course, tongues can become carpentry too. What do you think "Bike Boy" is? Or the Soft White Underbelly? Or "The Fool on the Hill"? Or "Surfin' Bird," the oh so awesome "Surfin' Bird"? Hell with the necessity of regularity elaboration and distortion, and get with it with the non-move. That Stones bummer, what's the name of it . . . oh *Satanic Majesties*, well that's the groovy totally inadequate break-the-spell-of-Beatlistic-tongue-enforcement that failed. The Underbelly won't fail, isn't failing, will never fail. As the tongue trail Bee Gees have said, you don't know what it's like. You know, music as avocado, but avocado as turquoise cardboard dead cat run over by ivory toe. Okay, here it is in a nutshell: 1. crystallization in flux, fill in or at least do something with empty-full spatio-temporal infinitesima in putty; 2. form as field, field as form, —— as ——, tusk as brutal face, brutal face as nasty vortex, nasty vortex as umbrella treatment scheme, but, all in all, umbrella treatment scheme as field qua field qua form.

Other kinds of tongues: the beef tongue, so named by Roni Hoffman. Obviously that's a real fat one. Used to be known as the mega-tongue. The first eruption of the theme in Jimi Hendrix's "Third Stone from the Sun" is a beef tongue. And Pearlman's turkey tongue is the irrelevance tongue of longer duration.

(Just as the realm of rock repetition easily copes with the experience of sameness, the several varieties of tongues can easily deal with the experience of apparently unbreachable disparity. To rock the distance between *Pride and Prejudice* and *Last Exit to Brooklyn* is no more than that between, for example, Magritte's "The Human Condition II," 1935, and his later "Les Promenades d'Euclide," 1955. Thus can "I Want to Hold Your Hand" and "Being for the Benefit of Mr. Kite!" be viewed simultaneously, as even "My Boy Lollipop" and "The Last Time" can be.)

The closest explicit resemblance of a rock conception of music to that of Schopenhauer is to be found in the Lovin' Spoonful's "Do You Believe in Magic?" They comprehend the sheer power of the "magic of-a rock 'n' roll" but internalize it as the most human of all musical experiences: "The magic's in the music, and the music's in me!" (But "don't bother to choose, if it's jug band music and rhythm 'n' blues, just go listen . . .") Earlier, Danny and the Juniors adenoidally stated their estimate of its power to transcend time in "Rock and Roll Is Here to Stay": "Rock and roll will always be,/ I dig it to the end./ It'll go down in history,/ Just you wait my friend." If Danny and the Juniors accept this as a final cause of music without any clearer specification, Chuck Berry is more perceptive in his "Rock and Roll Music":

> I got no kick against modern jazz,
> Unless they try to play it too darn fast,
> And lose the beauty of the melody,
> Until it sounds just like a symphony.
>
> That's why I go for that rock and roll music,
> Any old way you choose it.
> It's got a back beat you can't lose it,
> Any old time you choose it.
> It's gotta be rock-roll music
> If you wanna dance with me.

ROCK AND ROLL MUSIC by Chuck Berry. Copyright © 1957 by Arc Music Corp.

How foolish could Nietzsche have been to cite Wagnerian orchestral music as the metaphysical equivalent of the power of nature? Obviously, Chuck Berry has found more immediacy in the melodiousness of rock and may devalue amoral "nature" for amoral man. He pities the classicists who have died before the advent of rock 'n' roll in "Roll Over Beethoven": "Roll over, Beethoven, and tell Tchaikowsky the news."

Music itself has changed, and man's conception of it has perhaps changed more. From pure will it has become the selection of organizations of sound ordered either to follow the pleasure principle or extend it, or to jar one to the realization that this context exists and is responsible for music's "power." Thus, John Cage can produce modern symphony pieces full of conventional power using transistor radios, scratchings on glass, and silence. Sounds have always evoked images in the listener and the primary sense experience of hearing music has always led in reflection to relating the sound patterns to objective states of varying levels of abstraction. Even the musical experience of power or sadness or whatever is the sense experience of something external; granted that music alone allows for such direct sensation of such states, but it seems that there is still always a mental correlation of the state produced in the subject to one in the object world.

In rock 'n' roll, songs that have been purely instrumental have often been undeserving of lyrics. Among these have been "Raunchy" by Bill Justice, "Rebel 'Rouser," "Cannonball" and "Forty Miles of Bad Road" by Duane Eddy, "Walk Don't Run" by the Ventures, and the abysmal "Cry for a Shadow" by Tony Sheridan backed up by the early Beatles without Ringo (and with Pete Best). If words can be banal, and poetic words are to represent an objectification of will, then that music which can represent the freed force of sheer will can become awesomely banal in a manner whereby listening is tantamount to sheer drudgery; in such a case, expectations of operation along the lines of the pleasure principle are jarred. The cliché can exist merely on a musical level, as in the case of the reverberating twang of a guitar. After all, Vivaldi's musical output consists of slightly transformed carbon copies.[124] But the necessities of rock 'n' roll require more than sheer music.

Sometimes there is a compromise, as when the Tijuana Brass with its "Lonely Bull" and Johnny and the Hurricanes with their "Telstar" produce works of music that are powerfully crude references to well-known pieces of the objective world. Trini Lopez has seen the resemblance of surfin' music to surfing in the resemblance of cascades of guitar sounds to the rolling of the waves. Music has sometimes been used to refer to music itself, as with current uses of certain distinctive twangs to refer to twangs employed by the Stones or Eric Clapton.

But for the eclectic artists of rock 'n' roll the inclusion of the word, spoken and sung, is essential. True, the mixture of voice and instrumental sound produces one organized (/disorganized) fusion of sound, thus music, but it is important that words remain. Jan, of Jan and Dean, has remarked,[125] "If the kids can hear the words, they'll turn their radio down. We want them to turn it up. It sort of relieves a kid's anxieties if he can drown out his parents." However, Jan ought to recognize the *importance* of

---

[124] Well he was melodically inventive even if not so structurally. And, get this, the very notion of originality in art (that each work of art should break new ground or try to) is a rather late one in art history. In music it doesn't really begin until Beethoven (which is why, for example, he produced only 9 symphonies to Haydn's 111). In visual art it begins earlier—a key figure being Dürer. Anyway, such historic knowledge/ignorance provides (for rock) a convenient self-affirmation through negation.

[125] *Time*, May 21, 1965, p. 86.

words, even if to sound more obnoxious when ampli-
fied. No instrumental has been a number one song
in the past few years;[126] Ramsey Lewis' piano version
of "The In Crowd" is full of audible grunts and is
perceived as a purely musical rendition of something
for which words are already known; and Roy Head's
"Treat Her Right" contains a few verses of fine insipid doggerel to keep the attention of the listener
reaching for something to comprehend linguistically.
In the field of American "popular music," however,
both instrumentals and vocals can succeed (although
the "hit" does not apply as handily here), and often
words are added to instrumental songs and vocals are
instrumentalized with little loss or gain due to objectification or freeing of the will. An exception to the
general trend in rock 'n' roll is the Ramsey Lewis
Trio's instrumental recording of Doby Gray's (vocal)
version of "The In Crowd." The original proclaims:
"Other guys imitate us,/ But the original's still the
greatest." Thus the instrumental version must be
other than the greatest and hence less important than
the original. Rock 'n' roll has here inadvertently kept
its musical tradition implicitly intact.

Words *are* necessary, but, even more crucially, they
are *replaceable*. That is, it needn't be these words
rather than those, at least not at this stage. Take a
song like "Santa Claus Is Coming to Town." Even
if what you hear of it is purely instrumental, you sort

---

[126] "Love Is Blue," number one for an exorbitant number of weeks, wouldn't have made it without its infinitely
suggestive *title* which makes it music with infinitely fixed
domain of banality, something its music itself is incap-
able of accomplishing.

of gotta find it hard to listen without thinking out the words, and not just any words, but *the* words. There's a great deal of indelibility. Well, the rock tune set-up is more akin to allowing for more verses and doing without the ones the tune originally has, along with the notion of their past inclusion as both indelible and inviting indelibility transcendence (attempts).

In the musical phenomenology of the whole thing, here's the way rock can present it: a song with a tune at first seemingly not strong enough to back up and validate *any* set of words, with words not really discernible at first and not reinforcing of the strengths of the music anyway once you know 'em but which *have* to be learned on the basis of the whole (only partially discernible at first) total sound, the whole thing *being* reinforced in the word-learning and tune-remembering process; song whose appeal becomes even more opaquely mysterious as appealing at all once the words have become familiar and the tune is recollectable in the mind at any time in its sequential totality (and not just for its overall impact as a known package of goodies); and in the whole thing it gains power as an all-validating background for a set of words that need validating in their separateness and don't because they've never been separated from the music. One thing is good enough to do the acceptability job for the whole thing, and music is the (somehow) easiest good-enough unitary item, and one thing is often more than just good enough. And when you get your one item from more than one source (as two near-halves here, by simultaneous word/music unity grope situations), that's pretty big, man—the more absolutely minimal things get and the thinner and more independently interdependent you spread them the better. Which doesn't really mean keep things simple or say something through the fewest possible words, or less is more and more is less, or any of that. But it's a matter of having something or other, not necessarily a "most important" aspect, *deficient*.

And, of course, as always, the key figures in this vein are (no less than) the Zombies. The Zombies are not only the original linguistically (metamusically, dramatically, or whatever) "mysterious" group to practice opaquely mysterious musical proliferation and emerge and reemerge to illuminate their own (philosophical) relationship modulation within the field of empirical-conceptual indiscernibility as additional (non-essential) bafflement back-up of their initial merely musical back-up project; *and* here's the payoff: the Zombies fit in right there between the Beatles and the Doors (*and* right there between Dylan and Procol Harum too). How's that? Well . . . handle a few Zombies opuses just to familiarize yourself with the terrain, stuff like "Is This the Dream," "Whenever You're Ready" and the more recent "Care of Cell 44" and "Friends of Mine." Words, when they finally become discernible, couldn't be triter or conventionally profounder, words like "And life's not pretty, its ugliness will hide the sun." Music so untiringly gutsy, whatever the hell that can possibly mean, that it urges immediate audience increase in knowledge of the words as just more nearness to every ounce of meat the song could contain. Music that doesn't release you even then because then sing-along is so much easier and the drone of the sound

is so unencumbered by the cogent meaning swamp.[127]
And a vocal hesitancy and drowsiness and alligator
snappiness that puts the cogent meaning swamp right
up there. Etc. And thus, more or less, you're stuck
with "Yes It Is," "There's a Place," "Penny Lane,"
and "My Eyes Have Seen You" in the same bundle,
stuck with them the same way the Zombies stick you
with their songs. And there's even substantial surface
resemblance, there's the Doors' (Manzarek's) organ
reliance for both surface eeriness and structural mystery reinforcement, Morrison's outburst and his acceleration beyond constancy both by choice and
structural unavoidability, as well as a whole batch of
"Break On Throughs" and "People Are Stranges" to
subliminally verbalize it alongside. And the Beatles'
drone of the mere and clarity in the skies. And Dylan's organ (Al Kooper), even in "Ballad of a Thin
Man," is more soap opera than phantom of the
opera, largely because of the clarity of his slurred
words and the overt over-obviousness of their mention
of mystery opacified ("Something is happening, but
you don't know what it is, do you Mr. Jones?"). And
Procol Harum adding a piano to the now mere organ
and *super*charged post-Dylan absurdity to the words
and shoving it all through the Michigan State marching band. And Dylan coming back by means of Man-

---

[127] The Beatles' introduction of a complete set of
printed words for everything on *Sgt. Pepper* is a move in
the direction of additive nondisruptive (because you can
ignore the lyrics on the cover unless they're compelling,
which would be a reversal of the prior function of music,
hence disruptive) and disruptive verbal immediacy plus
assistance in building minimality of audience urgency
where it is musically absent. It's also a move toward
speed-up of the audience's ease-of-eventual-disengage-
ment move. Get it started, get it over with.

fred Mann and returning to traditional words in the air by proxy with (in "Mighty Quinn") "ain't my cup of meat." And now the Zombies might just as well be using themselves as proxy media after their prolonged public obscurity which encompassed a period that saw the Left Banke go through the same musical summation and then depart the same way. And the Shakespeare quote on the Zombies' *Odyssey and Oracle* is an appropriate dandy: "Be not afraid;/ The Isle is full of noises/ Sound, and sweet airs that give delight and hurt not./ Sometimes a thousand twangling instruments/ Will hum about mine ears; and sometimes voices." And they even (apparently) left off a comma (after "noises") and a period (at what comes off as the end). Nice.

And "Cell 44" even sounds like Keith's "98.6," like it's a·*numerical* suggestion, not just straight words. Words are *always* suggestive of similarity with the past, tunes not always so, but when they are they are particularly interesting 'cause like how do you (intentionally) miss and yet sound like (here where sound is what you sound like)? Words or verbal descriptions (as Martin Sharp's "Tales of Brave Ulysses") sure can (linguistically) *sound* like, but how 'bout when *sounds* sound like, particularly when it's sound in sequence and the whole sound variance thing is what music is about anyway?

Referring to songs by words (even if they happen to be the title), like the question of whether it's "Good King Wenceslas" at the end of the Stones' instrumental "Sing This Song All Together (See What Happens)" (rather than if it's ABCDEFG, which at least refers to linguistically labeled sound fragments) is a nice out-of-context move, which in rock combines with a whole slew of others more prevalent than you get in classical-jazz-folk-pop-etc, which is far more cautious[128] about (the seemingly) outrageous out-of-context move orientation but misses the point that this orientation is the most outrageous (and goody for it too). Imagine that: *talking* about *music* at all!

With the Grateful Dead and acid rock in general, *all* of mere music emerges as a lost chord. Hence, although the move is not totally "warranted" from within earlier (worded) rock, it is a standardly self-validating move, and a move in awesome juxtaposition with the rest of rock proper, almost like a first use of music ever, even though it's been there (geologically) all along: nice. And it's great that a new bare minimum has emerged, an instrumental one allowing guys like the Jefferson Airplane to avoid exclusive use of their worst, the vocal atrocity, and thus be okay.

And once mere musicality has been associated with the instrumental, Country Joe & the Fish are there on the scene to make maximum use of the instrumental move. Their "Section 43," packed with vaguely memorable San Francisco Beau Brummel archetypes and the Link Wray archetypes far earlier than those, is music plus length (7:43). "Masked Marauder" is music as edified expectation of la-la, the easiest musical common denominator this side of humming. "Thursday" is a song with so few words ("Some people they find each other, I found you") it couldn't make it on a word-copyright level, so it's even officially musical only, wantonly pretty like any favorite-

---

[128] Blind assertion, but at least it's blind.

day-of-the-week time attention delineation.[129] Chicken
Hirsh's brush introduction to "Eastern Jam" flows
right out of the preceding album cut, the lack of
conventional space indicating a special awareness of
silence and its replacements which makes musical the
previously collapsed (by *Sgt. Pepper*, etc.) interval.
And "Colors for Susan" sums up the whole silence-
interval thing *and* carries the natural masochism of
the rock extension into mere music far further than
anything else, employing interminable silences between single twangs and finally throwing together a
short series of twangs to delight the bewildered ear.

Duane Eddy's instrumental rendition of "There Is
a Mountain" has an audience reaction level (on record) so homogeneously noisy and undistracting that
it must be externally superimposed, particularly when
you figure that nobody would react that way to
Duane Eddy anymore even if he does perform live.
Obvious overdubbing of applause is a big step.[129a] I
once asked filmmaker Peter Kubelka if he realized

---

[129] As opposed to Arthur Lee, who says (in "Red Telephone"), "I don't need the times of day, any time with
me's okay," and is uncenteredly different musically from
Country Joe accordingly. Like Love, after Arthur's announcement to the live crowd at Generation in New
York (May '68) that they would do just one final number, finished with the 17-plus-minute "Revelation" as
their "one" last song, a real dispersion scene.

[129a] *Do the Twist with Ray Charles*, a twist-era an-
thologization of his earlier twist-appropriate album cuts,
used (modest mere) applause *between* cuts, presumably
so that respect-for-the-previous-cut reference would be
conveyed to validate anything not twisted to (accompanied by twisting) and so that post-shake-it-up moment-of-rest would be accompanied by applause and so
that having-danced-to-it respect would be further heightened and accompanied during moment-of-rest, etc.

that one of his films, which consisted of black frames
and white frames and only sporadic noises, actually
had the loudest implicit sound track of all his films,
since it summoned quite a bit of audience laughter
and endure-the-tedium chatter and get-away-from-it
door-opening at the exits. But he was just angered at
both the audience response and my question, largely
because it lost for him in his rejection of audience
heterogeneity of response (he wanted and expected
just silence and praise) the entire dimension of artist
control over his prey. All films have an implicit sound
track in addition to their own, but with just music
(as with just picture and silence) this imposition
matters most. So with Duane Eddy it's imposition as
independent superimposition and interference unre-
solvable as far as you want it to be (as a member of
the audience just faced with a non-homogeneous
sound that makes sense on at least two levels and is
capable of being aurally exciting/interesting on all of
them). And the awe-inflicting TV Batman theme is
the use of an irrepressible non-melody as exciting before it can be interesting, significant for the last TV
comedy without canned laughter (because it began
under the guise of adventure show before it became
straight comedy). Having something to do with all
this is Lee Michaels' "Sounding the Sleeping," whose
huge volume-level changes and whose beginning (so
minutely audible that you can't be sure if it has
actually started or there's something wrong with your
equipment or the recording engineer messed it up)
force audience compliance and heighten audience perceptual sensitivity.[130] To pay attention at all is to pay
attention a lot.

---

[130] Zappa's applause-denial on stage is sometimes so
dogmatically effective that his lighting of a match is
audible.

And, of course, the single-note fadeout of more than 40 seconds that follows a crescendo of equally unaccustomed non-rock harshness on the Beatles' "Day in the Life" is the biggest musical reference point of them all. Whether it's descent into silence and/or the sounds of the extra-record world (foreshadowed by the animal sounds at the finish of "Good Morning, Good Morning"[131]), or that followed by a reemergence of everlasting sound (the English *Sgt. Pepper* ends with a continuous band of gibberish that won't even be heard if the record is rejected on the turntable), the inclusion of this sort of thing on a record that will be distributed throughout the whole goddam world goes beyond anything Cage or any of those guys were ever in any position to do with the music-sound of the whole sound totality of the whole thing, officially decisively ending all art-non-art/music-noise distinctions forever, or until somebody forgets.

And then there is instrumental "Soulfinger" by the Bar-kays, so self-explanatory in its title and trumpet burbles that it becomes an actual definitive sex-music analogue, and what is sex without words like anyway? The Doors get vocal to split hairs and arrive at music as mere inexhaustive preparation (yet self-contained totality nonetheless) in "When the Music's Over":

When the music's over
When the music's over

---

[131] Not only does the slew of animal noises at the end complement/supplement the mere rooster crow at the beginning, but the sequence and motion is nice, with dogs speaker-to-speaker and physical-size-of-source relevance being neatly manifest by an elephant following a lion.

When the music's over turn out the lights,
   turn out the lights, turn out the lights
When the music's over
When the music's over
When the music's over turn out the lights,
   turn out the lights, turn out the lights
Well the music is your special friend
Dance on fire as it intends
Music is your only friend
Until the end, until the end, until the end.

The instrumental, when it takes on the proportions
of the instrumental freakout, gets subsumed under
the spectacular-dramatic as well as the merely musical. And the recorded instrumental freakout, even as
the instrumental "long track," becomes pale beside
the live instrumental freakout, not even in the sense
of live-is-more-immediate-than-recorded, an old cliché
borrowed from jazz and erroneous as butter. What
the "live" setup adds, particularly at outdoor festivals
which introduce immediate athletic-event analogies,
is *visual* (and environmental, etc.) accompaniment
to mere music and a space for it to fill and bounce
around at least merely metaphorically.[132] The "light

---

[132] The only guy to do just instrumentals all weekend
at Monterey was Ravi Shankar, who, ironically, needed
the (shallow) word route to undo it all, resorting to
his whole explanation-of-Eastern-music-and-why-it-isn't-
really-pop routine. And his biggest applause was for his
inadvertently humorous Indian scale exercises with his
tabla player and his "boss licks" references to George
Harrison. The only unconditioned response to mere
music was (the "ignorant" reaction) to his tuning up
(which he almost resented), and that was to music as
something alien.

show" is just the introduction of control and vividness, but often the control and vividness is so substantial and merely freaky that it becomes (positive
and/or negative) interference, and Country Joe once
stopped playing and ordered a light show off,[133] and
the Apollo Theater in Harlem sure don't need (but
now has) the excesses of the light show added to its
already everpresently full excess, but that's just accompaniment overstatement. Probably the best use
of the light show is by the Group Image, which is high
on both the instrumental freakout and the visual accompaniment gimmick qua gimmick. During a usual
50-minute Image stage instrumental at their bubble-
machine dance hall, the audience can use the Mickey
Mouse cartoon or Vincent Price filmstrip or photo of
Jupiter on top of STP sticker on the screen up front,
use it as groovy synchronized reinforcing accompaniment or use it just for a rest and pay no attention to
the music at all,[134] with the occasional strobe lights
(which even Murray the K has used) obliterating the
stage-screen motif and setting off everything everywhere there as the unavoidable scene-worth-watching-
and-participating-in (by turning everything into
spatio-temporal molasses and fragmenting the visual
even more rigidly than the auditory, challenging the
whole internal time-consciousness flow thing at least
conceptually). Well it *is* significant that rock reached
the light show at the same time that it began to take
on the long mere musical ordeal.

---

[133] Stony Brook 8/67. (Morrison frequently orders *all*
lights off, his optimum light show being darkness.)
[134] The Group Image's ex-announcer, Uncle Ray, en-
couraged another ritual transcendence of merely listening to mere music, the minimally physical hand-holding
circle dance, which he led.

And in your own home posters will help, but, since a black circular piece of plastic is just a drag,[134a] the album cover has to do a lot. It is not an accident that the first Grateful Dead album, which featured the first example of definitive acid-rock instrumentality, "Viola Lee Blues," had what was up to that time (spring '67) the most topically bizarre cover.[135] When the visual boys in rock learn about the whole history of art treasures, there'll be (inevitably) a blank white unlettered cover, some day, and a transparent plastic job[136] equally "freaky."

[134a] Fantasy Records used to have red discs, but their only peripheral rock hit, Vince Guaraldi's "Cast Your Fate to the Wind," came out as a black single (but then it was, in its time, an instrumental move qua move). Apple-labeled Apple black discs may be the reintroduction of the color move plus the introduction of a visual move in general, dealing with stuff like the symmetry of other-than-the-circle (the apple's a start, and you can cut it in half, etc.).

[135] Also, note this additional aspect of the Dead's musical structure itself. For a long time all the musicians in the group were really knocking people out with their unified effort except for Pig-Pen, the organist, who played what were regarded as hack r & b riffs in the midst of superproficient electric music. So Pig-Pen, the archetypal grotesque human masterpiece of Haight-Ashbury, actually enables the Dead to avoid the notion of perfection in their music, a specific "stultifying" aspect in audience encounter with the newly discovered mere music mystery, at the same time as he supplies the fattest visual focal point.

[136] Warhol has already contributed banana peel (*Velvet Underground & Nico*) and black-on-black (*White Light/White Heat*) album covers. As for white on white, Richard Hamilton did it for the Beatles' *The Beatles* cover.

And some other-than-just-music corequisites of just music other than freakier-than-thou album covers. Picture books: *Magical Mystery Tour*, which includes the Beatles' first instrumental, "Flying"; *Gorilla* by the Bonzo Dog Doo Dah Band, whose "The Intro and the Outro" is a list of members of the band ("Vernon Dudley Bohay-Nowell, rhythm pole"; "Eric Clapton on ukulele"[137]). Inconsequential-words-anyway: Steve Miller Band, *Children of the Future*, with the powerfully musical Steve Miller still "powerfully musical," since how could those words ever get in the way; musical after the fact by proxy. Transcendence of cuts: *The Beat Goes On*, wherein the Vanilla Fudge doesn't do much of a job delineating the tedium when they're alinguistically tedious, so you can easily disregard the whole thing.

Visual accompaniment is almost analogous to the music-printed page of notes relationship. Well, notes are in sequence and a picture by itself doesn't go anywhere—*but*, a picture being worth 1000 words (or 4 typewritten pages), you get something similar.[137a] And *Magical Mystery Tour* has lots of *pages*, so you can change up, everybody change up. With film, the connection is not easily eradicable (as the last twangs from George's guitar in the "I Need You" sequence of *Help!* with its green landscape and cannons, just twangs and a cannon, no Beatles), it's even more of a union than music with words (words are *assumed* anyway). And Beatle cards, photos, pillows, hair

---

[137] The music for "Roy Rogers on Trigger" sounds faintly like a piss solo.

[137a] The Fish Game, which accompanies the second album of Country Joe & the Fish, is a visual thing with directionality.

styles, etc., are always so noisy and also seemingly less word-oriented, and what does a yellow shoe have to do with words except when you consider both of them as shapes and functions. The brute feel and appearance of clothing and alphabetic[138] structures are more like noise than meanings.

And rock *is* (after all) responsible for the biggest clothing and hair moves of all time, that's the music operating—but any actual direction and shape (and relevance) for the clothing-hair move sort of oughta be molded by the words. But the conglomerate lump of the whole clothing/hair splash is music as a big indiscernible-but-obvious splash splash, with this- and other-worldly clothing/hair affinities based on both availability and search-orientation inspiration. And clothing move importance is made official (-ly major/minor) by the Stones in "Under My Thumb," basing root change indication on "the difference in the clothes she wears."

The vast number of head hairs, lengthened for emphasis/exaggeration, has always been analogous to the larger rock musical proliferation (as form, and to lesser/greater extent as content) (hence Little Richard, Jerry Lee Lewis and Elvis Presley even well before the Beatles and everybody else), whereas facial hair is amelioration/elaboration less relevant without prior or simultaneous hair length move. The Beatle topical mustache-beard (-marginal hair manipulation) move, as manifest in the photo below (with Brian Jones and Donovan on the left), multiplies relevant

---

[138] Jim Morrison, a revolutionary in the field of rock leather, even happens to speak of "secret alphabets" ("Soul Kitchen").

superficial superficiality facial-hair musical-analogy extension possibilities.

Drinking a toast and wishing luck to the new Grapefruit group, who make their disc debut this week (see picture and review on page 4), are (l to r) BRIAN JONES, DONOVAN, RINGO, JOHN LENNON, CILLA BLACK and PAUL McCARTNEY. The reception to launch the disc was one of the most lavish ever—not surprising, as Grapefruit are being backed by the Beatles.

(From *New Musical Express*)

More about the instrumental. It's the easiest way to produce the long track, or the longer track, or the even longer super track. A harp part makes "Sad Eyed Lady of the Lowlands" a longer *fadeout* for Dylan. Patient organ-guitar-drum back up Morrison's lapses of interest with the live Doors. For Zappa and the Mothers the instrumental is a tedium with less strain to perform (or maybe more), it is easy ano-nymity and easy mere membership card in the group and in rock itself; the Mothers' reed man Bunk is mere music's greatest anonymous transvirtuoso in a context where he's even less than that.

The Electric Flag, led by Mike Bloomfield, the traditional greatest-(white-) guitarist-in-the-world type of guitarist, is about the opposite of the usual rock instrumentality trend. Bloomfield must squeeze his super-role into a subservient voice, one which bears the burden of worry over out-shining the whole show and yet being buried enough by a real vocal

voice so that it's got the rudiments of a vocal show.
Only because Nick Gravenites doesn't pack enough
wallop on the Flag's first album, *A Long Time Comin'*,
does the Bloomfield overstatement (with all its big-
band associates) overpower internally, which is as it
should be. And only because Bloomfield has come to
short stuff and themes from the lengthy improvised
solo does it seem as if his theme leads are sudden
cliché immersions, as if the long stuff in its creative
majesty isn't as deep in the great easy-listening pit.
The Flag's "Another Country" has fallen prey to
musical-purity misunderstanding: "The number is interrupted by a cacophony of distorted noises, mostly
indecipherable—the whole thing is really unnecessary."[139] As if a guy who has produced only significant
sounds can't fool around with silly sounds in his first
opportunity to do so.

Blood, Sweat and Tears is supposedly a band to
answer the in-context dance band need the rest of
rock has generated, so it's swell that they have more
of a reason for being than they have for being abysmal. The fact that the group is a big band milestone
along with such occasional occurrences as Miles Davis'
1949 band or Gerry Mulligan's once-in-a-while affair
is nice too, since forefront jazz couldn't care less for
big band moves and rock is involved in such total
move plethora that Blood, Sweat and Tears is only
that, a milestone. It's a good thing that Al Kooper
ruins the instrumental efforts of the rest of the group
with his singing and that the best part of their first
album is the opening overture which is sufficiently
short enough to sum up their musical afterthought

[139] Barry Gifford, *Rolling Stone*, May 11, 1968, p. 20.

move quickly. And the Blues Project, which died and gave Kooper and Steve Katz to Blood, Sweat and Tears, ended up keeping Andy Kulberg and his flute (and he was their *bassist*) as the most un-played out jazz-or-rock element of either group, while Blood, Sweat and Tears confines its duties to anachronisms and the Blues Project refuses to come back into existence.

Another function of early rock albums was background makeout music. Sometimes voices louder than music by itself fill in the silences easier without a volume increase and still cover up anything parents in another room might hear. An outgrowth of this is sensuality on a "wider" plane (narrower) as the proposed graduation beyond mere programmatic makeout stuff; some (blues type) instrumental (erotic) stuff happens to be an available likely choice.

And all actual volume moves are nothing compared to the all-at-once summation job done by Blue Cheer, which plays so loud using only bass, guitar and drums that sound loses its significance as sound and becomes seismic vibration and pain shared with the audience. Their vocals are mere mouthings of sound and they are kept minimal so as not to make the ordeal more cognitive; their "Summertime Blues" substitutes for familiar vocal lines with instrumental fiddle faddle. Where other musicians bear the scars of prolonged playing only as calluses and blisters, Blue Cheer's drummer, Paul Whaley, is accustomed to getting bloody hands from his two-fisted onslaught and has recently resorted to gloves. The Velvet Underground's overamplified violin assault by John Cale and the Paupers' three drummers are just not con-

stant volume jobs but (lengthy) freakout punctuations of contrast.

But Blue Cheer *is* outdone cacophony-wise if not
volume-wise by Ornette Coleman's great *Free Jazz*,
which had eight guys (including the late great Eric
Dolphy at his most honk-oriented) just wailing for
half an hour and occasionally coming together for a
theme reminiscent of "Swinging on a Star" just for
polar contrast. The late great John Coltrane tried to
top this with his *Ascension* session but just about
didn't, so in this year of Blue Cheer *Free Jazz* is making its way into ordinary record store windows for
the first time (released around 1960/61/62). A letter
in *Downbeat* a while back angrily suggested that the
people buying Ornette-Dolphy-Coltrane stuff just
have to be teen-age rock and roll fans because the
chaos affinities were obvious, whereas the letter writer
himself, who had been raised on the tasteful bands of
yore, was still buying and loving good wholesome
Count Basie. It's nice to see such distance as genet-
ically possible within jazz itself. This easily generaliz-
able distance allegory just about makes jazz eligible
for consideration as not only a source of the music of
rock but as holder of membership within rock as a
foreshadowing and continuing subset.

In the annals of jazz and the big band there is (perhaps) no greater (officially visceral) bringer of fame
than the drum solo. Ginger Baker of the Cream,
whose drum solo in the 5:09 "Toad" was probably the
longest in rock since Cozy Cole's *de facto* rock hit
"Topsy," has really gone to work with a 15-minute
drum solo version of "Toad" recorded live at the

Fillmore, an exemplary rock contextualization of the drum claim to fame. Things like "rhythmic inventiveness" and "taste" are frequent criteria for judging the drummer on his own, the drummer being, anyway, the very base of the beat for the whole band, etc. So to say any particular instrumentalist is great and to particularly groove on his efforts when he's soaring on his own is stripped to bare minimum (/maximum) when the guy is a drummer, like he's summing it all up just by producing some noises with sticks, which just happens to seem more primally simple an act than plucking strings attached to some electric circuitry or blowing into a crooked metallic tunnel and doing some related yet different finger moves at the same time, etc. Hands and feet, true, but it's (in terms of the physicality of sound production) still a matter of absolutely similar percussionality in each case, it's a total limb move and it's loud beyond the all-around super-electricity. When Cozy Cole, an old traditionally great jazz-hand, made the rock move with "Topsy (Parts 1 & 2)," of which Part 2 happened to be the side of the single that was pushed, Alan Freed ran a why-I-like-Topsy-Part-2 contest; its strong different-worldly articulateness coupled with its contextually overstated nearness to the official big-beat basis of rock, plus its classy unworded topical sublety, made it strangely interesting to the rock audience. So you could say, if you wanted, that Cozy Cole was "great." Dino Danelli of the Young Rascals, whose stage performance consists of the constant careful selection of cymbals (there are *hundreds* on all sides of him) to tap with consummately detailed taste, is an all-the-time drum soloist for those close enough in the audience to watch him (even when the other guys are doing stuff or he's just being part of the whole thing as a unit), a visual analogue of the Cozy Cole mystique.

Well by the time Ginger Baker hit the scene the drummer brigade had been publicly categorized by an audience itself seeking the same level of trans-articulable "taste" as the scads of drummers it sought to make sense out of while claiming their "quality," like "He's sort of like Keith Moon" or "You can tell he's been listening to Elvin Jones." So in the midst of all that, there goes Ginger, Ginger the great at the Fillmore with a maximally extended minimum drum solo, devoid of even the exhibitionistic clichés of a Gene Krupa except the fact of exhibition itself, sort-ing out one fallible gimmick after another, emerging with the most minimal coverups for and changes in mere periodic repetition as grounds for rhythmicality, and once even doing two (!) things at once (high hat regularity with his foot or could it perhaps be one of his hands, wow gee that would mean so much slightly more wow!), and ending up so sweaty that it's a pity that that could have no sound implications, making even more an historical claim-to-fame than an at-the-moment personal experiential claim-to-fame. But above all he strikes the greatest rock blow within the tradition of the musical solo (solo as easy diminution/enhancement of overall group musicality,[140] whether

---

[140] And Eric Clapton and Jack Bruce, Ginger's asso-ciates in Cream, even have to stand around just like mere members of the audience and gawk or snicker knowingly. In this regard, the drum solo, above all other instrumental "solos" (in particular, Clapton on guitar), represents the guy alone without accompaniment (so

from "virtuosity" or lack of it) and the musical utterance in general.[141]

With the genesis of jazz from the blues, music proper switches its emphasis from analogy to nature to reference to human states. Human cries and squeals are "imitated" in a manner of playing an instrument calculated better to resemble the human voice than

---

the other guys don't have to endure with the soloist and take a back seat during the subsequent applause which they in part have produced), and Ginger, freaky hair and sweat at the Fillmore full of freaks and sweat, is doing the artist equivalent of the Group Image audience circle dance and gaining optimum recognition for it.

[141] In the pseudo-quasi-classic bag (classicism as a form of at-large rule-governedness) is Van Dyke Parks' *Song Cycle*, the most formidable dispersion of homogeneity through detail and the most formidable Muzak doing of all time. Its musical claim-to-fame is somewhere between (classical) obligatory quality response and (*Younger than Yesterday*) Byrds seductiveness (particularly around Hollywood as "never-never land juxtaposed" but even "amid a dash of influenza"). Hovering between rock immediate applause, (immediate) suspension of consideration resulting from (planned) obstacles to immediate interpretation (words on the cover are in true necessary libretto fashion, not Zappa neat pretentious aid with *Absolutely Free*), and . . ., V. D. Parks compulsion forces a "worst" possible response of "Swill," which is pretty good in (or out of, but particularly in) context, covering a lot of aesthetic room too. And the classical rigidity of in-my-own-timeness of urgency of acceptance as an important mere musical fact, smoothed over by all the "never made the grade" of "Vine Street," contextualizes the Bee Gees' "In My Own Time" (which can merely make the grade as pretender to classical nouveau dispersion), all without recourse to strict Muzak dogma, whatever that is. Although he could have used it.

previous music. Jazz is a freer[142] music than its predecessors while it simultaneously is more "objective"
than its predecessors. Rock 'n' roll is perhaps even
freer and yet more objectifying, although with an
epistemologically more ambiguous and obscure role.
If one measures negatively the increase in linguistic
objectification, one is losing the possibility of a con-
structive/destructive function for this development.
Man can produce more "stirring" art by reference to
"himself" than he can by reference to either "nature"
or "experience of the raw power of nature itself." The
mere appearance of man's objectifications themselves
can be incredibly aesthetic in their implications either
in conjunction with the original raw being or apart
from it. Consider the apparent fixity established upon
the unharnessed metaphysical power of music in
Chuck Berry's "Sweet Little Sixteen":

> They're really rockin' in Boston, in Pittsburgh,
> P.A.,
> Deep in the heart of Texas, and 'round-a Frisco
> Bay,
> All over St. Louis, and down in New Orleans,
> All the cats gonna dance with Sweet Little Six-
> teen.

SWEET LITTLE SIXTEEN by Chuck Berry. Copyright © 1958 by Arc Music
Corp.

This delineation of experience of an adolescent cele-
brating her birthday in a quasi-physical cavortion is
decidedly more powerful experientially than the mon-
umental insipidness of what D. Gerber calls "traditional American darkie music" (tracing its origin
from Stephen Foster), or than the physically discon-

---

[142] *Officially* in its own public jargon. More about this
later on.

nected real-world event(s). Berry's metaphor as a vision is more powerful than the raw music could be. I assume that a complete analysis would (foolishly) distinguish the power of primary experience from that of reflective experience, with music implying an original subject-object unity and linguistic poetry carrying an analogy of this into the realm of reflection. Chuck Berry's words are the objectification of that experience which would arise from his music; they are a reflection upon the monstrous proportions such experience can attain. This reflection is so much more important than its (hypothetical) primary origin that the distinction of Nietzsche and Schopenhauer is in a sense downright silly. Yet when considered as an objectification even further removed from primary experience, it is (capable of being) fairly exciting itself. Perhaps one of the finest examples of the coolness of concise linguistic objectification has been produced by a state boxing commission which made a profound announcement concerning a no-contest decision rendered when Sugar Ray Robinson's opponent suddenly fell down without provocation. As I remember it, the statement sounded like "From the evidence we have gathered, we are certain that he (the fallen fighter) did not put forth his best effort."

Mainstream Records first achieved prominence as a vintage jazz reissue company; it later attained obscurity through its production of albums by hack rock groups (Big Brother and the Holding Company is an exception but they went through a totally hack studio job to make up for it). Mainstream.

Jazz: same thing as rock music only it's implicit rather than explicit, and the fact of improvisation is a ritualized attempt to forget about plagiarism-after-thought before the fact; only reference to the fact of improvisation itself doesn't fit in itself except as inevitable mere plagiarism-afterthought (and that's the rock domain), and not fitting doesn't fit in jazz-as-art proper (but then there's the willing rock receptacle again). Conceptually begin with rock as the easy structural readymade receptacle and showcase of the out-of-context and you can't avoid jazz as music in-context slippery enough by virtue of its essential flux to be labeled *in-context ultimately out-of-context* and hence rock. Or easier and thus more ironically in-context is jazz-as-rock ontologically, by virtue of its *being* insofar as everything is inevitably (and originally) rock.

Whether it occurs as the result of awakened one-step-at-a-time art-historical awareness and the actual corequisite developmental moves along with it, or as merely structurally inevitable stumbling-upon, jazz and rock are going to come face to face from now on with increasing frequency. Or you can say that jazz has always been rock and that rock has always used jazz. To say that jazz uses rock too is to miss the point, because rock is more than the whatever-happens-to-be of the surface musical structure of all that has come to be labeled rock; rock's employment of anything whatsoever as afterthought (in any manner whatsoever) is itself a very crucial (ha) point of its superstructure, making jazz's apparent use of the rock readymade a use of only an infinitesimal speck, and only rarely an ironic use thereof.

Jazz is independently the high point in conscious cliché recognition before rock. Eric Dolphy, by merely playing his then strange-sounding bass clarinet on too-too familiar lines (as in Coltrane's "Spiritual" and "India") always knew where it was at and had a good thing going already.

In jazz the multitracked recording (such as Bill Evans' *Conversations with Myself*) and all the early reactions thereto have always been too opaque. So have all the big-band recordings with unlisted personnel and the traditional opposition to that too. The Beatles consciously and obviously have gone through this entire bizarre setting, starting with a pure John-Paul-George-Ringo recording arrangement and taking their time working their way through much of the array of possibilities used before and adding their own. "Yesterday" was the first obvious use of the external unlisted readymade for them, "Lucy in the Sky with Diamonds" their first announced twelve-track recording, although they had been done a million times before. Not just rock conscious of itself and spreading itself out programmatically, but positive appreciation of gimmick and anonymity all along the way.

"Captain Soul," the only instrumental by the super-musical Byrds, is also their only atypical song.

A distinct possibility, accompanying the loss of classical potency for music itself, is the word-sound as the unit of a new musical experience. In such works as "Come Go with Me" by the Dell-Vikings, musical sound and linguistic fragment are united to bring even closer together those levels of experience which might traditionally be reckoned as separable: "Dom-

dom-dom-dom dom-bee-doo-bee-dom/ Dom-dom-
dom-dom dom-bee-doo-bee-dom/ Dom-dom-dom-
dom dom-bee-doo-bee-dom/ Wa-wa-wa-wa-a/ Well I
love love you darlin'/ Come and go with me . . ."
In this form, such work is akin to the sound poems of
Tristan Tzara,[143] who sought to negate the traditional
significance of poetry by incorporating merely collections of letters embodying collections of nonsense
sounds since words are only conventional representations of sounds which conventionally convey meaning.
But this unit of rock music has been annihilated in its
significant role by a few factors. Songs like David
Seville's "Witch Doctor" converted these linguistically
meaningless syllables into syllables conveying meaning, even if abstruse. A witch doctor confronts the
story-teller with an aphrodisiac expression: "He said
that/ Oo-ee oo-ah-ah/ Ting-tang walla-walla *bing-
bang*/ Oo-ee oo-ah-ah/ Ting-tang walla-walla bing-
bang."[144] This is similar to the conversion of music itself to a referential role and the introduction of a new
reflective level to this raw experience by the unavoidable arrival of poetic ambiguity. The introduction to
the popular standard "Blue Moon," as recorded by the
hard rock Marcels, is in a nonsense sound-word form
that might at first indicate the possibility of renova-
tion of traditional music by the addition of this com-

---

[143] Yeah, Tzara (since his name is flashier and), since
he came to Dada sound poems from gesture poems, and
Raoul Hausmann, Richard Hülsenbeck, Dr. Serner and
Hugo Ball beat him there. So rather than being innova-
tive his "Roar" ("roar" repeated around 631 times) is a
lot of great dull noise.
[144] There's even the fully-conscious "Who Put the
Bomp" ("in the bomp-a bomp-a bomp") by Barry Mann.

ponent.[145] But this component is used by the Marcels to sound traditional in the realm of rock 'n' roll and thus is an expert implicit self-negation. It is a component which, when placed in with all other rock components, is doomed to an ever quicker self-negation than the others; it cannot become referential and "meaningful" through repetition and still retain its explicit overt importance, but as part of rock it must be repeated. "Rama-Lama-Ding-Dong" is the apex of the development of the nonsense syllable of sound embodiment in terms of both development and inevitability of sterility. When the Edsels sing, "I got a girl named Rama-Lama-Lama-Lama-Ding-Dong,/ She's always good to me, Rama-Lama-Lama-Lama-Ding-Dong," the group implies the possibility that even a crisis of identity can grow from (and be resolved through) language music, with the sheer joy of her name not enough to escape this trap (and far more than enough too). As a music with new-found conventional legitimacy, jazz has employed this component as it sees it in its musically energized role. The Double Six of Paris and the Swingle Singers have applied it to earlier works, the former to jazz standards and the latter to classical works.[146] Thus is a "legitimate" art able to incorporate elements which it can consistently apply in supposedly enriching its

---

[145] A great deal of traditional music, such as opera and soul music, works on an intermediate stage by over-syllabicative repetition of regular words. But no one is as brazen as Lou Christie with his "Two Faces Have I": "Two faces have I-I-I I-I-I-I-I-I-I-I-I-I ..."

[146] Scat is by itself just a neutral compromise between instrument and voice, hence its legitimacy in the midst of legitimacy.

structure, while rock 'n' roll eclectically decides when they are usable or necessary.[147] The word-sound might have so conclusively been the solution to many problems presented by contemporary music that it simply lost its relevance to rock 'n' roll. It is to be found today only in fragments of the content of songs, in the background, or, in rare instances, as the appropriate title of a new (in)appropriate dance.

With Pythagoras (the original Mr. Music) you get at least a known conceptual framework (celestial harmony) as a backdrop for music, so words are (if you really want them to be after all this dumb discussion) there anyway in the mind—in rock you get the blurting out of *actual* verbalness as an easy avoidance of meremusicalmasochism (conceptuality ain't enough dammit unless you want it to be). All the grunting in the build-up of the Stones' "Sing This All Together (See What Happens)" is exemplary end masochism avoidance.

And after all is said and done, there is an occasional "end primacy"[148] for the music music music over all else, the amazement that this can be so and that music can have any predictable effect at all, particu-

---

[147] Or, as in the case of the Beach Boys' "Good Vibrations," they may simply be employed as pleasantly decadent referential/structural elements of traditional enrichment.

[148] On possibly the last album the Lovin' Spoonful will ever record (*Everything Playing*) is their first instrumental, entitled "Forever," as well as "She's Still a Mystery."

larly as an end high.[149] And melody is still the trickiest part of the new song to remember, cause it's a totality, a unity, not just a bunch of fragments. And sometimes you can even "sing along" on first hearing[149a] and recall nothing but the initial awe.[150] And dammit if the song isn't sometimes easy as pie to remember on one hearing, isn't that a stereo-typical rock move? Right on down the recallability continuum are the likes of Zappa (make melody remembrance potential small as possible but use fragmentation to maintain enough interest to allow for acceptable giggling and boredom) and Autosalvage (fragment the entire melody structure and keep it nice too so the retention of small pieces is almost assured).

But, alas, as the Stones say in "Singer Not the Song," the great *ad hominem* move is even more basic to rock. Nice.

---

[149] Arthur Lee's "I believe in ma-a-gic, why because it is so quick" is easy access to the Schopenhauer primacy/finality.

[149a] In the early days of mass-printed rock lyrics (*Hit Parader*, etc.) accumulation of lyric-knowledge in terms of written reference material was always late in coming and wrong enough to be wrong. So first-time sing-along was even more significant and absurd and melody-grounded in light of the assured listening-groundedness of lyric-learning reinforced by the difficulty of an early obtaining of written lyrics (correct or otherwise).

[150] I've had a lot of trouble remembering such really catchy super-songs as Elvis Presley's "Don't Be Cruel" (I was so young that I got it confused with "Old Cowhand from the Rio Grande"), Donnie Brooks' "Mission Bell" and the Soft White Underbelly's "John L. Sullivan Readymade," whose *words* I wrote.

Bob Dylan's greatest initial dive into the rock 'n' roll domain, "Like a Rolling Stone," represents an attempt to free man by rescuing him from meaning, rather than free man through meaning. John Lennon's two collections of writings, *In His Own Write* and *Spaniard in the Works*, have shown his desire to denigrate all meaning and thus throw intentional ambiguity and straight meaninglessness into all domains of meaning. And very definitely *all* meaning is similar, beginning with the most "authentic" and continuing down the line. When told by Paul McCartney about a girl who told Paul that God had advised her to marry him ("I was trying to persuade her that she didn't in actual fact have a vision from God, that it was . . . ,"), George Harrison interrupted with "It was probably somebody *disguised as God.*"[151] Meaning by any other name . . . John and Ringo destroy P. F. Strawson's argument for separation into logical and empirical primarity:

> John: We're money-makers first, then we're entertainers.
> Ringo: No, we're not.
> John: What are we then?
> Ringo: Dunno. Entertainers first.
> John: O.K.
> Ringo: 'Cause we were entertainers before we were money-makers.[152]

Whereas James Joyce attempted to salvage meaning from semantic chaos, John would rather attain a cool semantic oblivion, and thus he has written two books intentionally inferior to James Joyce's works.

---

[151] *Playboy*, February 1965, p. 54.
[152] *Playboy*, loc. cit.

One of Lennon and McCartney's maneuvers is to present meaning in such a role that it becomes trans-semantic and/or trite. Thus is the use of "in spite of" in a positive sense reduced to triviality in "Yes It Is":

> Please don't wear red tonight,
> This is what I said tonight.
> For red is the color that will make me blue
> In spite of you
> It's true ...
> Yes it is, it's true.

The very spirit of the song, with its assertively positive title, presents a frightening ambiguity between arrogance and possession of a unique vulnerability. "When I Get Home" plays upon the mere appearance of a single word, "trivialities":

> Come on, if you please,
> I got no time for trivialities,
> I've got a girl who's waiting home for me
> Tonight.
> Whoa-ah,
> Whoa-ah,
> I got a whole lot of things to tell her
> When I get home.

In the midst of apparent "tragedy" in realizing a sudden revulsion at his semi-adulterous involvement with another girl, he can hesitate to give it the meaning "triviality". But the five-syllable word is so strange in such a monosyllabic context that it is rendered so incredibly inappropriate that the need for meaning collapses.

Barry McGuire's "Eve of Destruction" presents a plethora of such words: "coagulatin'," "legislation," "disintegrating," "regulation," "integration," etc. The very appearance of such "serious" subjects as war and racial stuff in a rock context is a denigration of their original significance. His absolute overstatement of theme renders disaster cool; his "Don't you know we're on the eve of destruction" is so affirmative that one can feel comfortable with such knowledge. England's banning of this song is a really fine misunderstanding of how McGuire has rendered Weltschmerz trite.

The Beatles' introduction of intentional ambiguities purely on an aural level has a similar effect. "I Want to Hold Your Hand" has a line which, as written down in sheet music, appears as "And when I touch you I feel happy inside./ It's such a feeling that my love I can't hide,/ I can't hide,/ I can't hide." However on record the second line often sounds quite like "It's such a feeling that my love I get high" and renders it an image of amorous elation. Vic Ruggiero (rock enthusiast and college dropout) has pointed out that the last word of the line could end with a "t" sound, thus making it "It's such a feeling that my love I get hot," and seemingly one of the most sexual passages in gentle-intention rock history (destroying the innocent front of the song already). Yet what I've finally heard increases anything in this direction: "It's such a feeling that my love I get hard."

"I'll Get You," with its merely hypothetical "likely"/ "like me" ambiguity, contains a passage in which two lines which are distinctly audible are simultaneously sung: "Well there's gonna be a time/ When I'm gonna change your mind" and "Well there's gonna be a time/ When I'm gonna make you mine." Meaning can be ambiguous in any given stable case and fulfill any of Wheelwright's considerations of resembling Heraclitus' fire, you know, *that* stuff. But John Lennon's shifting, juggling multiple ambiguities, which prevent any stable case for viewing a moment of this ambiguous cross-section of reality, are quite different. A case is thus given by the Beatles for the elimination of semantic enslavement for, after all, metaphor can become not only "flabby" and useless as Wheelwright notes, but (better still and better still for the sake of argument) also the source of enslavement, which Wittgenstein partially notes: "Anything —and nothing—is right.—And this is the position you are in if you look for definitions corresponding to our concepts in aesthetics or ethics."[153]

Okay,[154] rock contextualizes everything, but rock is also a matter of clichés, clichés not just in reference but clichés *per se*. That is, all art either manipulates clichés (i.e. old or new-passing-as-old cultural ready-mades) or turns—via the process of exposure to the public—its creation into clichés. Art is concerned with the overly familiar, what looks like the overly familiar and with turning things into the overly familiar. But the ability and willingness to (cognitively and non-cognitively) deal with the cliché as the sole source of viscera and as sole viscera itself is rock's alone. Disappearance of "credibility" and "applicability" of

---

[153] Ludwig Wittgenstein, *Philosophical Investigations*, translated by G. E. M. Anscombe, Macmillan (1964), p. 36e.
[154] Okay?

the cliché: the aesthetics of cliché manipulation in its
sternest confrontation with mere belief and relevance
comfort.[155] Cliché referred to, cliché understood and
used, cliché just used, specific cliché just used in the
midst of other clichés referred to and understood
and used, cliché possibility/inevitability ignored at
varying stages of the games, return of the previously
inadequate/adequate as crystallized cliché, cliché relationships of cliché to cliché, the mere possibility of
easy structural differentiation between the clichéed
and the corny (the cliché as the approach to the neutralized corny without recourse to overstatement),
cliché as readymade, reliance on the cliché of ready-
madeness, cliché of the non-cliché, cliché as the only
level of avoidance of the just-once metaphor, cliché
as unreflective (or merely non-cognitive) continuance
of use, ancient vs. recent cliché, something about the
cliché of the cliché that goes further than the definition of the cliché, cliché as trans-semantic endurance
for semantic molecules, cliché formation as the sur-
face-obvious whole with conceptualizations in the
process of crystallization and as receptacles and
media for containing the whole thing. It's as unavoidable as a mongoose.[156] When it's musical, a repetition

---

[155] Why not "resignation" to an assumed proposition
of "reality," the cliché, rather than "mere reality" itself?:
you get both an assumed reality and an assumed substitute, plus the formal excitement of the formally unlikely
(the logic of heaven rock, etc.).

[156] There is, further, an ambiguous multiplicity of
actual cliché generation points. Whereas it is only a few
days' familiarity that separates the artist qua cliché
monger from the audience qua cliché recipient—after
the moment of initial public exposure—the actual discrepancy of consciousness in relation to any set (or level)
of specifics in the cliché market can be covered up by

orientation helps and a repetition obsession is better-best. When it's linguistic, all you have to do is open your mouth or think for a second or two. When it's non-musically meta-linguistic all you have to do.

The biggest grammaticity-poeticity-spelling-vocabulary-etcetera[157] word moves of all time are within the confines of rock. With "Complicated," "Obsession," and "Cool, Calm, Collected," the Rolling Stones figure that familiarity with overuse of line-ending polysyllabic words will finally break the Barry McGuire jinx and shatter presuppositions about the overuse of Latinate words in rhyme, making poetic response greatly enough a matter of conditioning to refute empirically a few of Socrates' arguments early in the *Republic*. And the Stones are right enough, although these songs are not yet straight rhyme-songs but songs with a cool tension between acceptance as "straight" and rejection as just more "Eve of Destruction." " 'Sophisticated' " or "mature" self-negation! "Obsession" even has random polysyllabic words thrown in to confuse the setup "a little bit" (borrowed from "Think," the Stones' version of "I've Been Loving

---

the artist hiding in his present as a post-exposure past. Awareness of this time lapse can easily engender deeper, more direct cliché concern/disregard.

[157] A great deal of associations between "quality," "objectivity," and superficial rules are made in high school (and earlier) English classes: totally appropriate that the first great rock crowd was the high school set, to which "vocabulary words" like "adolescent" were affixed. The Stones' "We Love You" is about (inevitable) mocking reflection upon English class verbal conceptuality long after it has been shaken down (and long after inevitability has seemingly been exhausted): "We love you/ And we hope/ That you will love we too."

You Too Long" and the Seekers' "Georgy Girl"):
"objection" and "exclusively" (which don't even
rhyme where they occur). Rhymingness falls under
a raunch epistemology anyway. Also, "discretion"
rhymes as sung with the "-ession" words although the
spelling is different. This brings to mind "I love her
and she's loving me" in the Beatles' "Good Day Sunshine," which is prominent as an example of English
language grammatic construction which would disap-
pear in translation into a foreign language, making it
fortunate/unfortunate that polyglot rock ("Komm
Gib Mir Deine Hand" et al) has vanished.[158]

And you can play a great silly game with the first
letters of words grouped together in the Stones'
"Who's Been Sleeping Here?" (and don't forget
Shirley Ellis' "The Name Game," which even gives
explicit instructions for the same sort of thing all put
to music). The song goes to extremes to be "poet-
ically orthodox" in two ways (in respect to conventional poetry as an historical fact and in respect to
Bob Dylan the poet, whom the song puns) and is
successfully pseudo-poignant (words still have some/

---

[158] Wilson Pickett recently did something with Italian
in it, but he never would've if he hadn't been the big
American star at the first (fiasco) Rome rock festival.
Otherwise, there have been a few *de facto* polyglotifica-
tions of note. David Roter's "James Brown" is overindulgence in the s-removal of ritualized black-American
English: "Jame Brown, Jame Brown . . ." The Beatles'
"Michelle" is not only English and French ("Michelle
ma belle sont des mots qui vont très bien ensemble, très
bien ensemble") and a strange total vocabulary ("I will
say the only words I know that you'll understand, ma
Michelle") but also *de facto* over-crystallized overindulgence in Roterism ("ma" for "my" within a single
language, within subsets of a single language).

all associative associations) despite this and because
of this.

And spelling and the names of groups: Beatles,
Byrds, Cyrkle, Crome Syrcus, Surfaris. And the Fugs,
with "fug" itself being Norman Mailer's original con-
cession to censorship (in *The Naked and the Dead*).
And Them, taken from the movie where the little kid
could describe the giant ants she had seen only by
means of a pronoun. And the Lovin' Spoonful as the
first step away from straight collective nouns (Association, Syndicate of Sound) and plurals and the like
(We Five) on the way to singular concrete nouns
(Jefferson Airplane, Soft White Underbelly, First
Edition), abstract nouns (Love, Influence, Spirit),
adjectival stuff (the Lost) and After The Third
World Raspberry. And the Doors' insistence on being
doors that open inward/outward rather than revolving doors or sliding doors or any of that by being
harshly plural (and not even Doors without *the*) in
the face of all this.

Jimi Hendrix's "Are You Experienced?" pumps
new life into the whole verb-tense thing[159] with
"Have you ever been experienced, well I have," which
even manifests ease of convenient specific meaning
duality-etc. access through mere grasp of mere
(taken-for-granted) language "tools." And, for (in-
structive) fun, you can deal with the song merely in
terms of language stuff; he is/was being experienced
by someone else (and language-form thing is being
experienced therein too); he is/was an experienced

---

[159] And the verbal spelling move, Chuck Berry's "Reelin'
and Rocking."

guy (did have linguistic consciousness and now re-
members it and/or reiterates it).

Donovan's "There Is a Mountain" ("First there is
a mountain,/ Then there is no mountain,/ Then there
is") and the Beatles' "Hello Goodbye" ("You say
goodbye/ And I say hello") exploit parallel positive-
negative linguistic construction for all it's worth as
mere content. The Bee Gees do the same with the
language of specific objects, which has no such parallel vocabulary of non-objects and hence requires words
of generalized non-being (which might just as well be
non-being *process* words), in "Red Chair, Fade Away."
(V. D. Parks and disappearance of object qua subject's disappearance: "Palm Desert not fade away.")
The (pretended) non-being of appropriate non-being
words, and its intersection with the mere incidence
of words for wider-range categorization of being, may
be gleaned as a content from Love's "Red Telephone":
"Life goes on here/ Day after day;/ I don't know if
I am *living*/ Or if I'm supposed to *be*." In the same
song is the freshness of another obvious formula, this
time for the mechanics of (mechanical) variation
upon enumeration: "I've been here once,/ I've been
here twice;/ I don't know if the third's the fourth/Or
if the fifth's to fix." The Stones' "Dandelion" is just
extended enumeration as both mere counting and
numerical time: "One o'clock, two o'clock, three
o'clock, four o'clock, five, dandelion don't care about
the time."[159a] Love's "Seven & Seven Is" combines, in

[159a] Hey, Bill Haley's "Rock around the Clock," an
initial initial rock rumbling, makes use of numeration
("One o'clock, two o'clock, three o'clock rock . . .")
made possible through the coincidental rhyme of rock
and clock. Flip side, another number item, "Thirteen
Women."

sequence, the incomplete sentence (the title), "1 . . .
2 . . . 3 . . ." (numbers, words *in* sequence and *of* sequence), followed by music (numbers . . . numerical
sound forms) and mechanically constructable "Boop
bip bip" certified nonsense grunting. And "Maybe
The People Would Be The Times Or Between Clark
And Hilldale"[160] does just the incomplete sentence
move and goes on and completes 'em too, well a little
late.

Yeah, and getting semantic-poetic just a bit Arthur
Lee makes the big language-rock move of them all
(and the big language move of the last 17 million
years), all this in "¡Que Vida!" which starts by delineating the setup for the syntax-of-semantics-refer-
ence move: "With pictures and words/ Is this com-
municating(?)/ (The sounds that I heard,/ The
drowning voice then fading)" and from then on it's
the restoration of literalism in the context of rhyme,
the collapse of all distinction between jargon and
mere naive vocabulary, featuring words which rhyme
and yet totally avoid pretense ('cause so naive):
"With nickels and dimes/ You soon will have a dollar," devoid of doper implications of measure, "Am I
in your time(?),/ I see no need to swallow/ Or catch
a plane to travel,/ My mind's not made of gravel . . .,"
an old-line atomist mind/container.[161]

---

[160] A two-title title (with conventional *or*) which would
be a nice mess if you followed standard capitalization
procedure ("Maybe the People Would Be the Times or
between Clark and Hilldale"). Another Love composite
title all in one word, "Andmoreagain" (a chick, "you will
see you in her eye").
[161] A lot like Donovan's "elevator in the brain hotel"
in "Epistle to Dippy," his biggest extravaganza during
his period of snappy Dylanesque formula "plagiarism"

And, to acknowledge the direct source by quoting
from any obvious Love fragment ("She Comes in
Colors"), the Stones (who just might have been the
direct source for Love[162]) stick it in "She's a Rainbow," which does a whole bunch with color listing:

> Have you seen her dressed in blue?
> See the sky in front of you,
> And her face is like a sail,
> Speck of white so fair and pale,
> Have you seen a lady fairer?
>
> Have you seen her all in gold?
> Like a queen in days of old,
> She shoots colors all around

---

for contents already overripe in afterthought imagery,
with the run-on sentence being his addition, as with the
line "such a tiny speculatin' whether to be hip or skip
along quite merrily." A cornerstone of doper and post-
doper mere imagery generation through mere word-
phrase conglomeration, this move is used by the Beatles
in "I Am the Walrus" only after it has become so ripe
that it has spoiled. In it the whole thing gets gutter-
ally joyfully forced ("Yellow matter custard dripping
from a dead dog's eye,/Crabalocker fishwife pornographic priestess boy you've been a naughty girl you let
your knickers down") to the point of "GOO GOO GOO
JOOB" and degeneration into the viscera of thousands
of simultaneous messages as the song fades into some
stuff from *King Lear*. At the same time there's "everybody ha ha" and "everybody smokes pot" and "everybody's fucked up" and more.

[162] And who knows whether or not the biggest hard-
language repetition song of them all, the Beatles' "All
You Need Is Love," isn't also with *Love* in mind? And
Peter Albin of Big Brother has said that Love should be
called Hate (they're nasty and beat guys up), good.

Like a sunset going down,
Have you seen a lady fairer?

So structurally sound as a sponge that they can throw anything in. And they do, "She comes in colors everywhere,/ She combs her hair,/ She's like a rainbow," never missing an opportunity to be repetitious with their grocery list.

Hmm and isn't that where Dylan was playing golf just before his motorcycle accident opened up a year for everybody to structurally fill in and articulate and improve (by leaps and bounds) the Great Dylan Grocery List Story Song (since the dictionary was always open so wide to him)? Yeah, so when Dylan finally gets around to coming back, everything he *knew* everybody else *assumes*[163] and the best he can do is to "get back in the race" with "moon's gonna shine like a spoon" ("I'll Be Your Baby Tonight"), working out in the nth (or n + first) time around mere fact-of-rhyme category, which Dylan had originally plucked out of rock as an explicit easy-as-pie rock-poetic gimmick qua gimmick. So after the start of the seclusion it's Dylan the unseen influence chain producer, so you can finally just talk mundanely and simply as possible about the Dylan rock-move corpus (and reiterate undigested by time—since digestion is what his quasi-disappearance got too poetic in suggesting to all the hacks).

[163] "Younger Generation" by the Spoonful: "And then I'll know that all I've learned my kid assumes." A father-child easy analogue to Dylan and his implicit/explicit followers.

The folk spirit of Bob Dylan never fully embraced rock 'n' roll except on his *Bringing It All Back Home* album, itself his major turning point,[164] until the awesome majesty of "Like a Rolling Stone." Previously he had masterfully written and sung (ironically) unique works of social protest, including one of the most frightening visions of war ever perceived, "A Hard Rain," eventually to be trivialized by Barry McGuire. Rumors had pervaded his folk singing career that he had been an inauthentic folk person, that he drove his XKE with a snarl through unemployed mining areas of West Virginia. Then he emerged as a full-fledged "authentic" rock singer with a vast backlog of his own serious work to destroy (and the Newport folk fans booed him to help him along).

This situation can be compared to what Allan Kaprow senses was the direction of the work of Jackson Pollock, toward self-destruction. As his work dealt with (if ya want it that simple) affirmation through negation, Pollock was in the process of affirming his own life (which he was traditionally drinking away) when he was killed in a car accident. But Dylan's sentimentality is far removed from Pollock's intense enactment of life through art. Dylan's destruction is only a trivialization, a saying of "So what?" to one's own creations, devoid of any explicit tragic overtones.[165] Beholding the absurdity of truth through language in "Gates of Eden," he ends with "Sometimes I think there are no words but these to tell what's true/ And there are no truths outside the gates of Eden." In its place he substitutes coolness through

---

[164] "I ain't gonna work on Maggie's farm no more" is an indicator.

[165] Dylan: "a crushing yet meaningless blow."

language with cascades of meaningless (or overly meaningful enough to be granted meaningless) but great sounding poetic images. Sung in such a way that several (at least ten) hearings are necessary even to discern most of the words and accompanied by conventional nominally vulgar rock instrumentation with pseudo-revival-meeting organ[166] and coupled with a newborn striving for number-one level acceptance, this is the initial culmination move of "Like a Rolling Stone."

Upon first hearing one is deceived into expecting the song to contain nascent profundity, perhaps with the intention of protest against the bourgeois society which has apparently forced Dylan into abandoning the sincerity of folk music for rock. But meaning is to be found only in fragments and it reveals instead a newfound joy at the meaninglessness he has been given and has sought out via his own such move. Some of the sounds that are transcribed into words from Dylan's song are seemingly senseless. For instance, "bumps-a-chime" could be a combination of the bump and grind and the rock dance called the monkey shine,[167] "juiced on it" usually sounds more like "choustinit," and "mystery tramp" first struck me as "mystery trend" (which is alluded to in *Hard Day's Night* as "the clue to the new direction"). The only reference to expected Dylanesque prior "meaning" is the mention of political disillusionment; this has been removed. The person spoken to has been robbed, desensitized, deenergized, misdirected, and is now generally metaphysically lost, but with a new oblivion

---

[166] Last heard in Walter Brennan's "Old Rivers."

[167] But, lo and behold, it turns out to be "threw the bums a dime."

where there is "nothin' to lose" and no one to "get your kicks for you." Life can be a "vacuum" and "invisible" and only thus can man be resurrected from the nightmare of finite meaning given by "Fingertips" and "Land of 1000 Dances," which sum up to enslavement realized with the full incorporation of particles of meaning suggested by Chubby Checker. Only at the moment of rock 'n' roll's greatest official burst of initial profundity could such a statement of profound *unprofundity* occur. Here is at last a nihilism that is packed with joy, that demonstrates the awesomeness of triviality and the triteness of such unbounded potency (and that is public and official). And that refers to the Stones as well as Benjamin Franklin.

Dylan set the pace for a group of performers to attempt to interpret his approach and emulate it. The Byrds, with "Mr. Tambourine Man" and an entire Dylanesque first album, have completely spoofed Dylan as he has done with his own earlier work,[168] and the Turtles have accomplished a fair butchering of Dylan's "It Ain't Me Babe." Folk singer Joan Baez has had released a single track recorded years earlier, "There but for Fortune," which is endowed with the quality of a Duchampian ready-made in its new rock 'n' roll context. It bears a sharp resemblance to Marianne Faithfull's "As Tears Go By," which itself had been, seemingly, an insipid reference to Baez, thus without being changed it is altered by its new added rock pretensions. Bobby Vinton, a natural falsetto-resembling singer whose five previous songs all had

---

[168] Jim McGuinn of the Byrds even just about taught Dylan what to do with the Dylan vocal and Dylan's *Blonde on Blonde* is saturated with McGuinnized Dylan raw mere vocality.

"lonely" in their titles, then recorded the folkish "What Color Is a Man?" and thus went in a direction opposite Dylan's, that of attaching "seriousness" to a career basically banal, difficult for him since he could not possibly understand his own unintentional banality (but, just the same, he later did the inadvertent peace song, "Coming Home Soldier," with its ambiguous "my land"). And Sonny and Cher, a husband and wife team, have created something interesting by adding to their Paula-and-Paulaesque routine the Dylanesque (prior) folk sincerity and degeneracy (Sonny wears feather jackets and sounds almost exactly the same on record as his wife).[169]

And *all* the big pop folkies of the time, who could easily have made it directly into the folk-rock mainstream without much mere change, missed the boat. They just couldn't face the prospect of pertinence being just anywhere at all, which is a start, and certainly not the authenticity of inauthenticity or, better still, straight unbridled mere inauthenticity (since that's implicit/explicit everywhere anyway too). And poor Peter, Paul and Mary took years just to become passive partial *fans* of rock. At least they wouldn't admit it until "I Dig Rock 'n' Roll Music" (quite a while after the whole thing switched nominally to *rock*) which had its reservations in fact: "The message may not move me or mean a great deal to me but hey it feels so groovy to say (. . . I dig . . .)" and "They[170] got a good thing going when the words don't

---

[169] And Tiny Tim sings *both* parts on his recording of their "I Got You Babe."

[170] The Mamas & the Papas, a pack who made the folk-rock move using what Peter, Paul & Mary can't see as P,P&M readymades (or maybe it's just that folk is for everyone).

get in the way." Man, and where else did *their* words ever fit in except by the most insipid (great) rock aesthetic (except for their version of Dylan's "Don't Think Twice," which made it big before Dylan did only because they were stylistically lame enough). And the Kingston Trio, always plagued by qualms about authenticity and commerciality, ceased to exist, period, while ignorant of their potential place in rock.

But the pop (folk-pop and pop-folk) move in all its grandeur has found an entrance into rock, by way of the Jefferson Airplane.[171] One steadfast pop folk criterion is professional persistence (but not *too* overwhelming commercial success; hence, some retention of "amateurism") before a mass audience with pretensions about your ability to communicate and stuff like that. The Airplane is the prime example of ever-lessening professionalism (but ever-developing means of hiding it) through longevity (so success can never get in the way of innate amateurism, a naturally professional natural amateurism[172]), all flowing from readymade mere inclusion in the last dying embers of the folk-rock scene proper by way of a bit of bandying with acid (which started as fashionably folk before

---

[171] And then there's the great mere move as change of scene performed by guys like Gene Clark, who was in the New Christy Minstrels but can't be found in the listings on any of their albums, and Jim McGuinn, who only played (guitar) with (and did no singing for) the Chad Mitchell Trio. Great minimal establishment of minimally minimal folk authenticity credentials. A real Move Move if there ever was one.

[172] Marty Balin (leader and founder who held auditions for the original group) was once greasy-haired singer for the party-by-the-pool Town Criers, so he's got lengthy credentials as genius of this scene.

Says Elvis: "I remember this blond girl girl in Atlanta. She came to three different shows. She sat in the front row and screamed all through all of them."

"One night she grabbed me and tried to come up on stage. A policeman pulled her back. 'Let me at him!' she yelled. It tickled me and broke up the house."

Skip Spence of Moby Grape. Somebody said Skip had a wife
and six kids. I don't think he does. (Photo by Ken Greenberg)

The greatest thing that freedom
brought to MICK JAGGER
after his nightmare trial — and
two days awaiting sentence after
being found guilty — was being
with MARIANNE FAITHFULL
again. He is pictured with her
on Saturday — and how happy
and peaceful she has made him
feel.

(From *New Musical Express*, July 8, 1967)

Tommy James battles cystic fibrosis for you and me and this Christine.

Both Morrisons. There were only two. (Photo of Jim, at right, by Ken Greenberg)

Chuck Berry.

Double dynamite: Four Seasons (above) and Soft White
Underbelly. (Photo of Underbelly by Jeff Richards)

Bo Diddley

B. B. King
(Photo by Ken Greenberg)   **Otis Redding**

Howlin' Wolf

it was fashionably rock, and pop folk is often concerned with fashion or at least such mere fashion
predicates as *neatness*). All three of their albums
*(Jefferson Airplane Takes Off, Surrealistic Pillow,
After Bathing at Baxter's)* are simultaneously their
best, so any direction of evolutionary quality can be
derived from their total output just on records.

And, of course, they've had the added specific in-
gredients of, for example, the first major recording of
the Dino Valenti love-scene classic "Let's Get Together" and "meaningful-to-the-young" lyrics (which
were finally *in* for the past in rock and now engendered with the additional validity of stuff like the
notion of "groping") like those of "She Has Funny
Cars": "Every day I try so hard to know your mind
and find out what's inside you"; "Your mind's guar-
anteed, it's all you ever need, so whattaya want with
me?" And on the matter of communication, Marty
Balin has always been throwing around some line
about not *singing* but *making love* to his audience,[173]
a remark belittled by the Airplane's great cynical
bassist Jack Casady as being just a bunch of F. Scott
Fitzgerald tripe.

While guitarist Jorma Kaukonen's controlled feed-
back opening and ending to their biggest masterpiece,

---

[173] As seen in stuff like "Let Me In" ("Thanks for
nothing") and "Don't Slip Away" ("Almost a year now
since we've been together"), the Airplane's forte is the
transiency of the love intersection. Good old Marty once
had a thing going with a lesbian chick (who was able to
attract teeny bopper fan type chicks by telling them all
about their hero), figuring that it would enable him to
extend his love into domains not directly accessible.

"The Ballad of You and Me and Pooneil," set new
horizons for the electricity of what had become, if
folk at all anymore, a folk-technology and technological folk of the cosmos, the cosmos became familiar
enough and an electrified cosmos became just another
diaphoric juxtaposition of superstructure common to
all folk with cosmic pretensions; but because the import of "Pooneil" is so (topically doperly) overpower-
ing the direction is still folky: from electrical folk-rock
to a folk-rock of electricity to the rock-folk of electricity to mere electrical rock-folk, which easily reduces to rock-folk or whatever. And even electricity
as both a unification and focal point of professionalism has turned into a mere positive-negative rock
mere fact: it's still all electric even now that it's in-
strumentally not awesome enough to cover up the
Balin-Grace Slick-Paul Kantner vocal mild atrocity
(inadvertent folk sloppiness, inadvertent folk vocal roughness-but-really-just-a-bummer-and-certain-
ly-not-to-be-confused-with-raunch[174] all rolled into
one: great and mechanical and mechanically great).
And the "When I die"/"When I'm high" freakout
near the end of "Pooneil": *hidden* dope references,
particularly those which might have some depth are
corny enough to be hokey, and almost hokey enough
to be folky, since folky is already so hokey anyway.

---

[174] In the early days of Dylan, the vocal repulsiveness
move was in full flight, but, through lots of time and intentionally reinforced conditioning, Dylan's voice came
to be palatable and good and great and even actually
great long after you had no way of telling whether it
really was (or caring). The Airplane falls into this long-
dead (hence readily available) rock-vocal difficulty-of-
orientation scene, and what's better (now), it's an outcome of talent rather than insight: perhaps their greatest
folk non-insight.

And since, as Marty has sometimes revealed, he has never had an ego loss (high-die intersection).[175] So in the song, the "inappropriate" utterance of "Armadillo" at a nexus is Marty's only appropriate moment of glory: the Airplane's greatest show in the "taste" framework. And it's another big move for Spencer Dryden not to do any drum tap stuff at the very end of the "Spare Chaynge" jam; jazz tastefulness when they don't even have a taste for jazz.[176] And, more of that, Grace's "rejoyce" uses an inadvertently non-original other-than-the-ordinary Coltrane readymade, the McCoy Tyner piano monotony move and quasi-Elvin Jones cymbal gimmick.

"Wild Tyme (H)": "doing things that haven't got a name yet" and they're all minor and that's the grandeur of the Airplane: potential new designations, but all posthumously describing something that wasn't much at the right time (inadvertently folky temporal hokum), labels galore. Also, association of name and fame, and any origins of the Jefferson Airplane name and its initiation of the group name move.

And the United States of America has got-ta be the rock equivalent of the Serendipity Singers, whatever they were, whatever they are. Any group that calls itself United States of America instead of Mustard or Tusk, The Vanquisher (only a marginal distinction), sings "Love Song to the Dead Che," uses John Philip Sousa without previously building an excess of *ad*

[175] Airplane master publicity man Gary Blackman once replied, "If you ain't had no ego loss, Marty, you ain't ever had a trip!"

[176] Jazz, even lousy jazz (as a public object), requires specific proficiency.

hominem pressure or being Van Dyke Parks is in on some sort of serendipity scene, super-scenewise. Last of the definitive non-hack quasi-folk-rock bands. All that remains is hacking it out in a folk topicality direction from the rock hack substratum, as the First Edition does with "Just Dropped In" ("to see what condition my condition was in"), or pouring out a thick-as-pumice talent overstatement from the folk side, as with the Stone Poneys' "Different Drum." Period.

Oh yeah, forgot about Janis Ian, but who would wanna know anything about her?

And Simon and Garfunkel as the intersection of folk and poetic clarity with easy listening. And their use of "Silent Night" as easy listening juxtaposed with the harshness of a radio news report about all the tried-and-true atrocities of the day: they want real "message" stuff to be beyond the realm of easy listening, they'd rather have it shock, but the easy part of it is more than contrast, it's continuance of accessibility. And the whole act ends up (after all these years) as folk anyway: stick around and be pertinent once in a while, have no fear of (hitwise) dry spells. Their first hit, "Sounds of Silence," was a sleeper for them originally but it took off to launch them up and down. Their (2 yrs. later) scoring of *The Graduate*, which gave transpoetic vividness to their already old "Sounds of Silence" (it showed not only the sounds uttered by silence but the silence derivative from sounds themselves; with just the words and sounds Paul Simon happened to use, their lengthy dry spell of comparative silence in the form of unlistenability could not have been directly postulated, but the film's additions made it more obvious) and spotlighted their sudden biggest hit, "Mrs. Robinson." Someplace in between S & G did "I Am a Rock" (". . . and a rock feels no pain"), which without its Dylan-type nouveau rock band would have been almost serious about alienation. And Paul Simon's authorship of the Cyrkle's "Red Rubber Ball" left no doubts that his forte was writing for all occasions, just like the hick hero of *Mr. Deeds Goes to Town*.

Pete Seeger has never succumbed except to see his "Turn, Turn, Turn" become the Byrds' biggest hit and sit around on his ("educational") TV show and gawk at a sitar with Donovan acting bored and saying as little as possible. Such superficial paradigm humility really distinguishes him as a rock guy.

Burl Ives, once a co-worker of Seeger's, made his rock splash well after "Big Rock Candy Mountain" but also way before folk rock: "Mr. In Between" and "Little Bitty Tear."

And, come to think of it, Jimmy Rodgers' "Kisses Sweeter Than Wine" came from the version Pete Seeger did with the Weavers which stole its rhythm from what Seeger once overheard Leadbelly do on a twelve-string.

Phil Ochs has always been taylor-made for rock, being totally shallow of form and nothing but (political) content and intent. Bring in Joseph Byrd (of U.S.A.) to arrange and, pfff, his *Pleasures of the Harbor* is a rock album with a misunderstood censored hit cut ("Small Circle of Friends") about drugs and things.

When it first appeared the Kinks' "Well Respected Man" was surely the harbinger of eventual total folk-folkrock-rock fusion/dissemination. Afterwards no content would ever be overly social enough to be, on the basis of that alone, ineligible for immediate rock takeover. The Beatles' "Taxman" was in its time still regarded (as pretentious enough to be) "folk rock," and the Mamas and the Papas were dealt with the same way from the formal side of the coin, but soon all salient distinction collapsed. Finally, any work (claiming to be) from within straight folk has come through the strainer as *rock-folk* or *folk qua rock* or *folk qua folk qua rock qua folk* etc. This now goes for the likes of the Incredible String Band and ethnic ambiguous pop-folk-classical like the Bauls of Bengal. And in terms of traditional social analogues, rock as the form of the hippies and folk for the beats is an easy out. And Donovan (Tim Buckley), because of his hair as much as his music, has become a viable total substitute for Dylan if need be: personal charismatic interchangeability.

A survey of the evil done by rock people themselves is vastly revealing. With Leadbelly there is almost a straight unity between the content of his life and his songs, although he often exceeded "in life" anything he would have described verbally, even if his "Ella Speed" mentions "first degree murder with a Colt 41." A rapist and murderer, he was more publicly evil than Genet without the latter's objective glory (while still young) and with much less merely literarily enviable punishment. In "Rock Island Line" he half-jokingly bewails the triviality of his tragedy: "Jesus died to save others' sins,/ Glory to God we're gonna need him again." This could almost be a laughing reply to Joseph Wood Krutch, who opines about tragic man, "His passions are important to him because he believes them important through all time and all space; the very fact that he can sin (no modern can) means that his universe is watching his acts; and though he may perish, a God leans out from infinity to strike him down."[177]

Chuck Berry is later able to surpass Leadbelly, for he can do no better than commit a violation of the Mann Act with a fourteen-year-old Apache girl. For a long while rock 'n' roll, motorcycles, and juvenile delinquency were correlated as part of a common evil. Movies like *Blackboard Jungle* and *Rock & Roll Generation* reported and created this connection and were even impressive.[178] Elvis Presley and such groups as the Elegants easily could be labeled "evil" in appearance. Teen-agers beat up adults and fought with policemen outside Alan Freed rock 'n' roll shows in the middle and late 1950's. But even with the eventual diminution of evil in rock, the summer of 1965 saw a crowd outside the Bridgeport, Connecticut concert of the acceptedly innocent Herman's Hermits throwing rocks at cops, who by this time had become the new evil; a cult of innocence is now perfectly within rock's context.

---

[177] Joseph Wood Krutch, "The Tragic Fallacy," from *The Modern Temper*, Harcourt, Brace & World, 1929, on p. 180 of a xeroxed anthology. The Bonzo Dog Doo Dah Band's "Death Cab for Cutie" is the rock contextualization of both Krutch and the old tragic cats: "Someone's gonna make you pay your fare."

[178] One remnant of this era is the record series entitled "Mr. Maestro's Bad Motorcycle Golden Oldies," a proper consideration for original context without diminution of evil.

MARTHA & THE VANDELLAS

But leading up to this eventuality is a period of sociological reduction in rock, in which the evil one is viewed as the victim of circumstance. The Crystals' "Uptown" and "He's a Rebel" are Manhattan sociology of a Michael Harrington variety, viewable as significant only for their destructive effect upon the visceral quality of rock evil. Martha and the Vandellas revel in evil but somehow see the need to rely on sociological apology, as in "Wild One" where they rant, "You're the victim of circumstance." Fortunately the new (and new-old) wave of rock 'n' roll has brought with it a system of random ethical values, of even a system whereby sociological protest can be cool, just as Dylan makes (real-live) hate cool in "Positively Fourth Street."

Sociology, all the way up to Zappaesque articulate babble about sexual repression and Hank Ballard and the Midnighters,[179] is an obvious functional drag, particularly when it subverts the move qua move by means of opaque non-magical causality. The Stones have always had a super-easy time mocking this dilly-dally and all linguistic manifestations of it. On *Between the Buttons* three tracks, "Something Happened to Me Yesterday:"

No one's sure just what it was
Or the meaning and the cause . . .
He don't know if it's right or wrong,
Maybe he should tell someone;
He's not sure just what it was
Or if it's against the law

[179] Zappa, "The Oracle Has It All Psyched Out," *Life*, June 28, 1968, p. 85.

"Let's Spend the Night Together" ("But I just can't
apologize, oh no") and "Ruby Tuesday" ("Don't
question why she needs to be so free,/She'll tell you
it's the only way to be"), go to the point of kicking
rationalistic ethics in the groin, rightfully demonstrating that philosophical delineation and actual moral
ascription are radically divergent problems. And
metaethics too comes into play, with explanatory
metaethical grounds varying from track to track. In
"She Smiled Sweetly" it's "nothing in why or when."
"Something Happened" asserts "Someone says there's
something more to pay/ For sins that you committed
yesterday," using perfectly clearly two ambiguous ref-
erents (someone, something) while being convinc-
ingly "superstitious." "All Sold Out" angrily rejects
reductionist psychological ethical groundwork. Inconsistencies, eclecticism. But above all, dilly-dally before and after the entrance of the ethical language
game convention, ritualized chaos-and-back with the
omnipresent over-riding assumption of the ritualized
what-the-hell-does-evil-innocence/good-bad-mean-
anyway?[180] So of course the reentry of just these
terms as presenting the most obvious crucial (dippy)
inapplicable meat of all.

And on an even more invulnerably flimsy level is
the extension of ethical whimsy to intra-art interpretive byplay, as is manifest in the Stones' "Ride On
Baby":

> You walk up to me an' try an' look shy,
> The red round your eyes says that you ain't
>   a child,

[180] In "My Back Pages" Dylan uses this as an obvious
backdrop for the clarification of assumed out-of-context
clarity: "Good and bad, I defined these terms, quite
clear, no doubt, somehow."

Get out and ride on, baby, ride on, baby, ride on,
   baby,
Well I seen your face in a trashy magazine,
You know where you're goin' but I don't like
   the places you been.

If you could only recapture the times when you were just a creep and your responses to other creeps were just creepy, man that's where primal innocence is at. Go back to the days when you could really get something out of "Can I Get a Witness" and "Walkin' the Dog," an innocence that you still had all the way up to "Last Time" but not "Satisfaction," when you spread it on too thick and lost your vulnerability. Innocent even when you knew *completely* where Cassius Clay was at and even Feuerbach but *not* Feuerbach as a *post*-religious guy. Man once upon a time you *knew* that the Cowsills ate it but somehow could be listened to, you knew it *without* resorting to calling them a pack of freaks. Man the Stones were *always* happy don't you see? But now you see the Doors are like Cowsills and their world view is irrelevant. And the rest of this mamby pamby nostalgia (A PRIORI NOSTALGIA, EASILY GENERATED) only makes it when the flash is gone and the recollective penis is limp and silent. But like there were the days when you wanted to be Hud and now you respect him as a freak and deal with yourself as implicitly about the same as the guy, and who knows where *that* is at?

Okay, if Stones have always been happy more or less, here's their first noncynical album call it *that* Jack. And they do it all: not high school as content-by-external-imposition but high school qua high school in all its purity, senior sing and all ("Sing This All Together"). Friends sloppily fuckin' around with Steve's brand-new tape recorder. "Empty Heart Empty Life" is a little tough to match but there's always "Citadel" and what high school bathroom singers these days or those days are up to "Citadel" except for their social studies paper and where else if not precisely there? You even got adolescence as mere dumb over-crystallized rock ideal in reverse, instead of adolescence as the postulated bullshit ground for rock it's rock as the ultimate in adolescent drag.

For Beatles it's not high school but childhood-senility-childhood, which sure as shit comes out as unclarifiable wistfulness for the standard fornicating and prefornicating teen-ager. *Magical Mystery Tour*'s stuffed with childhood-senility dispersion-trip rhetoric, but it's never self-conscious cause Johnny Lennon has always been 5, 10, 15, 20, 25, 30, 35 (hey, remember when they used to say he was a seasoned professional of 34?), 40, 45, 50, 55, 60, 65, 70, 75, 80, 85, 90, 95, 100 . . . only self-conscious if ya wanna say he is just cause he is if he's on Mars and he's singin' about Mars which is okay if ya say it, okay? "The Fool on the Hill" is one hell of a fool and so are the unnamed creeps in the song and all the guys singin' and playin' it and you and me and everybody *knows* that everybody else blows, he just knows it Jack and that's valid if you're any kind of real philosopher, and particularly if you're a fascist and hate fuckin' commies and peace creeps or you're a peace creep and hate fuckin' fascist pigs or if you transcend any of it instead of or in addition to the rest. If you have earphones listen to "I Am the Walrus" in stereo and you'll hear "Everybody's fucked up" repeatedly near the end. If you're a little kid and your mommy or daddy or babysitter is reading this to you now just take it from me that the whole thing is a great just-before-bedtime goodie just for you. And ask somebody to help you find the page where George is giving the finger but don't ask what it means just stay primally innocent as far as that goes man.

Now, on to Herman the even greater paradigm. Originally recorded by an obscure female (group?) known as Earl-Jean, "I'm Into Something Good" is an insipid song of the birth of a platonic relationship. Sounding every bit as innocent, Herman's Hermits recorded the same song but by simply being males using the same words they created something at the same time contextually evil.[182] The arrangements of both recordings are basically alike, even to the insertion of a hackneyed piano break about three-quarters of the way to the end: yet Herman's reciting of "Something tells me I'm into something good" and "I knew it wouldn't be just a one-night stand" is radically different from the original. Subsequently, Herman (real name Peter Noone) recorded something else in the same vein, "Show Me Girl," with its subtly demanding refrain, "You've got to show me girl, show me that you're really mine." I've since been expecting them to revive another song by a female group, the Sensations, "Let Me In," which opens, "Let me in wee-oo, oo-wee-oo, wee-oo, oo-wee-oo wee-oo," and later begs, "Let me in . . . I thought you were my friend" (the old friend-lover distinction toyed with[183]).

---

[182] Minor mediocre sexual digression being enough to be evil, with masking it in criterion-contextual innocence heightening the evil even more.

[183] Other instances: Jackie Wilson's "A Woman, a Lover, a Friend," and a recent group called Friend and Lover.

Then came more innocently sung works such as "Can't You Hear My Heart Beat," which proclaims, "Every time you're close to me,/ I get a feelin' that's so oo-oo-wee," and a revival of the Rays' classic naive rock 'n' roll hit, "Silhouettes": "Let me in or else I'll beat/ Down your door." Next came Herman's biggest and purest hit (it even abandoned already non-raucous rockness for school-boy whatchamacallit), "Mrs. Brown You've Got a Lovely Daughter." Herman has clearly placed in all his works a transcendental innocence, a technique Memphis Sam Pearlman has named Herman's Contradiction. While stylistically the antithesis of Leadbelly and Elvis Presley's motorcycle followers, it reveals a vast magnitude of experience possible in this very innocence, a character at once free and self-sustaining and simultaneously merged with the universe of passion, lust, eventually even evil in a universal sense. First of all, Herman has transformed a school-boy innocence (already an instance of Herman's Contradiction if we rely on more familiar school-boy stereotypic conceptualizations) into a workable metaphysical experience and, next, has made it manifest as a mask covering an omnipresent eruptible evil and serving as a base for its eruption. Possibly all innocence is hiding the tragic image of man; therefore, in a Jungian sense, an analysis of this innocence could reveal man's greatest potential for tragedy, however (boring) we are to take this category. Thus Herman's naive message to Mrs. Brown suddenly evolves into a passion, indicating the hubris he can maintain even in an utterly frustrating situation completely lacking any original arrogance. That man must learn to sin and suffer as a precondition of Nietzschean tragedy is here subtly avoided totally.

With this foundation already set, Herman was then able to embark on his most profound (and profane) work, which along with all his previous works he had no role in writing, "Henry VIII I Am": "I'm getting married to the widow next door;/ She's been married seven times before,/ And every one was an 'Enery." Herman, singing for Henry, is here a seventeen-year-old obsessed with entering into the utterly repetitious routine of someone obviously old enough to be at least his mother. He has moved from Mrs. Brown's daughter to the equivalent of Mrs. Brown and is an analogue to Oedipus. But Herman's Contradiction implants a fundamental innocence in the entire relationship; for he has traveled from a natural innocence to one which remains pure merely through its (epistemological) naiveté.[184] In this current involvement with the widow next door, he is almost (so) foolish to remain with such an emotional outlook that (he) stifles his lust (minor-league and merely transcendentally presupposed) for her. The nature of his innocence is thus trivializing to his experiential out-

---

[184] There was a competitive innocence-rock rivalry in the making between Herman and Freddy and the Dreamers, who were older by far and had to resort to (more excessively contrived without contrivance conventions) maneuvers like a dance called the Freddy. On TV once, Herman, upon hearing that Freddy would be the special guest the following week, parodied the Freddy (simulated physical equivalent of a simulated parody of Herman) to everybody's laughter. And such (acknowledged) exclamation of superiority (hence, the *sophistication* of referentiality and superiority through cognition of postulated/actual inferiority) removed none of Herman's purity, purity as fundamental unspoiledness (aesthetic purity) coupled with slightly spoiled (hence further unspoiled) ethical purity.

look and simultaneously it is awesome if it can mask such a blatantly active manifestation of this outlook.

Yet he shows a joy of engagement with seemingly unavoidable repetition, a self-destruction strikingly powerful. Thus could universal conventionally tragic characters reveal themselves through such a repetition. And this repetition is the natural outcome of the evolution of rock 'n' roll made conscious of itself. From Chuck Berry's cognition that "it's got a back beat, you can't lose it" the glorification of music turns to a recognition of redundancy: "Second verse, same as the first," as Henry (Herman) VIII announces. From a primary joy at repetition, Herman comes to a feeling of monotony, which while an orgasmic monotony still has its feeling held in abeyance by his Contradiction.[185] In such a way are Parmenides and Heraclitus reduced to one viewpoint.

Cognition and perceptual mentation are repetitions, just as Plato's ideational universe most assuredly is a form of duplication. Aristotle could not accept this duplication for all the thunder it was. St. Augustine's view of man could take into account the potency of the orgasmic monotony of such duplication in memory (like how could he still have wet dreams all those years after renouncing the flesh?).[185a] Jackson

[185] In later Herman, Herman's Contradiction disappears from the opaque content and becomes merely an interpretive tool or focal point for ironic reeruptive specificity (as in "No Milk Today").

[185a] On the other hand, the double-flesh move, the Doors' "Love Me Two Times" ("one for tomorrow, one just for today" in potentially endless successions of overlapping two-day sets): duplication as forced oversufficiency ("Love me one time, I could not speak, love me one time, yeah my knees got weak, love me two times, last me all through the week") structurally induced.

Browne's "The Painter," recorded by Steve Noonan, presents, in the guise of apparent epistemological distinction, inadvertent after-the-fact duplication: "He sees no line between what he's imagining and what he sees with his own eyes."[186] To Berkeley, the epistemology of mind-things is dependent upon just how potent man's mechanism for internal repetition is.[186a]

Buber has viewed Kant as representing man's limitation of being tied to phenomena; either man has internally imitated the external universe or his universe is an echo of self. And Aristotle's treatment of art as a formalized imitation seems to indicate his displeasure with being confined by the universe. Bob Dylan has remarked in "It's Alright Ma—I'm Only Bleeding" that "it's life and life only"; in other words, an experience can be looked upon as everything of which it consists and as only that of which it consists. If life is to be the accumulation of echoes, man's reaction can be to choke or to rejoice or to ignore. In "Eight Days a Week" ("I luh-uh-uh-uh-uhve you") the Beatles rejoice in a limitation which, if expanded, will be a louder echo of its original form.

To Nietzsche, "universal" aspects of man are actualized in his Dionysiac revelry; he becomes fused with the hyper-personal. *A priori*, the very first notion of rock 'n' roll is that of a Dionysiac experience. Yet viewed through the image of Herman, the Dionysian rock experience is that of engagement with this thun-

---

[186] "If I Fell": "when she learns we are *two*," meaning *one*.

[186a] And with "resignation" to an assumed mere proposition of "reality" (the cliché) *as soon as* to mere "reality" itself, you get both assumed reality and an assumed substitute.

derous repetition qua repetition. Apollonian is also possible/probable/inevitable, first the elementary role of the eclectic grid of the rock artist, and next the totality given by society, world, critics, history, etc., through such media as the formation of conventions of association and reaction habits of both artist and audience. To attach the category of Platonic music to any music with regularity is to overlook the regularity that is a basic part of all music, even Wagner's or Dionysus'.

Two situations. First, overcoming the massive proportion of Apollonianism that is external (in origin or form of origin), since the readymade form is such a huge supply (ironic: trans-personal as Platonically universal intersected with the empirical transpersonal), all this *if you want to* (just in case) as a rock move. Next, locating anywhere the definitive Apollonian tendency which is not merely an over-regularized Dionysian move (good irrelevant question because it functions Apollonianly anyway from the Apollonian side of things and is reduced to definitive irrelevancy from the Dionysian side: so introduce it only to ignore it) and which doesn't undo the meat of the externality scene by means of its (when clarified) innate over-clarification potential.

The Byrds are so Apollonian throughout that it never gets in the way in spots. While with their words Apollo is almost the whole show, words are only half the whole show. And the music's only half Apollonian too, a Dionysian showcase for the Apollonian and vice versa—awe of form, form of awe. And music is only half the show. Balance keeps balance from showing.

With Pearls Before Swine the over-all balance becomes meticulous enough so that the intrusion of the
words is/isn't an intrusion, even before the fact of
any particular words. Because the words can be pearl-
like but not swine-like although aided by the imposition of the title-clad swine-word, words/meanings/
metaphors are never a hindrance, even when they
are. So as *mere* becomes clear as *meager* plus *sheer*,
their "Another Time" becomes not only definitive
Apollonianism but the constantly expansive Apollonian escape from Apollonian expansion:

Where have you been to?
Where did you go?
Did you follow the Summer out
When the Winter pushed its face
In the snow?
Or have you come by again
To die again?
Try again another time

Did you follow the Crystal Swan?
Did you see yourself
Deep inside the Velvet Pond?
Or have you come by again
To die again?
Try again another time

When you set to shape the world
Was the shape the shape of You?
Or did you cast enchanting glance
Thru the Eye that all men use?
Or have you come by again
To die again?
Try again another time

Did you find that the Universe
Doesn't care at all?
Did you find if you don't care
This whole wrong world will fall?
Or have you come by again
To die again?
Try again another time

Did you ever capture
All those jewels in the sky?
Did you find that the world outside
Is all inside your mind?
Or have you come by again
To die again?
Try again another time

ESP-DISK', catalogue #1054 and #1075.

The structural imposition of the merely mere metaphor is never crucial in any particular instance because the merely mere form of the merely mere
metaphor in its universality is never crucial.

In listening to and watching possibly the most
Dionysian of all rock 'n' rollers, James Brown, socio-
musical commentators have always attempted to ascertain the exact nature and source of the unbridled
force. Exhibiting some of the powers of the satyr on
stage, he has been labeled by Pearlman as "authentic,"
used in this case to have all the intentional ambiguity
it could have in such a cognitive reference. Eva Dolin
of *Rock and Roll Songs* has said this of him:

> James has won national acclaim not only for his ex-
> citing performances, but for unbelievable endurance on
> stage—unmatched in the world of showbusiness. He has
> been known to sing and dance a single routine or song

for over forty minutes, electrifying not only the audience, but the musicians in his band. In a typical James Brown show, the audience clamors wildly for encore after encore of a breathtaking dance or for the voice of a thousand trills and quivering sounds. His ardent fans are amazed when, instead of a finale, the pace quickens and the James Brown talent explosion continues on and on and on. (Eva Dolin, " 'I Give People Their Money's Worth' says James Brown," *Rock and Roll Songs*, April 1965, p. 22.)

He is even the paradigm of completeness by the standards of Cassius Clay,[187] who feels that Keats and Shelley died so young because they never trained. For Eva Dolin continues:

> However, today, he gives credit to his early boxing training, footwork drills and swinging pitch on the baseball diamond as being responsible for his unique dancing style on stage, and unbelievable endurance.

Of course the purely physical aspects of James Brown and the action painters among the abstract expressionists alike differentiate them from more passive artists. Yet their performances are enjoyable chunks taken from conceivably enjoyable lives and labeled as art;[188] a satyr would not label a selected moment of life as art, but still he could not be called authentic as Pearlman intends the term to be used.

"Papa's Got a Brand New Bag" presents James Brown and his Famous Flames extolling the virtues

---

[187] These days James Brown succeeds to the explanatory obvious (before and after the fact) on stage by announcing that he's about to do the Ali shuffle, triggering reverential and non-reverential automatic audience physicality of response.

[188] And there's that famous documentary film on Pollock at work.

of a new setup embodying a new briefcase metaphor with the statement, "Ain't no drag,/ Papa's got a brand new bag." Yet he can praise the newness only in a manner premeditated and basically prescribed by the course he has previously pursued. All his use of an unbounded energy in his earlier work leaves him with no chance of radical manipulation; he can only use everything. His frequent proclamation, "One more time," repeated several million times during the span of a single song, has been interpreted by Don Nielsen of the Fount to mean continuation to infinity. Nielsen's very own rendition of "Kansas City" is replete with this phrase, which suggests the reverberation of an echo as long as physically possible. But Nielsen is not "authentic" either. Somehow there is a nervous power to a James Brown performance that is lacking in one by someone structurally similar, such as Little Stevie Wonder. Perhaps the Heraclitean fire for which the sounds of his orchestra are metaphors, is a James Brown secret, and secret powers are after all more in keeping with man's emulation of the divine. Or maybe it is part of a reverse empiricism with its measure of primary heat accomplished through "authenticity."

Besides being, on obvious face value, ability to groove awesomely and stretch grooving into every nook and cranny, soul music is an endurance move, a mere endurance move. Thus soul is basically an erotics-of-potential move: the potential to endure as mere potential. Rock is the brute actualization where all earlier art is potential. Thus brute soul groping, even in its most "unstructured" forms simultaneously most reverent and merely reverent, is just one short easy step removed from use as a rock readymade and full incorporation in a transcendental rock system: use of the move move, externalization of the move move and internalization of *that*.

Rock soul (as opposed to a hypothetical rhythm & blues soul) would be potential to endure as one specific object or subject or subject-object rather than as many or all (or vice versa) where infinite expansion (and/or generalization, universal implication, systematic totality, variety-totality, or any of that sort of stuff) is indicated more or less explicitly as an inevitable actuality. The byproduct of this is the *why-bother soul substitute*. Like why bother to complete what can be easily (or even difficultly) completed, particularly where completion as a potential is overly obvious. Thus the move here is toward retention as mere potential no longer to be concerned with as an endurance problem: why actualize even if you get the chance since your soul/endurance move so far has already conceptually dealt with it all. Jim Morrison comes in as soul man after the fact, showing that he can exude so much (mere physical) energy[189] that he can outdo the prior empirical examples of soul incarnate without being soul incarnate itself and, to the contrary, merely a soul role atomist. And, unlike Sam and Dave, who, in "Soul Man," "learned how to love before I could eat," Jim wreaks havoc with the inadvertently farcical but soul-necessitated juxtaposition of loving and eating by being already mature and dealing with a so-young girlie ("Little girl, what school do you go to?") in a subject-object intersubjec-

---

[189] During his prime, around March '67.

tive mere unification of these two levels of being ("Little girl eat me . . .") in an occasional live performance of "Gloria": mere ontological easy transcendence of pure soul ontology (like it's implicit and explicable everywhere baby).

(In all fairness) soul implicitly deals with an *all* independent of its own *all*, a *totality* of insulation etc. and other standard goodies. But actualization (in life content expressed in art, in stylistic program for all future increments of additional development in the medium of the expression, etc.) is (and *may be* if you want) as much an *a priori* conceptual drag as it is an *a posteriori* work problem (for the artist-plumber). And the mere intentional/unintentional mere insulation aspect of the cosmos of external stylistic organization really makes it from both sides of the drag: drag-generating from within, drag-reinforcing from without. Nice.

Actual *musical* trans-soul solutions (for example, Aretha Franklin's "Natural Woman," which on-the-ball Jonnie Landau says "lost the brothers" by, as a matter of fact, being a little too greedy in its use of Ray Charles acceptability of soul transcendence readymades) can, from the internal soul standpoint, easily be a *drag after the fact*. Eric Burdon suffered greatly, even leading himself to live with good old (authentic) John Lee Hooker whenever he was around his neck of the woods (and go out with spade chicks in Harlem and marry a white chick his mother reputedly put him up to marrying), until he actually made it out of that by abandoning soul-inferiority through acid (*Winds of Change* being the delivering bummer). It's sort of silly (rock silly-usably unre-flectively merely silly) and ironic (rock ironic too) that the ins and outs of soul inclusion should them-selves present a readymade soul-content problem. For Eric, this has taken the form of minor-league darkie imitation necessitated by ignorance and semantic dif-ficulty and pushed to the point of desperation, finally subsiding and settling comfortably in "San Francis-can Nights," where there *are no* such things (usually) as "warm San Franciscan nights" and only the salva-tion of inadvertent Heraclitean semantic flippancy covers up the factual error professing to the doings of his ignorance. Contrary to the "you don't need a trip to" convention about the attainment of real soul, Eric just seems to have found the somehow right trip that has intersected lameness with soul (cause they *do* have affinities, just too bad Eric didn't see 'em early enough to be an official soul man).

The juxtaposition of a traditional soul content with something external (such as Charlie Parker with strings, Ray Charles with strings, Drifters with strings) is different from the standard rock externality set-up. It is generally one of the acceptance and manipulation of background for the purpose of nearly pure perform-ance against it as intentional merely different limiting ingredient to work against. The emphasis is on accept-ance as move from without with self-motivated primary manipulation of the initially external kept minimal. There is loss of control with, consequently, only uncon-trollable incidence of increase in purity-by-contrast. If one refuses to occupy both ends of the apparent mere contradiction he in fact loses the boundaries of his own definitive polarity as mere standard overstatedly ob-

vious meaning through no-more-definite (except simpler) specificity. Phil Spector enters here as musical
eclectic capable of inhabiting both ends (and throwing
out more ends and even being a straight dialectician).
Jimi Hendrix handles it with science-fiction. Beatles,
Stones, etc. handle it by taking the whole simplicity-
necessitated non-control of externality as positive and
(Beatles with "Flying" and "She's Leaving Home"
and "Nowhere Man" as the paradigm of all non-satiri-
cal non-contradictory pretentious devaluation of the
pretentious; Stones with "Back Street Girl" and un-
announced guest appearances by the Beatles in "We
Love You" and by unannouncables in their instrumental with mutterings "Sing This All Together (See
What Happens)" and with "She's a Rainbow" where
only Mick's voice indicates that the Stones are there
at all) preferable as beyond control anyway. And of
course the pure soul pros inevitably make the move
(as merely a subtle change of focus), as exemplified
by the Muddy Waters-Bo Diddley-Howlin' Wolf collaboration on record *(The Super Super Blues Band)*
gleefully performed as a great so-what mere collaboration on record for some guys who obviously want
just a mere collaboration on record expressing itself
as more than mere collaboration; but this is an example more of intrusion by an external (economically
relevant) general context for performance in general
rather than by external *style* in specific. Jimmie
Soul's "If You Wanna Be Happy" sure is calypso
(external of sorts) and it is also merely calypso (just
like the George Harrison sitar move, in "Norwegian
Wood," of incorporation of the merely exotic and
superficially exotic) but it is also Jimmie Soul's only
major hit. Hence, more (and less) than juxtaposition
with, even indulgence within, but still not *change*

into. It was his only hit, right? Thus, no indications of change. Ha ha.

Well it seems as if soul superstructure takes on a really tight classical legitimacy/validity/(purity) trans-reference. If this is rock, it is rock qua rules. It is rock qua embodiment in a specific concrete specific (object) with a plethora of explicit interrelation(s) of object and meaning taken for granted. This interrelation is not only conditional and conditionable (that is, merely preferential to a mere public mass and transitory even if on a non-obvious time scale) like everything else but it is only *absolutely conditional*, not even *conditionally conditional*: monistic sell for a less monistic plethora.

Original Beatle (and Beatle-Stone) purity and consistency, beginning with the return to musical accompaniment by the group itself plus audience familiarity with each of those involved in the totality of the group sound, is merely the first discernible stage in the programmatic purity-transcendence system of the Beatles and the Stones. The imposition of the (stylistic etc.) external is a chief device, operating beyond the stage of enhancement by the challenge of the unaccustomed. Where the strength of Ray Charles' *Modern Sounds in Country & Western Music* lies is that he overcomes the string arrangements and choral icing, the meat of the Stones' "Something Happened to Me Yesterday" is that it succumbs to, and even patterns itself around, some Dixieland swill. And the Dixieland section of "Something Happened" is a blast by mere association with a Stones record, even independently of its enhancement by specific location in the continuum of the song, just as is the trumpet flutter in the nearly contemporaneous "Penny Lane" by the Beatles. But these two instances are merely exorbitant developments stemming from the Beatles' addition of strings to a previously spotlessly unembellished group sound in "Yesterday," and the Stones' subsequent great insipidation of even that, in "I'm Free." What is so striking is that superfluous sounds, which always had their place in rock anyway, are here strictly part of the sound of a performance to which they are also strictly external. It's as if Bill Wyman, or even the peripheral Jack Nitzsche, were playing trombone when obviously neither one could be. Importantly, this reaches to extremes of the outside-in-the-rain readymade that Duchamp could never have coped with (revealing him to be a mere soul scrapper). And everybody thought that Dixie-land was trash or camp at best. And it is too. See what a little *ad hominem* glorification can do?

Back again to soul proper and the *ad hominem* across-the-board acceptability move is strangely minimal. True most Motown albums are packed with waste tracks and the plague of the not only external but white-oriented in specific; sure the Temptations don't mind singing (non-funky) Broadway stuff and lots of brothers gobble it up. But when the chips are down (and they're down easily of course) art as getting-away-with comes into focus and the audience deigns to challenge directly even the most strongly affirmed personal showcases of deceit and substitution of product. In January 1968 superstar Wilson Pickett was assaulted by standard boos for performing peculiarly, for peculiar meant shoddy. For rushing into his finale with this ready-to-be-passionate-with-a-little-preliminary-preparation audience unprepared he was called white. Spade stuff consequently intrudes upon spade soul stuff and illustrates that you can't get *ad hominem* enough even at the first level of physical performance: too much charisma of office unless you contextualize it the James Brown way by going overboard as an indefatigable super-crowd-pleaser with a regal cape.

Boredom is actually the greatest automatic soul-endurance move, coupling mere endurance with the enduring of the mere. The next easiest quasi-automatic soul-level move is the escape from the primary experience of confrontation or subsequent boredom by merely inserting mere change (interest) into experience or imposing eruption through/beyond it: *rejection* as the second great easy (nearly automatic) aesthetic displeasure move. The issue here is the dispersal of heavy increments of soul throughout the entire artist-audience population: why the pretense of one as an "artist"?[190] In fact the maintenance of this pretense is at the expense of the right of the artist to reject and be bored with (and by preference to bore and be rejectable by) an audience. With this type of quality enforcement and basic separation (at least by phase) between the evaluative inhibition/exhibition of the artist and audience, artist-audience "unity" is not ever symmetric except through the further edict of audience responsibility in its own quality enforcement. Unity attained is thus only

---

[190] In the film *Point Blank* there's a bonafide soul group, the Stu Gardner Trio, whose specialty is sticking the mike in the faces of nightclub audience individuals, one at a time, aesthetically forcing utterance (and presenting the "hey hey," "yeah" and "feel alright" ready-mades periodically as fuel for obligation).

ritualistic unity pushed to the level of "actuality"
only by further coupling with accident and non-
ritualized concurrent moves. But, greatly enough, accident and anyway are what rock is all about.

But, just for the record, the soul subset of rock has
received a little unrequested completion assistance
just about here from Jim Morrison. He has single-
handedly introduced a mutuality of performer-audi-
ence exchange which takes on the dimensions of a
new rule-awakening (but rule as influx of exteriority
qua influx). In his significant super-soul move, Morrison during his prime days would get so bored that
he would fidget with his belt and play with low ceiling
boards and just sort of stand around getting an erection by focusing his attention on a specific chick, all
during a performance. He would yell at and stare at
and sing, "When you laugh, you laugh at yourself,"
in response to anything from inappropriate laughter
to mere inattention; the stares have been particularly
telling on an audience, and hesitations extended far
too long for an audience's patience have been big too.
Even fear: audiences have been frightened by his
leaps and the other Doors themselves have gone in
for being nervous before a crowd. Morrison has even
worked out an internal group move of physical harass-
ment of the rest of the boys on stage, pushing men[191]
and instruments alike. And an off-stage skirmish with
cops in New Haven once precipitated a later on-stage
precipitation of police-state horrors. Once the quasi-
parallel construction of relationships to the audience
and the other Doors was jarred by *ad hoc* and *de facto*

---

[191] Jimi Hendrix is famous for having wrestled his
bassist Noel Redding to the ground in the midst of a
performance.

reversal as he showed his contempt for audience inattention by picking up drummer John Densmore's fallen cymbals rather than continue to stand dramatically at the front of the stage. And part of his whole thing is the ironic partial reintroduction of the (black jazz) struggle before an audience abandoned for its overly introspective overtones devoid of innate visual ritual. And, since he has gotten tired of his own ritual of getting tired, Morrison has come to frustrate (brutally) an audience ready and anxious to face his barrage.

And Donovan's (insipid) farewell of "I love you and you love me" to Lincoln Center patrons was his own comment on the extension of rock concert reverence to eventual audience lameness, for rock has taken performance from the doldrums of Murray the K communality of repulsion to utilizably engendered overpoliteness and overawe. Nice to be able to use the unaware senseless masochism of the guys buying yours.

And the first American encore by the not yet known (English) Crazy World of Arthur Brown was something intentionally vastly duller and more annoying than anything during the body of the performance. Appropriate even more since most of it was second-hand soul devoid of any ritualistic implications to this particular set of seated observing creeps at the Fillmore East. (Less relevant)

And the Chambers Brothers, who are black and use soul tunes as Byrd-type readymades, do this stage routine (generally before non-soul audiences) which mocks both camps with "Do you wanna hear the psychedelic sounds, lemme hear you say yeah." (Less relevant)

And there's always Zappa of course. Miscellaneous weaker versions of all the rest but so many of them and sometimes they're funny. (Irrelevant)

Etc. (Dull)

See? Verbalized mere actual superiority is dull if you want it to be. Even if you want it to be. Let's now take a gander at how soul's own conception of superiority operates. And how its soul hierarchy system compares with the heaven rock hierarchy system. Well, all great soul stars, like heaven rock stars, are obviously so, obviousness incarnate. Attaining their natural aristocratic status, rather than by matching some sort of spurious-unassailable Platonic style form, gets its import from a missing of the mark, a transcendence of the taxonomy restricting "defining" the soul star in general.[192] Where sometimes in soul there may be a raunchy, sloppy match, and hence a mismatch from that direction, the standard customary procedure (enhanced by the building up of archetypes and filling up of archetype banks over the years) is neat classical matchup of the secondary-primary Platonic miss-match form.[193] The mere star of soul is a readymade titan of soul (already imbued

---

[192] Landau's comment on Stevie Wonder's "Made to Love Her," that it transcended being Motown and became "art," is evidence of the Motown Millstone Move in particular.
[193] Smokey Robinson's "I'll Try Something New" is both soul and heaven rock.

with sufficiently ritualistic reverence), whereas the heaven rock aristocrat's level of divinity is dependent upon the audience's species of divinity conceptualization (and there is both lack of responsibility and specificity here). Actually the reverence form of heaven rock is a focal point for viewing soul reverence form and total rock reverence form as conveniently polar. Total rock has its hierarchy both within and beyond the soul type of hierarchy: both reverence and trivial reverence, no matter where you locate each type. And since *all* is so obvious, so is *transcendence* and it, as well as godhood, is just as easily a useless (great) and pretentious (nice) distinction too: dig the Beatles in *Help!* with a "ho, ho, ho" down their sleeves in response to Ringo's cosmic realization, "There's more to this than meets the eye." If you want it that way.

Definitions and definitiveness are both high and low. Both (conceptual) clarity and confusion are both (conceptual) obstacles and liberating forces in the rock universal-particular game. So soul makes it big from this perspective within rock as a focal point with *obviously-functioning clarity-confusion fusion* and *clarity-confusion confusion.* Within the experiential realm, dig stuff like an Otis Redding-Eddie Floyd hierarchical mismatch perpetrated and hidden (by selection of tracks) on Stax-Volt European tour live albums. From the mere rational standpoint, check Chuck Berry's totally articulate anecdotes between (traditionally pseudo-illiterate) numbers at concerts. And, obviously, billions of far better, far more appropriate, far less obscure examples are all over the place. Find them.

So (wow), on the *avoidance of soul hierarchy* move. *Run-of-the-mill soul move* (Archie Bell & the Drells, Jay & the Techniques). The *even actually predictable & inevitable run-of-the-mill soul move-after-the-fact* (white guys like the Soul Survivors, the Box Tops, and even Paul Butterfield especially when he tries too hard). And the *almost intentionally inauthentic soul (bummer) move* (Frank Sinatra's version of O. C. Smith's "That's Life"). All are great (inadvertent or otherwise: better as inadvertent, since soul-wise inadvertency only works for the top straight soul guys) move-avoidance moves, with ascendancy the result of accident, unconscious conditionability (vulnerability to conditioning just like all the rest, but taken here in context as mere as you can get it) and exposure to the real (experiential) fluidity of preference underlying apparent system. And if the public acceptance move turns out in favor of rejection by proper soul people anyway, there's enough marginal acceptance possible from the super-conditionable segment of soul marginality and outside it. After all, they are the soul people who can survive being labeled unsoulful. The Soul Survivors are more than mere pun.

None of this is particularly traditionally soulfully simple, but soul has an overassumed simplicity anyway. Simplicity's a dumb abstraction anyway too. (And but stuff like the Soul Survivors simplify things most with the nice soul self-generating functional quasi-non-paradoxical ability to endure non-possession of soul, etc): (thus, soul comes through, simply and simply enough, as a great mere abstraction after all, capable of experiential import because of stuff like conditioning to it as a mere symbol after all) . . . (clarity-confusion paragraph)

Lou Rawls constantly manipulates the soul symbol (at Monterey he noted that T-Bone Walker had so much soul you could call him Ham-Hocks and introduced "sock it towards me" for people tired of "sock it to me"). To Arthur Lee, the great trans-soul spade trans-spade of Love, the soul symbol is a tool (imitations of Jagger imitating primal soul spades), but merely one among many, including the show music symbol, the orchestrality symbol, the plagiarism symbol, the language symbol, the symbol symbol, others too. Many of these hack symbols are equivalently hack trans-soulfully manipulated at random: black soul in a sea of many equivalent souls, and even "You made my soul a cell."[194]

I'll just get comfortable now and tell ya a little story about Jimi Hendrix. But I gotta build up to it with detail just as Jimi Hendrix himself hadta. Okay, there's the whole soul-as-punctuation thing, an aspect of soul that extends itself throughout its entire internal fiber. And where the song as soul unit is randomly applicable in brutal specificity to any life temporality, the internal standard Ray Charles "Don't it make you feel all right" or "Pray with me boys, please pray with me" hangs in there with optimum necessity, really justifying the whole previously assumed necessary connection between soul and music outright. It took Wilson Pickett quite a while to be able to cast out his "I feel pretty good" with particular relevance and intra-temporal urgency. It took Jimi Hendrix more time and work than that, and less too, before he could get things precisely in the proper punctuation slot, but when he got there he under-

---

[194] "Live and Let Live."

stood the slot and not merely occasions of its appearance and use. If you don't need a trip to attain soul you can easily take a trip and/or avoid it or catch it on the way back or further on or further in. Beginning with mild soul (performer) potential (he once won at an Apollo amateur night, etc.), Jimi Hendrix debarked for England[195] and acid and discovered the freak potential of soul and everything else and the soul potential of freakiness and everything else. He has become soul's greatest master of space and time if he wants to be and space-time's greatest master of soul if he ever wants to do anything with that. But instead of being the soft shoe dancer alone he is Pythagoras the Cave Painter and master of names and other proper nouns. Any base for ascendancy is okay: unverbalized subtitles from classic explicit philosophy and great exciting hack science-fiction and any brand of once-upon-a-time you can name punctuate his move, they always continue to fill in and enhance his silences and moments of hesitation (and negate them as well—goody) and his everywhere else, and what's even better is that he never has to formulate them in sound and meaning himself. Go.

First: *Are You Experienced?*

New questions. New questions? Really? Old philosophers, played out even then, novel even now. But just hear, and hear and listen to the beginning *before* you conceptualize the possibilities for the question "Now that you know who you are, what do you want to be?" actually to be a question as opposed to an

---

[195] With, of all people, Chas Chandler of Eric Burdon's original Animals.

even-though-you-know-what-you-know-I-know-that-
I'm-ready-to-leave. Gargle with mercury but if you
don't know what's coming off you'll never realize that
"Third Stone from the Sun" is the *D.C.* version of
the Silver Surfer on an asphalt trip: that is, you sure
as hell have to be arrogant even if you don't particularly groove on ego trips.

Many are the means of allegorically expanding it
all and summing it all up. Remember Plato's myth of
the cave bit? SEE THE SUN FREE! And Nietzsche:
groove on murkiness and Dostoyevski's vaginal pit
extensions thereof. And more or at least a few, to
name a few. But what happens when everybody has
seen the sun and wallowed in the shit? That doesn't
mean hey *Time* and *Newsweek* have written up the
hippies even though John Canaday still doesn't understand Rembrandt or Andrew Wyeth. Or Genet is
welcome in *Family Circle* and *Family Circle* is welcome in your own home so what do you do now, now
that Janis Ian has taken STP and avoids Clearasil.
But: Well you just gotta be better in your all-encompassing bit and think and know that better is worth
something and worthiness isn't a drag and that infinite regresses are okay. Enter: Jimi Hendrix, standing on his head and knowing what that means too.

Afterthought is a different slightly different story.
Inches can be miles if you want them to be, and the
ground between the Beatles and the Stones is far
greater than that between Jan van Eyck and Hoagy
Carmichael, the development from "Dandy" to "¡Que
Vida!" is awesomely greater than that bridging the
gap between Hans Memling and Marcel Duchamp.
Irony is ironically important, and ironically these pro-

portions hold ground anyway. The Byrds *sing* "Eight Miles High"; the Beatles, Stones, Doors and Jimi Hendrix (and the Byrds) *are* far more than eight miles high, and, with the way up and way down being one and the same, they cover a lot of space, traversing it without moving. Still one place to go. Lastly through a hogshead of real fire. But come up the years, too, perhaps. Perhaps.

Okay, let's work on a logic of ascent/descent that's more fun and less fun than Fitch proofs or Nelson Goodman or even the famous Aristotle. Man like we can be so high that the high is irrelevant and so systematic that system crumbles so we might as well be structurally ready and readily structural so we can guarantee a good time for all total awareness freaks. Of course A and not-A. Of course, of course. Although she feels as though she's in a play, she is anyway. I can pick your face out from the front or behind. It really doesn't matter, if I'm wrong I'm right. And some people like to talk anyway, like Paul McCartney in *The True Story of the Beatles*:[196] "John propositioned me. He told me that he thought the group could do nicely and anyway it was a lot of fun. He didn't talk about the possibility of turning professional. It was me, I think, who realized that skiffle could easily lead to some useful pocket money so that we'd be able to date the girls and maybe get a few clothes for ourselves. Remember, though, we were very young . . ." (a peculiar quotation for a paragraph on logic). Enter: Jimi Hendrix, pre-literate, post-

---

[196] By Billy Shepherd, Bantam Books, New York 1964, p. 15.

articulate, proto-logical, bi-lingual (at least English and American), plurisignative. His major logical connective:

(A *pubic hair* B)

All you've got to work with at any time is your bank of memories and the state of the world as it is under all sorts of internal and external interactions and things like that. "I Don't Live Today." Okay. Right. Present progressive time sense goes out, future-oriented past and past progressive come in. Jump from speaker to speaker, alternate sounds and silences, you're finally conscious of all the implications of musical spatio-temporality. Fine. And hey there go the Stones 55 seconds into "Take It or Leave It" sliding through "then you go, now you're back." Spade rock was three years ago or now or the year of the iron sheep? So? It's also in Jimi's "Fire." And a real blues, "Red House," isn't even spatially on the American album, so you have to wait (forever or a few months) for the English *Are You Experienced?*

Law of identity fanaticism? Marvel comics too hung up on the avoidability of the identity of indiscernibles; D.C. knows that if you live on the planet

Xzgronl#m you can tell your kid at the ninth meal
of the 67.3-hour Xzgronl#mian day that here on our
planet Xzgronl#m we eat purple potatoes and groove
on bizarre tautologies. Jimi Hendrix, in "Third Stone
from the Sun," grooves on the earth's "strange beautiful crescent green" with its "majestic silver seas" and
"mysterious mountains" which he wishes to "see
close." And somewhere guitars hum like bumble bees.
And "may you never hear surf music again." And the
Silver Surfer is a Marvel guy.

All this and déjá-vu transcendence too.

Double-standard science-fiction rock too. Byrds
have to be uninsulatedly "open" but not if they really
knew that openness means inevitable openness to insulation. Paul McCartney suggests merely fixing a
hole in David Crosby's jewel forest closet "Mind
Garden," and Jimi Hendrix wonders if maybe this
chick's made of gold or something and asks her quite
politely, man there are still some standard precious-
ness metaphors man.

Are unknown tongues still possible? Sure, but they
might just be about as significant as bottle caps.
Bottle caps might be significant however too. The
world is music but what is music but what is the world
too. And monism pluralism monism pluralism too too.
One of the alltime great traditional unknown tongues
occurs early in "Third Stone" at the first eruption of
the theme played at a random speed which just might
be 45 or 33 rpm I guess. But that's not the point about
the Hendrix tongue relevance board of directors (get
your mind together, there are a whole bunch of you)
that should be made to relate to post-Beach Boys

ethnomusicology in general. For, along with Schopenhauer, we know that music is the metaphysical equivalent to all the nitty gritty power of nature, but along
with Johnny and Brian W and Jimi we know that
music is also like the *World Book Encyclopedia* article on Brazil. Obviously Heraclitus contains Anaxago-
ras, but crystallization out of flux in music or in
subway-car stability assertions might also be a different scene too. "Waterfall, don't ever change your
ways" in "May This Be Love" is not only perfect
Anaxagoreanism in a nutshell but even the perpen-
dicularization of Heraclitus' river. The anti-tongue
fadeout of "Foxey Lady" is the death of a guitar
string. Best quotation tongue on the album: the Who-
like beginning of "Love or Confusion." But how 'bout
the beginning of "Hey Joe," a quasi-transitional passage which would be an awesome internal musical
thingamajig in any Airplane context? That's nice too.
And the first utterance of "Are you experienced?" is
without doubt *the* definitive jack-in-the-box tongue.
Morrison says, "Everybody loves my baby," right
there in the middle of "Break On Through," right
there conspicuously out of place. Lennon tells you in
this book at the movies that he'd love to turn you on,
right there where grass smells like World War II English newscasts. But Jimi Hendrix puts the question in
the question slot, oh but where did the question slot
come from and how did it get there?

"And the wind cries Mary" and "The Wind Cries
Mary" sounds old, in a manner that peculiarly makes
the whole album sound old for a while, not old in
archaic or old like good-time music but old like a few
years old. But just for a while, whatever a while is.
And it's essentially appropriate that this actual real

world introspective psychological time thing has the
ring of "Queen Jane" by that groovy temporally
aware Dylan guy. Oh yeah, but on the other hand
"May This Be Love" is reminiscent of great American
Indian hits of the past as performed by the Crests. It
could easily have been a hit as a direct followup to
Johnny Preston's "Running Bear" or as a release
within six months before or after the Beach Boys'
"Ten Little Indians" or as the track before "Tomorrow Never Knows." Anyway, a grandiose *specific*
past-oriented temporal tidbit. Open your mouth and
you are referential, play a guitar and you are trans-
referentially a reference guitar scientist too. Fall
asleep and you are lying on an archetype. Hear "move
over Rover and let Jimi take over" (in "Fire") and
you might just believe you've heard a brand new big
dog-little dog variation. "Manic Depression" is a post-
label salvation song. "Manic depression is a frustratin'
mess": labeled content already old hat and no longer
solution; neat tension between former label as subject
and latter as enunciated experiential predicate. Byrds
vs. Yardbirds in "Purple Haze" shows you that any
polarity is usable, any dualism is okay for two minutes or so. And "not stoned, but beautiful" is an
excellent spur-of-the-moment neo-eternal I-don't-
want-to-tell-you-this-so-I'll-tell-you-that readymade
dualism. "*That's* what I'm talkin' about, now dig *this*"
(in "Fire") was ironically written on the same soil
as all that Russell-Moore constipation!

Music-noise pleasure/displeasure conditioning is a
funny thing. By changing my seat at a Jefferson Airplane performance in Boston a few months ago I discovered that all guitar sounds, down to the merest of
guitar sounds, sounded okay from behind the guitar,

on the same side of it as the musician. Now I can listen to Jorma on record as if I were in his guitar position. Jimi Hendrix presents a multi-faceted problem with his guitar pluckin', one so vast that it ceases to be a problem as such on the same plane as mere irritations like the sociology of knowledge or medium-message stuff and it merits whole new conceptual schemata replete with matching jargon shoelaces. Like Roland Kirk. Like Jasper Johns. Hendrix's spatial relationship to his guitar transcends any standard finite batch of prepositions. It even requires a few new sexual position-process metaphors, like synchronized cunilinguo-copulation, since he's obviously capable of playing notes with his teeth while outdoing the whole Bo Diddley-John Lee Hooker mild-mannered exhibitionism with his crotch.

In the case of listening to a standard guitarist on record, the actual audience-artist spatial relationship is epistemologically irrelevant, and aesthetically relevant only, in a rather limited setup. Required is a mental picture of the guy facing you and occasionally moving around; in conjunction with this you visually change the situation and sit behind him or turn the stage around, or you put yourself right in his shoes. This requires a tunnel view of space with enlargement-contraction due to imagined distance and 180-degree reversals. Or you can give yourself an *a priori* behind-while-in-front-of sort of compressed tunnel space. But the ambiguity of the actual spatial relationship between you as a person positioned all over the place in the world and such items as the guitar cat at the moment of recording and the hi-fi speakers as apparently flat in front of (as the case just as well might be) you while you're listening x hours later is never much of a concern, simply because it is never much of a concern. Most people, even psychotics obsessed with 180-degree reversals, simply couldn't care less about getting additionally hung up with the problem of determining (or being gripped by the impossibility of ever, ever determining) their *actual* spatial relationship to this guy far over the mountains years and years ago who happened to have recorded the original raunchy version of the tune they happen to be humming while they're facing east, right now (or is it north by northwest and some time other than now, since the *en soi* and *pour soi* just can't get together). Just think about this: Jimi Hendrix makes this new realm of aesthetic psychosis tenable, not only tenable but groovy. You can *care* about it because his space is not tunnel space but PAISLEY SPACE. Not just a cylinder of relevance or a cone of relevances extended to a sphere of relevance, but a *paisley*, metaphorically wondrous and elusive enough to be even more all-encompassing without the "of relevance" attached. Implicitly, the record-listening experience has *always* been far more complex than the in-person experience. The Beatles always knew that. Reversed fadeouts and multitracking even scared some San Franciscans into a preference for live performances. Now Jimi Hendrix has thrown it all into everybody's faces, even the faces of those who have never heard him live or on record and those who never will and those who are frogs.

Yeah .... and sort of on with *Axis: Bold as Love* just for the hell of it just because it's next in history and there's some real live real stuff going on meanwhile in the merely real world.

No mystery in *Magical Mystery Tour?* Oh really, where's the mystery in *x* if not in *y* too, and where's the science-fiction in Mars? And where's magic and where-magic?

Dealing with the audience as dancing sparrow (not to mention dancing fornicator) (in the wake of Fillmore as theater without seats and Group Image circle dances just to keep things minimally other than stationarily seated or stationarily standing), okay, but deal with it also as nearsighted deaf guy who has seen and heard it all and never cared much about his legs .... you really should some time.

Soul as mere survival, soul as intensification, mere survival of mere intensification. But what about background music and forgettable drivel?

Wubba wubba ggggg, huh? Reversal: musicality of criticism. If saying anything about singers is already a drag while they're still singing, what's gonna happen when the singers just talk? Oh no, is that happening now? Yeah. But a drag in music is a drag anyway. Anything said (or not said) about Jimi Hendrix's second opus, *Axis*, fits it automatically, embellishes it, dulls it, appreciates and understands it. Where his first album, *Experienced*, has implicated all modes and directions of consciousness as thought (as experienced), his second does the same for all audience responses as *spoken*. The mere critical consciousness bit didn't work in this context, something (remotely) like his comment (in "Ain't No Telling") "Oh, Cleopatra,/ She's driving me insane,/ She's trying to put my body in her brain." Criticism as return in kind. Yelling: yelling, etc. Remotely obviously sexual like anything else in the land of Hendrix.

Standard magic, mystery and science-fiction as conceptual order have generally been associated more or less with such stuff as the unknown, the unknowable and the bizarre. As categorical aspects of art they have been applied to whatever the strange and freaky could topically encompass. But once "magic" has been overtly manifest everywhere as at least an epiphenomenon (with Donovan as presiding angel and Morrison as super-demon) there can no longer be as much topical interest in just a part of the everywhere. (Like "Spanish Castle Magic.") Some creeps have scoffed at the Beatles' *Magical Mystery Tour* because it didn't have the spunk and sparkle of *Sgt. Pepper:* but magic must be found in the *merely* topical too (and merely untopical too), all over again as afterthought. And the black-magical implications of the title of but a part of the Rolling Stones, *Their Satanic Majesties Request*, are a form of this same move, only in reverse: the conversion of the magical whole into a topical apparent mere part. And Jimi Hendrix began on the "Third Stone from the Sun" and has here come to investigate the science-fictional implications of Mere Earth: Van Dyke Parks of the ordinary and sub-ordinary, technician of mere pumice and, better still, mere technologist-technician of mere pumice. And (as he declares in "If 6 was 9") "Now if 6 turned out to be 9, I don't mind, I don't mind."

Listening to the rhythmically unfamiliar and/or unfriendly (?) is often too much of a superimposition by external time upon the listener's internal time sense for him to withstand it without mechanically tapping along. This establishment of a minimal common denominator between one's own spirit flow and that of the music is itself at least inertially present even in the standard orgiastic experience of fused personal-musical flow. The "soul music" experience is thus one of both rhythmic endurance and rhythmic ecstasy: enduring enough to get into it, getting into it enough to require further endurance, merely getting into it, merely enduring, grooving, merely grooving, grooving on endurance, endurance of grooving, mere etc. Part of the accomplishment of the blues is the extension of its rhythmic code to the curse of eternal monotony which one can easily bear—as orgasmic monotony. R & B carries this basic structure into the slightly more easily accessible aspects of soul temporality, removing a little basic inertia (or perhaps just introducing sufficient motion to work with it), introducing more readily comprehensible—and hence less merely subtle—frenzy. Rock is musically a more rapid development, a drive toward total summation at once: total readymade accessibility including the relevant/irrelevant inaccessibility resulting from such easy universal immediacy that the foreground becomes mere background. Rock is the fusion of Muzak and the blues and everything else for that matter. And Jimi Hendrix right now is the most obvious visible summation of the entire mess. Where *Are You Experienced?* is focused at the stars from the peak of rock proper, *Axis: Bold as Love* focuses at the same target with the implicitness of the most advanced. Soul as mere soul is the neutralizer of mere freakout, but the readymade potency of its neutralizing action is freaky in its easy negation. Particularly when the temporal superimposition of his concrete summation results in that superimposition upon words known as "talking" or "just talking." The album begins with a radio message on U.F.O., the most singerly track is by bassist Noel Redding ("She's So Fine"), and Hendrix himself freaks his way through the inertia of music itself (and on *Experienced* it's "music, sweet music" only by analogy plus a cymbal ending, in "Manic Depression"). And with printed lyrics included, you can even visually, visibly follow this music as merely unanticipated emphasis. It's easy to track down the elusive.

Dancing? You should have been dancing with your *mind* all along—and not even just dancing to the danceable; that was always the transcendental prerequisite to the bodily anyway: now it's time to be an athlete of the transcendental only. And genitals are easily trans-physical, so you don't even have to abandon them.

But what about actual discrepancy—like cover-content discrepancy (opulently exotic cover, homogeneously rustically substantial innards in this case) —after you've realized all along that it doesn't—that it never did—matter? Atlantic Records, with lots of meat in this field and with Hank Crawford's *Soul Clinic* album as the primal early example, was always the pioneer in this direction. *Pioneer* only because once upon a time it did matter, so it was just a prehistoric pointing. Jimi Hendrix's *Axis: Bold as Love* is the optimum statement of the absurdity of pointing with arrows: it is still minimally discrepant despite the merely historic negation of discrepancy. Now that sticking out like a sore thumb is the thing, Jimi Hendrix is the pioneer-in-something-else who has come to be the over-under-over-healthy sore thumb/green thumb. Helps you keep your fantasies as fantasies instead of ruining them by fulfilling them. Relationship = intersection in two places, at least, sometimes, or anything else. And relationship or anything else in sequence form with one grocery list item after another = (in "You Got Me Floatin' "): floatin' "round and round" and "never down" and "naturally" and "float to please" and "across and through."

Hmm and another apparent entrance of "being" in the soul artist-audience preference framework. There is not merely a disparity between systematic preference and mere preference and no preference but between all of that and all of that as embodied in the soul object as if part of the object. Not only is the parameter of its objectification easily remote from that of its original rise, but its object-linking is taken as its most significant manifestation (which it thus may easily become since it isn't). With tensions all around, those thought of as embodied in this eventual superobject are the focal point of all apparent aesthetic tension incarnate, as if the tension were incarnate in the soul object's *being itself*, not just in (the whole) conception. Here's Heraclitus by way of the introduction of public referential permanence to the intimations of objects themselves: overstatement of revealed Logos, revealed religion (what a coincidence), nothing possible *except* overstatement—not even overstatement *by choice* anymore, and that's nice, man.

Speaking of referential, on to the only reference-tongue-field group to be intentionally so almost all the time, the Kinks. In answer to the spades, who are constantly plagiarized from without and only plagiarize (themselves) from deep within and take only entire discernible unmodified units from the outside world, the Kinks reply that to discover that you've been stolen *from* and not to have retaliated in kind and/or become cynical (not just *more* cynical, but aesthetically-artistically cynical anew) is laziness or overwork. Singing a hack show piece like "The Impossible Dream" (the Hesitations do it) is neither plagiarism nor intentional burlesque, but borrowing and use; it's neither underhanded nor incorporative and certainly not plagiaristic qua plagiarism. Ignoring *is* the only full refutation of an argument in dialogue, since response is acknowledgment that the argument merits response and contains minimal coherence and interest. And ignoring being stolen from may also be a step beyond bothering about it (yelling or avenging), but it is also a step *before* the non-necessitated revenge-anyway move. Whereas in dialogue form if you have with your original move caused (influenced) a theft the first blow has been struck in your favor and pulling out is at least a one-blow dialogic advantage (victory maybe), soul dialogue ought to be discontinuous.

Discontinuous enough so that ignoring may result from ignorance (insulation) and revenge may occur as intentional theft but only accidental revenge. And by being obscure enough so that the entire dialogue is never visible or knowable, the Kinks are kings of both intent and accident. They are the only group to use the reference-tongue field so blatantly and yet still be obscure as such to the non-archaeologist. Let's see, their "You Really Got Me" is taken from the "La Bamba" pit, the Stones' "Take It or Leave It" is stolen from their "Ring the Bells," stuff like the Beatles' "I Feel Fine" and "Lovely Rita" bear unknown origination relationships to Kink stuff (and the latter song might even be in the Who bag, setting up a Kinks-Who derivational ambiguity), Kink stuff (nothing specific comes to mind right now) once in a while has the same sort of ambiguous but obvious derivation, and oh yes their "Party Line" led to the Stones' "Connection" or maybe it was the other way around, and right their name and earliest style come right from the Kingsmen. And the Kinks' "Where Have All the Good Times Gone" is (as nobody knows) the densest reference-tongue field known to man, just stuffed with familiars like "yesterday" and "time was on my side" and "get your feet back on the ground" and more . . . this is boring so I'll just dump the rest of my notes on you . . . the Kinks, the Who Sell Out and the Mothers are big on readymade non-dialogical theft (beyond readymade *influence*): incorporate best of both: ignoring + free incorporation . . . soul plagiarism inside soul seems like an act of respect, put in context by the Impressions' loose use of the musical opening of "Soul Man" in their charisma-oriented "Movin' On Up" . . . Chuck Berry move: self-plagiarism + respect avoidance which must itself be respected, as by the Stones, who, after having a Chuck Berry oldie slot on most of their albums, wrote their "own" Chuck Berry song, "Amanda Jones," after they had given up directly using anybody else's material . . . and move from within soul to ignore thefts is only a continuation of show-of-strength against non-metaphoric instrusions *by* the external: but the more this is done the more internal repetition density increases and keeps parallel with external plagiarism moves... some application of the Cassius Clay move ought to do it somehow (arrogant non-assimilative whatchamacallit) ... Brenton Wood uses Country Joe (David Cohen) style organ on "Gimmee Little Sign," not plagiarism, not reference (because nobody inside would recognize), but appropriation as a useful commodity, a *cop* ... Jimi Hendrix internalizes whole soul hierarchy generation principle; it has close affinity to the self-freak expansion move... easy to be honest using somebody else's garbage, just as it's hard to be honest doing your own thing etc.... and a tedious quote from Dylan's "Absolutely Sweet Marie" would be "To live outside the law you must be honest" but so what and what if... the paragraph is over right here.

Some nonsense:

In the standard archaeological grab into the pit of prior non-art-labeled super-groping the basic basic question of all science-fictional analysis of the external becomes pertinent. Does the current obviously channeled move-orientation of Batman indicate the same intrinsic move-orientation move in early Batman? Does the internal understanding of a move add to the surface of the move any more than as super-added simultaneous or prerequisite understanding focusable as surface and as vision articulator and director in the potential acts of creation? And isn't the potential field of future creations delineated more by

instinct (a brute given) than by vision as understanding, thus granting more likelihood to a delimitation
of (archaeologically relevant) understanding anyway? Etc. But, y'know, then you get to well etc. as
long as you get to see instinct through time as style
and instinct as tending to be (in manifestation
through habituated *style*) more or less monofaceted
etc. So more-than-instinctive understanding comes
off as the potential for manipulation of style and
choice of other styles. The *will* sort of comes in with
the ability to fuck around on the style-style tran-
scendence-style avoidance continuum merely postulated by the trans-instinctual/non-instinctual understanding. And then there's all this interplay: will
style, understanding of the will, etc. Yeah, big shit.
So you get all this crypto-Kantian-Nietzschean not-
yet-evaluated metaphysical psychology on the verge
of the meta-metaetc. Without even any of the details
at all but vastly detailed already. Making a real implicit soul cosmos move but not quite. So, back to
wherever it was, with the soul move as being (in
varying degree) a natural erotics of philosophy move.
But probably also a step behind (or in willful avoidance of) the meta-meta-metaetc move, which you
could call the rock move proper. And folk is somewhere around meta-meta-land too, but generally
closer to mere meta than soul, and even sometimes
very pre-meta but never really meta itself or totally in-
stinct-oriented meta-meta and meta-meta-meta *only*
by instinct if at all (whereas soul is meta-meta-meta
by understanding affinity *and* instinct): that is, folk
would cease to be folk proper if understanding (scene-
comprehension) entered and it became rock, soul is
still soul no matter how it makes the rock crossover

when it does: nice smooth insulation move by soul.[197]
Etc. And then there's folk soul with Leadbelly and
Son House and etc., sure a lot of strange land there
once it's in the public scene. Right, the public move,
the actual public move, the mass move, whatever.
And show music and show biz. And show biz soul with
Lou Rawls and folk show biz soul with Louis Armstrong. And etc. And preferences from the instinct-
understanding-will bag and how they determine part
of the scene mobility move too. And how "Penny
Lane" and "Strawberry Fields" (the whole form/non-

---

[197] The (factual/definitional) album notes of *The Otis
Redding Dictionary of Soul Complete & Unbelievable*
make Otis rock by way of additional meta in terms of
supporting material (if) not immediately: meta-itself so
triple-meta!:

Ou-yea (ū′ yā′) adv.	to give in: a reply to get what one wants.
My-my-my (mī) poss. adj.	no longer yours; goodby three times.
Ou-ni (ū′ nī′) adv.	to hurt so good.
Ni (nī) adv.	to do very quickly.
Leetle (lēt′ l) adj.	just enough to make one want more.
Ou (ū) n.	ouchless excitement.
Yea-ni (yā′ nī) adv.	an agreement to give in very quickly.
Oh-mi (ō′ mī) interj + adv. (comp.)	to get it very quickly.
Weel (wēl) n., v., aux. v., v.t.	desire to give it or get it.
Gotta-Gotta (gŏt′ tă) v.	not able to do without it.
Give it (gĭv′ ĭt) v. + pron. (comp.)	absitively posilutely not.
Oh-naw-naw (ō nâ′) interj. + adv. (comp.)	to let oneself go. under any circumstances.
Fa-fa-fa-fa-fa (fä) phrase	sad song.
Ou we ni (ū′ wĕ nī) phrase	getting gooder by the minute.

form psychology of creation summation for jazz) are meta-scene. And more galore. And sociology too, only sociology is both opaquely irrelevant to rock and flamingly irrelevant (if ever articulated) to soul, that is, sociology as inertial stimulus to creation and inertial creative surface (social psychology preferable in creation move?). Yeah but also it's only an articulation problem with soul and only an irrelevant one (qua irrelevance) with rock. No mention of soul *qua soul* in that portion of the sentence just for the sake of unnaturally persistent apparent descriptive parallelism. And oh balls that's a drag. And soul knows that well for whatever that's worth. And soul knows that well. (And so did Elvis Presley.)

The rise of cognition in rock should not be viewed as a factor in strengthening its Apollonian tendency at the expense of stifling its Dionysian dimension. The Beatles have juggled the strict James Brown conception of the rock performance to produce an entire show with less physical and emotional output than even one of his numbers; at Shea Stadium the Beatles sang twelve songs in roughly half an hour.[198] Yet, possessing their own secret solution and also a calculatedly mechanical method of musical construction, they can fortify any song with an inimitable intensity.[199] Their act from life is, up to this point,

---

[198] That's 2.5 per. Roughly.

[199] Pearlman has felt that the Beatles have used the greatest word expansion since Yeats; this achievement, while not doubted, is dwarfed by the sheer sonorous impact of their words. Note the unbelievably intense expression of the word "love" in "If I Fell" and the agonized screech of the word "don't" in the final phrase, "My baby don't care," at the end of "Ticket to Ride."

fuller, by means of tricky minimal metaphoric volume manipulations, than merely the great brute Dionysian ritual of a James Brown or an Elvis Presley, both of whose audiences could rival the Dionysian tendencies of Beatle audiences. While not quite as "authentic" as Brown, their Shea Stadium versions of soul staples "Dizzy Miss Lizzie" and "Twist and Shout" far exceeded minimal Dionysiac needs.

The Righteous Brothers represent a cognitive move to conquer soul as an already overworked and weakened Dionysiac field. As "blue-eyed soul brothers," Bobby Hatfield and Bill Medley (with Phil Spector as their guide) have used their r&b-rock formula to create the orgasmic splendor of "You've Lost That Lovin' Feelin'," full of thick orchestral suggestions mixed with a down-home earthiness. But the melody of the song is derived (or derivable) from "Tara's Theme," pompous theme of both *Gone with the Wind* and *Million Dollar Movie*, first prepared for rock 'n' roll use by the Duprees with their "My Own True Love."[200] With such illustrious imperfection to start with, their song became the first Caucasian song to become number one on several Negro hit ratings.[201]

---

[200] The Bee Gees do for overworked (Apollonian) symphonicity precisely what the Righteous Brothers have done for soul. And maybe Van Dyke Parks has picked up on the demise of this, even though it's never had its day, even though it's never had a moment of definitiveness. And "Wild Thing" by the (pre-Bee Gees) Troggs dealt with the doubly dead *soul* aspect itself, and it had it's day as such blatant overstatement that the concept of double overstatement was unnecessary.

[201] Slightly different from the earliest Presley discs, which were a big hit with Negroes before *any* whites began listening to him.

"To reach a closer understanding of both these transcendencies, let us begin by viewing them as the separate art realms of *dream* and *intoxication*, two physiological phenomena standing toward one another in much the same relationship as the Apollonian and Dionysiac. It was in a dream, according to Lucretius, that the marvelous gods and goddesses first presented themselves to the minds of men."[202] Perhaps this is so, but rock 'n' roll's view of the dream is often more extensive. The Majors, through their "Wonderful Dream," weaken the potency of Nietzsche's dream world with what seems to be a limp homoerotic fantasy (even) immensely banal as they moan, "Last night I ha-ad a wonderful dream," in possibly the highest pitched male voices ever recorded. "The person who is responsive to the stimuli of art behaves toward the reality of dream much the way the philosopher behaves toward the reality of existence: he observes exactly and enjoys his observations, for it is by these images that he interprets life, by these processes that he rehearses it."[203] Yet in his "115th Dream" Dylan senses that the corrupt illogic of his waking hours has finally crept into his dream imagery. His unrestrained but unintended laughter at the opening of his song is evidence that he can no longer hold the two realms separate; otherwise he could have kept them separate by having a recording engineer remove it. In "Gates of Eden" Dylan finds the dream of paradise no more comfortable than real-

---

[202] From *The Birth of Tragedy and The Genealogy of Morals* by Friedrich Nietzsche, translated by Francis Golffing, page 19. Copyright © 1956 by Doubleday & Company, Inc. Reprinted by permission of the publisher.

[203] Nietzsche, *op. cit.*, pp. 20–21.

ity,[204] no more lucid for interpretation of life. Here one encounters the hostility that such a situation presents to analysis: why should a soul writ large be more readily open to analysis than a soul; why should a subset of the human irrational be more understandable than the total human irrationality? In "Talking World War III Blues" he is actually bemoaning the utter predictability of reality through dreams, if as an artist his sensitivity implies something as corny and final as ultimate destruction.

About the state of intoxication, Dylan comments in his original version of "I Shall Be Free" that it "Levels my head and eases my mind/ . . . Catch dinosaurs,/ Make love to Elizabeth Taylor . . ."[205] Quite naturally Dylan abhors retreat from sober (even Quotidian) reality to see the mere world through mere rose-colored glasses. Sandy Fadin of the finally

---

[204] One of Jim Morrison's loud stage exhortations is "Wake up!!! . . . . I can't remember where the dream left off . . . . the snake was pale gold, glazed and shrunken and we were afraid to touch it . . . . the sheets were hot dead prisons . . . . and she was beside me . . .": acidic muffling of actual physical dream-reality marginality. "Day in the Life" approaches this scene from the opposite direction with the additional shocker of clarity and distinction: "Found my way upstairs and had a smoke, and somebody spoke and I went into a dream . . ." The Spoonful's "Daydream" disperses dream fully throughout waking reality: "What a day for a daydream." And the Electric Prunes' "I Had Too Much to Dream Last Night" is a dandy instance of dream *as* intoxication. And the Who's "Whiskey Man" is intoxication as dream.

[205] The mere alcohol metaphor was once a big deal in its so-what sham wide applicability before being supplanted by drugs and non-alcoholic mere frivolous poetry.

defunct Tuckets, grandson-or-something of Man Ray, has made one of his goals that of viewing a rose through world-colored glasses. Intoxication, while apparently an experience of freedom-or-something, can become a troublesome cliché of a necessity. The Beatles see even the less-than-necessity cliché as a drag in "I Don't Want to Spoil the Party":

> I've had a drink or two and I don't care,
> There's no fun in what I do if she's not there.
> I wonder what went wrong.
> I've waited far too long.
> I think I'll take a walk and look for her.

Nietzsche (Plato too) exclaims that music is architectonic in determining what state a person is in. When one talks about music its power is lessened, it loses its effectiveness. The smallest loss due to verbalization occurs in tragedy, says Nietzsche. Thus, unless he wants to consider his *Birth of Tragedy* as a work of tragedy, his objectification of all the undercurrents of man's tragic/musical experience represents an inconsistent failure. Seen by rock 'n' roll, Nietzsche's fine distinctions lose clarity in such a (ready-made) hazy universe. Opposing tendencies do not always appear in opposition if at all. Nietzsche wants to find power for human experience; it is a pity he seeks it in something so classical and time-honored. Power is everywhere, it is to be found in orderings of experience which somehow are (merely) viable, and my silly objective labels, such as orgasmic monotony, are as applicable to that which is viable as are Nietzsche's silly objective labels, tragic, Apollonian, Dionysiac. Nietzsche fears the nausea of confrontation with the Quotidian world; rock 'n' roll ignores it, inhabits it, spreads it, enhances it. But most definitely rock has expanded man's potential to experience in this realm, where all objective analysis is equally applicable and equally wrong. It is to Nietzsche's credit that I have so distorted his system (a proto-rock anti-system[206]), that I have in fact so misinterpreted him.

During the period roughly between *Help!* and *Rubber Soul* rock was historically at a point of momentary hesitation.... The Beach Boys had descended from their original peak, and were settling at a moderate level of creativity and success, but they eventually condescended (or perhaps ascended) to star in a Walt Disney movie, *The Monkey's Uncle*; surf-drag music was consequently then at its low point. Motown was descending from its peak achieved by the Supremes and their followers (com)piled on top of the earlier achievements of Smokey Robinson and the Miracles. The introduction of Detroiter Marvin Gaye at the Beatles' 1965 Shea Stadium concert was rock 'n' roll's equivalent to the ringside introduction of retired ex-champions at title fights. Blue-eyed soul had become stagnant, necessitating the Righteous Brothers' "soul" version of "Unchained Melody." Which didn't have much trouble in sinking things further.

All of English rock maintained its being alongside the Beatles,[207] and the Beatles could conceivably con-

---

[206] Dylan: "Systems fled by confusion boat, mutiny from stern to bow."

[207] What about the Stones? you ask. Well, their generation-of-mass-interest level has always (without exception) been dependent upon the contemporaneity of their releases with those of the Beatles. During the above-

trol the development of their facet of rock 'n' roll until they literally became "eighty-year-old Beatles." However the quest for innovation can become stale, especially if you possess the solution to all problems of art. The problem of maintaining the self-contradictory key to such eternally absurd problems as the resolution of the one and the many can become stale more quickly than the original problem itself. Perhaps any possession of knowledge destined to become self-defeating is superseded in quickness of exhaustibility only by the possession of this exhaustibility.[208] Consider Nietzsche's possession of the following perception: "Consider the consequences of the Socratic maxims: Virtue is knowledge; all sins arise from ignorance; only the virtuous are happy—these three basic formulations of optimism spell the death of tragedy."[209] If primary knowledge and happiness have such an effect upon the human potential to experience, then what will the effect of such secondary knowledge and joy of mental possession have upon Nietzsche's own future range of experience? This seems to be just the realm to which a recent D. Gerber statement is applicable. If the former state of tragic impotency is, in the words of a time-honored cliché, a fate worse than death, subsequently the latter can

---

mentioned period the temporal matchup was always close, but slightly later the Stones missed the very top with "Mother's Little Helper," "Dandelion" (/"We Love You" and "She's a Rainbow" largely because of the absence of near-vicinity Beatle hits, while "Jumpin' Jack Flash" made it big both by affinity to diverse recent rumblings and its temporal concurrence with the Beatles' "Lady Madonna."

[208] Doors: "Try now we can only lose, and our love become a funeral pyre."

[209] Nietzsche, *op. cit.*, p. 88.

be described as "a fate worse than life," with no epistemological certainty intended.

But the question remained, is the actual total rock demise possible, can the whole thing collapse for real? Eric Burdon's "Story of Bo Diddley" reflected upon an earlier rock crud-consistent hypothetical abyss, one sort of earlier analogue situation, that period during which Bobby Vee ("Take Good Care of My Baby") had hits.[210] *Highway 61 Revisited, Rubber Soul, Aftermath, Blonde on Blonde, Pet Sounds, Revolver, Between the Buttons,* etc. were super-duper gap fillers that just scratched the itch. Donovan's first full rock album, *Sunshine Superman,* appeared, and its "Celeste" offered the focal point of nonobjective private vulnerability to mere whim (which might easily be generalized to the level of public as widespread private).

Rest became a move, replacement of the expected periodic reappearance of official crud. For the Beach Boys it was resignation to and systematic acceptance of utter peace in "Wouldn't It Be Nice." For Dylan it was the systematic preference for repetitive Muzak structural laziness. For the Beatles it was "I'm Only Sleeping" and the return of surrealism to the dream qua sleep. But for the Stones it was "Mother's Little Helper," the pill illustration of the close proximity of

---

[210] Sure enough, prophetic-in-reverse non-affinity-minded Eric Burdon is fortunate to have been forgotten for his analysis by the time of the reemergence of Bobby Vee, at the very height of the *Sgt. Pepper* return-to-infallible-quality hoopla. But then, Eric gloried in Bo Diddley's rejection of the Animals' version of the latter's old stuff, so if he knew about the return of Bobby Vee he might snicker.

death to relaxation. And the Yardbirds' "Farewell" is a comfortable suicide song *per se* or at least a "farewell to future days" full of insulated rest.

Then there came the Grateful Dead and the Doors. Doors and willingness to die, lose, etc. Not just obsession with the inevitability of death or speculation on laying the groundwork for future necrophiliac moves, but the need to do some killing. "The End,"

> This is the end, beautiful friend.
> This is the end, my only friend,
> The end of our elaborate plans,
> The end of everything that stands, the end,
> No safety or surprise, the end.
> I'll never look into your eyes again.

ends all Doors performances, with the final line being "This *is* the end!" There's a "Father, yes son, I want to kill you" section in it and a big "Kill, kill"[211] chorus. There's a Tristan and Isolde type revival of the sex-death relationship plus a willingness to succumb to it. And "I Looked at You" ("You looked at me, I smiled at you, you smiled at me, and we're on our way and we can't turn back"): an end to directional options. The Weill-Brecht "Alabama Song (Whiskey Bar)" was chosen for the Doors' repertoire most likely because of the death ("surely we must die") and mother[212] ("we've lost our dear old mama") refer-

---

[211] Sometimes it sounds on the recording like "Care, care" but that's certainly close.

[212] Of the twin life principles, mother and father, only the mother affords, in eventual sexual union, further conventionally repulsive/wholesome death/consolidation moves. The father can only be killed outright.

ences. And "Moonlight Drive," the nihilistic topper of "Patches": just a little join me for some suicide (we're *both* still alive) down at the wild old ocean (tide and all that, not a dirty old river), "Come on baby, gonna drown tonight." And "End of the Night." And "Take It as It Comes," which chops up "Turn, Turn, Turn" into a nonpolar non-preferential list: "Time to live, time to lie,/ Time to laugh, time to die." And, of course, "When the Music's Over": take the end of anything pertinent as the opportunity for turning out the light. Death as the end metaphor, and death *of* the end metaphor, for a while.[213]

And Dylan's earlier but finally becoming pertinent narrow escape from death on his motorcycle.

Then along came the Beatles again with "Strawberry Fields Forever" with an important forever on top of the Doors, signaling the death of past actual eternities, closing off the non-nostalgic present and stuff like that. And the death of certainly-all-over-the-place for a while, or at least the dream-location of it, which in this case heightens confusion (which doesn't mean *obviousness* is lessened) both *a posteriori* and *a priori* or something like that. Sleep as a surefire actual conceptual death/closure, etc.[214]

---

[213] But the Velvet Underground sure forced the issue. "Black Angel's Death Song." "Heroin" ("when it shoots up the dropper's neck, and I'm coasting in on death"). "Venus in Furs" with non-death-oriented sado-masochism: *persist* in self-negation.

[214] The abundance of "that is . . ."—like construction in "Strawberry Fields" is the most overt clarification and simultaneous non-formalization of raunch epistemology ever, indicated by such masterfully fluid knowledge

The growing awareness that there was an American-shore multiplicity/variety lots-of-new-groups move taking place (Mothers, Airplane, Love, Buffalo Springfield, Moby Grape, Grateful Dead, the hint of Big Brother & the Holding Company) both heightened the tension and made it easier to bear. But Tim Buckley, part of this wave, confided in me[215] and everybody else that he wanted to see the Beatles come back (their album absence was getting longer and longer) and knock him out one more time, and *really* knock him out this time: he thought them dead what-a-pity, for that would mean that in a way the *whole thing* had died without an official time of death.

Then "New York Mining Disaster—1941" by the Bee Gees! Right, the Bee Gees. That just had to be a pseudonym. It sounded too much like *Revolver* period Beatle stuff, and Brian Epstein was the Bee Gees' manager too. But then photos of the Bee Gees appeared. So hunger for the actual became greater than it ever was for the possible.

So, as expected, it had to be the Beatles themselves to do the job of (one-more-time) summing up the recent by summing up the whole thing in a soft cata-

guidelines as "it must be high or low" and "all wrong, that is I think I disagree." "You know I know and it's a dream" or "You know I know when it's a dream" or whatever that is is a perfect reversal of Platonic-Cartesian certainty for being awake knowingly only when you are actually awake. The last prior time this type of philosophical reversal occurred was in "I Want to Tell You": "It's only me, it's not my mind that is confusing things."

[215] February '67 in Memphis Sam Pearlman's car, with Noonan and Jackson too.

clysmic combination of death, sleep and multiplicity/
variety, as if they hadn't done it before (every album
beginning with *Beatles '65, Beatles for Sale* in England, or maybe it was already going on album-wise
with *A Hard Day's Night* or earlier), so this time it
would have to be a *really real* decisive end-of-culture/
end-of-the-world thing. And that's precisely what
Sgt. Peppers Lonely Hearts Club Band was/is. Bringing with it the consequent death of art forever (until someone forgets) and subsequent everybody-in-
fluenced-by-everybody-but-particularly-the-Beatles-
and-Sgt-Pepper,[216] eventually dispersing it everywhere
and thus inevitably devaluing the specific Sgt. Pepper
focal point. "Beatles" nearly became established as
an official category rather than "rock," with Johnny
Rivers referring in a song of his own to "Sgt. Pepper's
Lonely Hearts Club Band" as an (the first) actually
quoted album fact, and the Stones (on their *Their
Satanic Majesties Request*, their move directly and
indirectly to obliterate the Sgt. Pepper concept which

---

[216] For even *everybody*, including Baltimore art teach-
ers and proverbial grandmothers and clothing merchants
of the world and established music morons like Leonard
Bernstein (he has named "She's Leaving Home" something like one of the three great compositions of the
century, ha!). And apparent dissonance has enabled fans
to regard the Beatles as having gone "underground" or
"sold out to respectability" or anything else. And not
very ironically, the slow-fast onslaught of the greatest
rock-sound homogeneity (conditioned raunch epistemological readiness and the abandonment of perceptual
acuity have been contributors) since the '50's. And the
biggest mere group plethora (Ultimate Spinach, Grapefruit, Dada, Lemon Pipers, Elephant's Memory . . . . .)
of all time.

was already self-obliterating) use somebody or other to garble "Beatle show."[217] Enough said.

John Lennon focuses upon the dead end toward which all solutions, although utterly successful, may move, in a two page cartoon in *A Spaniard in the Works*.[218] Shown on the left hand leaf is a very thin blind man, standing upright upon a cane with a trumpet at his lips and a pot of coins at his feet. Even his seeing-eye dog is cadaverously thin and also furnished with a pair of sunglasses like those of his master. He has only two toes on each foot, and his tragic despair is evident in his upright resignation. His "I am blind" sign is his only objective label. Opposite him on the right hand page is someone who has seen beyond the inadequacies of tragic authenticity and bears "I can see quite clearly" on his chest. He is fat, has three toes on each foot, owns a well fed, smiling dog who is roaming freely at the end of a leash, and from his jovial expression and carefree, slovenly stance, he appears quite successful for one endowed with the limitation of sight. The creative genius of the second trumpeter has carried the tin cup experience about as far as it can possibly be extended both artistically and financially while still toying with an ambiguous level of authenticity. Although he has a great solution, perhaps the only viable one, standing on a street corner will reduce to sheer boredom for him in about three hours. He has seen and rejected the tragic

---

[217] Whereas the Stones' appearance on *Sgt. Pepper* was on a "WMCA Good Guys Welcome the Rolling Stones" sweatshirt on a doll on the cover. (Whereas?)

[218] John Lennon, *A Spaniard in the Works*, Simon and Schuster, New York 1965, pp. 58–59.

possibilities of blindness and would not wish to build a mythology under which the state of blindness, with all its metaphysical and poetic implication, would generate a new potency for man, as a Nietzschean trumpeter might. But now he is about to become simply bored, so he may pack up his earnings and pay the debts he owes his brother-in-law.

The genius of Sisyphus might eventually produce a scheme whereby he can scratch pornographic drawings with his thumb while rolling his rock up the hill; after fourteen or fifteen successful attempts Sisyphus would then finally get bored by this newly found experience. But Sisyphus is entrapped by his situation: he cannot completely say *so what* to his fate worse than death-or-something. But the seeing trumpeter and John Lennon share a fate worse than life-or-something. They can become fully bored; this capability limits their ability to sustain aesthetic expression while it simultaneously allows them an escape.

Cognitive "solutions" can be more awesome in their manifestations than Nietzsche imagined, additionally awesome because they are doomed to burn out as brilliant sparks awaiting a non-cognitive or post-cognitive rekindling. Writer for children Dr. Seuss has given insight into a related aspect of solution: " 'If I ran the zoo,'/ Said young Gerald McGrew,/ 'I'd make a few changes,/ That's just what I'd do.' "[219]

The Shangri-Las could (have) offer(ed) rock 'n' roll its next opportunity to throb for a while, with a

---

[219] Dr. Seuss, *If I Ran the Zoo*, Random House, New York.

solution neither cognitive nor anti-cognitive nor non-cognitive, but quite likely a-cognitive (here can be seen the inadequacy of an antiquated dependence of artistic analysis upon useless linguistic categories). "So Much in Love," originally recorded by the Tymes with seagull calls, is rendered by the Shangri-Las without birds—but with human audience reaction; and, as Legs Forbes has supposedly said, "All people are birds" (see page 3). Their "Twist and Shout," without birds in its original form, has Trini Lopez-Isley Brothers bird calls interspersed by the Shangri-Las. But their enormous hit "Remember (Walking in the Sand)," replete with birds in its original form, is not even included in this collection. Their "What Is Love" takes its title from the innocent adolescent love of a song by the Playmates. But from its start this song makes it evident their love is not play. (Incidentally, one member of the group does not appear in the album cover photograph; according to the evidence of Dennis Kelly, who has been chasing her unsuccessfully, she had been absent from the photographing because she was pregnant.) At precisely ten o'clock on the evening of August 16, 1965, D. Gerber announced that this song showed the Shangri-Las to be "Something other than female; I don't know if it transcends it." The girls' "Leader of the Pack" is a fusion of literally every overstated theme ever developed in the realm of rock, complete with motorcycle sound effects and the amazing sound of a death-dealing accident. "Give Him a Great Big Kiss" is more of the same with the great absolutely abominable "good bad, but he's not evil" cluttering its already trivially ambiguous ethical structure. It's even an improvement on the dialogue section of "Leader of the Pack."

(But of course, after the "Hush little baby, don't you cry" of "Never Go Home Anymore" and the re-tolling of "When Johnny Comes Marching Home" in "Long Live Our Love," *that was it* for the Shangri-Las. That was that. Or that was that until Shadow Morton himself reentered as the producer of the Vanilla Fudge. . . .)

But (also), to digress from the grammatically temporal fun of apparent multiple presents and get into the now-wow sequence of up-and-coming possible grooves, here's another pseudo-prophetic offering (Autosalvage). Prophecy requires for fulfillment a period of non-acceptance and even forgetfulness: otherwise, you get merely fulfilled mere prediction. So gaps are important, but so the drama of the inevitable build-up (and the likelihood of total memory loss) doesn't get tedious small gaps are best. And an embarrassing plethora of at least temporary nonfulfillment around the rest of the scene is a corequisite requirement and everpresent phenomenon there for background use anytime. Okay, thus: Autosalvage.

Stuff you could laugh about in the days of the Shangri-Las is about equivalent to the stuff you (can) take seriously this particular now, like Autosalvage (which is even funny and the Shangri-Las weren't).

Autosalvage is a view of entropy at the peak: ". . . today in the junkyards are the fifty-nine Fords, and the sixty-one Fords, and the sixty-three Fords./ What kind of person owned a fifty-nine Ford?" Rock is the greatest intentionally organized junkyard multiplicity with possible recovery of anything as an

element in the crud; and yet the whole thing itself is
on the same level as anything hidden for now or fore-
ever or a week or just gone or just there on top or
wow on top or almost visible through the dead goat's
mouth (the whole landlocked Yellow Submarine without seagoing mobility).[220] Words out of step with the
phrasing, but phrasing just sort of sorted out from
the musical debris, no line-to-line consistency, no
maintenance of the integrity of any individual parts,
words given on the album cover to only six out of
nine songs, words clear enough only when on their
own and never when fulfilling their conglomerate
function, pairs of transitionally indistinguishable songs
clumped together as "medleys," etc. And lots of manipulations and ameliorations of junkyardness itself,
like entropy-decadence and the choice of the Mc-
Guinn vocal readymade and/or the impossibility of
avoiding it; and the coarse laziness inevitable in the
vocalizing of any language trash with its tiredly
freshly exuberant trappings of inevitably tiresome
cosmic flow ("Oh the moon is rising and the stars're
flying through the air, but the sky is falling, yes and
we know where, then someone was done in, you know
he was calling for you" sung sarcastically ever-so-
lazily at the start of "The Great Brain Robbery").
And "The Great Brain Robbery" even ends with the
end of the near-the-end instrumental of "The End,"
weakened and disguised in the rubbish of its weaken-
edness. And the relative newness of the usable portion
of the corpse of the corpse-referential "End" comes out

---

[220] Only in a junkyard will all possible nature-artifice
interplays and interferences occur. Pollock only ap-
proached this when he included pennies, nickels and
cigarette butts; César, reconstructor of actual junkyards,
gains access fully to the universe of Pollock's intent.

in the unguarded homefront as junkyardlike source (in Autosalvage's "Burglar Song"): "I can't say but I think that I know for sure/ Whose house this is but I think I know it's yours/ With your furs and your jewels and your TV sets./ You know I'm going to take just what I can get my hands on." Autosalvage is the last decadent outpost before the total accept- ance of Grace Slick, but that can only be understood in another garbage bucket. Autosalvage, with its over- ly clarity-prone philosophic crystallizations of univer- sal muck and with its conventionally RCA-ugly green- blue face first album cover. So this entire super-system will stagnate and grow healthily upon a new crutch. But it might happen or not happen in some utterly different manner. Off the junk heap: called-for un- called-for caution-to-the-winds caution.

No longer *wow* but *hmm.*

And no longer *so what?* but *so?*

Epílogue

An epilogue adds to a body of writing what occurs temporally after the main action or what occurs to the writer after he has written about the main body of action. Often it is the summation of all the excess energies still residual after this main body has been explicated, but necessary to explain it fully. Actually, an idea should be quite visible when first mentioned, and continuous attention to it should beat it to death. Thomas Mann's novels contain this type of idea expansion and elaboration. Thomas Pynchon's first novel, *V.*, whose main character, Benny Profane, envisions himself as a yo-yo, proceeds like a yo-yo to expand and elaborate the idea that it is silly yet essential to expand and elaborate to infinity. Pynchon's epilogue, quite naturally, is a flashback to an event forty-six years before the time of the main action.

Often an epilogue can contain what would have been too boring to develop in the preceding body. John Lennon's self-descriptive epilogue to *In His Own Write*, entitled "About the Awful," states the following gibberish:

I was bored on the 9th of Octover 1940 when, I believe,
the Nasties were still booming us led by Madalf Heat-
lump (Who only had one). Anyway they didn't get me.
I attended to varicous schools in Liddypool. And still
didn't pass—much to my Aunties supplies. As a member
of the most publified Beatles my and (P, G, and R's)
records might seem funnier to some than this book, but
as far as I'm conceived this correction of the short writty
is the most wonderfoul larf I've ever ready.
                   God help and breed you all.

George Harrison, in *Hard Day's Night*, remarks upon
boredom as the preclusion of continuity of expression
in his description of a television personality: "She's
a drag, a well-known drag. You turn down the sound
and say rude things."

An epilogue should be an afterthought on afterthought. "About the Awful" appears on the back
cover of the book, a perfect mechanical epilogue. "Mr.
Moonlight" and "Everybody's Trying to Be My
Baby," the two most trivial of the songs contained
in *Beatles '65*, appear last respectively on side one
and side two, a perfect mechanical incorporation of
essential triviality. The Beatles' trivialization scheme
has often been this reflexive afterthought.

The Rolling Stones' trivialization scheme has been
more elusive. Although the Stones appear timid in
the face of a creative universe of triviality, one which
the Beatles and Dave Dee, Dozy, Beaky, Mick & Tich
visit frequently, they have allowed a truly trivial
American, Joey Page, to accompany them on tours.
His distinctively abominable television performance
on *Hollywood à Go-Go* exonerates the Stones: they

are unafraid of triviality, at least by proxy. And this significant key to a great mystery of the Stones remains invisible to the American follower of rock 'n' roll unless he is either degenerate or sophisticated enough to appreciate the unique experience of this television program. Here we have an empirical approach not dependent upon dispositions of human perception but upon dispositions of human sentiment. The Rolling Stones have not relied upon reflexive afterthought.[1]

---

[1] Oh come on, that's a lot of crap; so a footnote all about the Stones:

Emily Dickinson's "I Heard a Fly Buzz When I Died" is a high point in death buffoonery, and she's just a little girl writing about lots of things, sometimes death. Those Stones, now they go ahead and build up a reputation for being primarily a death or post-life-as-a-conceptual-framework morbidness group, so when they go in for death buffoonery afterthought they're goosing a lot more things even without intending; that is, you can easily pick up on it and use it in that bag (a *dead* bag in fact). "The Lantern" must have both Emily Dickinson and Brian Epstein turning over in their graves.

> We, in our present life
> Knew that the stars were right,
> Then if you are the first to go
> You'll leave a sign to let me know,
> Oh tell me so,
> Please carry the lantern light.
>
> You cross the sea of night
> Free from the spell of flight (plight) (trite);
> The cloak it is a spirit shroud,
> You'll wake me in my sleeping hours,
> Like the clouds,
> Please carry the lantern high.
>
> Me, in my sorry plight,
> You waiting every night,

So what?

At the close of Plato's *Symposium*, Socrates has
clinched complete control of the situation and has,

> My face it turns a deathly pale,
> You're talking to me through your veil,
> I hear you wail,
> Please carry the lantern light.
>
> The servants sleep,
> The doors are barred,
> You hear the stopping of my heart,
> It never parts,
> Please carry the lantern *high*.

In death not only freedom from flight but everything
topically entailed by such a suddenly current (in doper
cosmic research linguistically staple terminology): astrol-
ogy, the Doors (their whole death takeover, Robbie
Krieger guitar, John Densmore drums), heart trans-
plants, post-Byrds church music *objets trouvés*. And
your cloak is even a readymade spirit shroud (as opposed
to mere corpse shroud) so you're all set.
    Stones in "2000 Man" sing "Oh daddy, proud of your
planet,/Oh mommy, proud of your sun" as if it were
"proud of your granny, proud of your son." Double
decker trivialization, and nowadays only the Stones
could reintroduce such a safely trivial terminology.
    "In Another Land" hands you everything blue
(hey, all the way back to "Yes It Is" but so long afterwards that you probably forgot) until it all turns red.
And there's all the usual Donovan-Lucy in the Sky
goodies (breeze, trees, sea, sky, feathers, grass growing
high, your hand). Then the sledge hammer falls: "Then
I awoke;/Was this some kind of joke?/Much to my surprise,/I opened my eyes." But further trivialization steps
in in the form of elaborate reconstruction (since there's
ample repetition of the awake insight), such as the addi-

by keeping his listeners on the verge of boredom and sleep, forced them into acceptance of anything he chooses. "Socrates was arguing with the others—not that Aristodemus could remember very much of what

---

tion of explanation within what is now clearly a dream (hmm, Stones kicking around "Strawberry Fields"), "The sky turned red when I accidentally said that I didn't know how I came to be here not fast asleep in bed." And the sequence mixup-or-something in the "awoke"-"joke"-"surprise"-"eyes" eye-opener throws it all back on intentional poetic inarticulateness rather than rationality as a dud. Nice going, Bill (it's Bill Wyman's song and Cole Porter is one of his favorites). The greatest trivially reflexive poetic inarticulateness poem of all time; since versification makes meaning alien to form, you might as well make it irrelevant and work your way back (and forth). And the greatest irrelevance tongue proliferation ever. Morrison by way of the Association.

Getting ever more trivial by the day is the fact of poetry in the Stones' "Ruby Tuesday." The timing of the verses of "Ruby Tuesday" fully transcend the standard stock of devices used for discussing rock meter. Taken as rock it has the raw potent impact of, out of nowhere, a poem read from a printed page! While in an ordinary poem the temporality of music itself is only implicitly part of what is going on, this is a poem from the other side of the fence, with overt but utterly subtle musical accompaniment and implicit "poetic" time sense, whatever that is. This is just what written poetry is, superimpositions of time senses upon a bunch of words. "Here, There and Everywhere" was the first "perfect poem" to appear in rock proper. "Ruby Tuesday" is the first poem qua poem to hit the rock scene, as well as being the first rock song to contain more overt writtenness than the rock songs of Tim Hardin.

In the annals of political and religious rock, nothing is more important or importantly trivial than the Stones' "Sing This All Together": vision without move intimation, no, but overintimation of "political" importance

he said, for, besides having missed the beginning, he
was still more than half asleep. But the gist of it was
that Socrates was forcing them to admit that the
same man might be capable of writing both comedy

---

contained in the stylistic superstructure of the song and
album (*Satanic Majesties*, which didn't have, but was
supposed to have, a picture of the crucifixion of Mick
Jagger). Albert Bouchard, drummer of the Soft White
Underbelly, took acid and listened to it before going
down to his draft physical, which he was finally kicked
out of but not freed from as insane.

> Why don't we sing this song all together
> Open our minds, let the pictures come
> And if we close all our eyes together
> Then we will see where we all come from.

Albert took this to be the nth primal overstatement of
religious insight (it's all inside your head, man, it's not
up in the sky, that sort of thing). And that must surely
be its first appearance in rock proper. Big Bill Broonzy
once said about Ray Charles' mixture of the blues and
gospel, "He's got the blues he's cryin' sanctified. He's
mixin' the blues with the spirituals. I know that's
wrong." Okay, so all you got here with the Stones is
blues-from-the-other-side-of-the-fence not only dumping
its purist split with mere divinity but also with the conventional transcendental ground for it. Wowee that's a
lot. And it's not even remotely new, but, sure enough,
new as an overt rock move. Senseless masochism afterthought afterthought and not even that cause it's too
easy. Yummy.

And there's "Sittin' on a Fence" too. It sums up a lot
of this side of the Stones and even sets it on a counter-
side perspective with only one possible alternative side.

> Since I was young I've been very hard to please
> And I don't know wrong from right
> But there is one thing I could never understand

and tragedy—that the tragic poet might be a come-
dian as well."² Socrates here has spoken of tragedy
and comedy alone as a matter of pertinent drunken
brevity. John Lennon in a similar position would

> Some of the sick things that a girl does to a man
> So I'm just sittin' on a fence . . .

Indeed, especially after "If there's one sort of thing in
this world that I can't understand it's a girl" ("Sad
Day") in all its powerful contextual powerfulness. So
let's see, it's gotta be the Stones working with simple
trivial-content afterthought knowing full well the absurdity of *any* explicit fixed relationship between an object
and the triviality grid of analysis. Double check the song,
there's all that mandolin playing so maybe it's just "children's music," yeah, maybe, that's back in vogue, and
that's some association, isn't it? But then

> All of my friends in school grew up and settled down
> And they mortgaged up their lives
> One thing's not said too much but I think it's true
> They just get married cause there's nothing else
>   to do

sets matters straight (what does it set straight?), it's
adolescent music, so it's not kid stuff, and already you've
got another one-more contextual trivialization. As if that
couldn't do the job itself, on rushes the finale:

> The day can come when you get old and sick and
>   tired of life
> You just never realize
> Maybe the choice you made wasn't really right
> But you go out and you don't come home at night

and the confusion grid comes in. Who's he talking to/
about? Himself? Where's *that* at? All the trivial ques-

group together many more things, likely tragedy, comedy, pornography, melodrama, structured philosophy, mathematics and psychology, history, geography, limerick, babble, garbage collection, plumbing,

---

tions. You had to ask them just to figure out what was going on. You had to assume them just to be confused. And the whole how-much-does-Mick-believe-of-what-he's-saying? bit actually reerupts years and years after you've conveniently dismissed that whole (what-does-any-innate-or-otherwise-word-message-relationship-matter-anyway?) thing, and the Stones were in the vanguard of the boys that set that whole business straight for everybody anyway. So, additional perplexed (anew) wonderment about any sort of objective embodiment of triviality at all, and that's only a problem because the Stones aren't ever exclusively silly (they laugh, get arrested, make fun of Ed Sullivan) so there goes any topical silliness-triviality relationship and you're left with only sloppy affinity and the dismissal of topicality. And what about trite, banal and all of that? You can forget about them too and take the Stones' basic unity as being somewhere around the constant collapse and renewal of all that _____ (it's more basic to the Stones than "power" and power's just as trivial as unity) (both conceptually and objectively).

So on with the show: the Rolling Stones' programmatic trivial object (whatever that could mean) trail:

"Take It or Leave It": "La la *la* ta, ta *ta* ta, la *la* la la."

"It's Not Easy": "All of the things that you used to do,/If they're done now, well they're done by you."

The irreverence (?) of *December's Children* and the reverence of *Aftermath* combined spiritually (and ambiguously) (on *Between* the *Buttons*) in the trivial nullification/enhancements rendered by the introduction of strange instruments (all at once, not like the slowpoke Beatles who only did it about 36 years before) in "She Smiled Sweetly," "Cool, Calm, Collected," "Miss Amanda Jones," "Ruby Tuesday," "All Sold Out," and, actually, maybe everything else. Whistling, bizarre organ, Brian's recorder, and kazoo put the listener all over the comfort-

cookery. Dulled beyond speech he might still indicate
his conception of the One as dullness beyond speech.
Mick Jagger actually offers a variation of this position
at the conclusion of the Stones' "Walking the Dog,"

---

discomfort continuum on the first hearing and make
eventual comfortable familiarity almost a matter of "self-
education" (ha). Trivialization of "novelty."

The entire *Got LIVE if You Want It*, some of which
("I've Been Loving You Too Long" and "Fortune
Teller") is just old recordings with overdubbed applause
on one stereo track, misses even a moment of the
bummer label due to awesome *ad hominem* pressure
greeting this first live album by anybody big and English, even though it's all simulated amphetamine-rage
dullard doings (or is that what it's *supposed* to be?:
trivial questions again). So the Stones lightly skip over
dozens of shallow levels of *de facto* trivializations, emerging trivially unscathed (and Keith Richard once got
jolted by some on-stage circuitry during a real and true
live performance, or maybe it was dope that did it: more
gleeful metaphysical trivial hypothetical tinkering). And
the guy who introduces them ("Ladies and gentlemen,
it's all about to happen, let's hear it for the fabulous
Rollin' Stones!") to an Albert Hall audience sounds
pretty American.

Or in the old days (1965 and earlier), boy-girl hokum:
"Gotta Get Away" ("I can't stand to see your face, you
understand me now, I got to get away, gotta gotta gotta
get away"); "Grown Up All Wrong" ("You was easy to
fool when you was in school, but you growed up all
wrong"); "Stupid Girl" (ends in roller-skating organ
and it's '66, why give up a good waste of time qua waste
of time?)

Or in that old (live) TAMI show with Mick substitut-
ing "hurt my nose open" for "hurt my eyes open" (only
one nose, physiological reinforcement of mere quantita-
tive reduction in accompaniment to mere content shift)
in "It's All Over Now" while Bill Wyman chewed his
gum and blew occasional bubbles.

Glorified glorified superglorified minor sniveling ac-

babbling, "Duh-duh-duh-duh-duh . . . just a-walkin'."
Struck by profound revelation, he is ambiguously
wounded and relieved of his power to speak coherently
or so awestruck that coherent speech is no longer
necessary. Anyway, he just babbles.

On this note, I begin my epilogue.

The Angels' "My Boyfriend's Back" presents the
entire panorama of the arrival of Orestes. The Beatles'
"Follow the Sun" contains the transitional element
"Oh, oh," present in *Prometheus Bound* as Io's "O O."
Barry McGuire's impassioned "You can bury your
dead, but don't leave a trace" is a reference to An-
tigone (and/or Cowboys-and-Indians scalp stuff).
And the following passage spoken by Artemis in *Hyp-
polytus* is a foreshadowing of rock 'n' roll:

> Do not bear a grudge against your father.
> It was fate that you should die so.
> Farewell, I must not look upon the dead.

---

complishment: "Under My Thumb" ("Under my thumb,
her eyes are just kept to herself,/Under my thumb, well
I, I can still look at someone else"): sniveling minor
accomplishment glorified glorified superglorified. And the
animal qua pet metaphor ("Squirmy dog," "S-siamese
cat of a girl") before before *before Pet Sounds.* "Ain't it
the truth, baby": borrow trivial soul punctuations and
make them trivialer.

And "Lady Jane" in retrospect: *the* source of Bryan
Maclean style vaudeville (Love's "Old Man"). Too awesome at first to be belittled in any way; two years later
it's even more impressive and finally acknowledgeable
as trivial as hell.

And the Mick-Marianne Faithfull juxtaposition.

[2] Translated by Michael Joyce, Everyman's Library,
London and New York, 1935.

Speaking of foreshadowing, Ricky Nelson's "Teen-age Idol" foreordains the future presence of the Rolling Stones: "I wander around/ From town to lonely town/ I guess I'll always be just a rolling stone." Chuck Berry's "Rock and Roll Music" predicts in 1957 the later outbreak of African nationalism, "It's way too early for the *congo*,/ So keep a-rocking that piano." Buddy Holly's last recording before dying in a plane crash is "I Guess It Doesn't Matter Anymore." Chuck Willis' last released recording before his death from cancer is "Hang Up My Rock 'n' Roll Shoes." And the name of Ringo Starr's firstborn son is Zak, the ending of "muzak" (Muzak), the union of "muse" and "Zak," possibly a clue to the new direction.

The sudden unexpected appearance of a new recording of the Beatles' "You've Got to Hide Your Love Away," this time by a group known as the Silky, is at first outrageous. After all, nobody can duplicate the four magnificent renderings of the yell "Hey!"[3] Secondly, the superficial harmony of the Silky ruins the fine single-voiced Lennon version.[4] But for the Beatles to inspire a need to be classicized by ardent admirers is a trick they must fully understand. Certainly the Beatles (Stones, 1910 Fruit Gum Co., etc.) are unassailably the finest, but the absurdity of their situation, just like that of Cassius Clay, calls for a clear view of the habits of association which go into

---

[3] Lennon's own "Hey!" is bitter, and he's not often bitter, so it's special.

[4] The Silky happens to be composed of some studio technicians who recorded the Beatles. *And* a Beatle or two is in there *playing for* the Silky. But who's *recording* them now that they've graduated to *singing*? So even the recording quality is deficient before they even get started.

labeling even obvious greatness. And surely the Silky
version should not be inferior, but it inescapably is.
If you want it that way. So to say that something by
the Beatles is bad is to miss one of the biggest points
around: rock is the first in-context revealed religion
incarnate ever.

Similarly Bob Dylan, leading man to oblivion in
"Mr. Tambourine Man," capitalizes on these same
inevitable reactions to acceptable art. "I promise to
go wanderin'" is the guarantee to the artist of his
security with paths of calculable reaction. As Wordsworth maintains the joy of poetry to be the satisfaction of certain patterns of association, Dylan sits
amazed at the poetry of the cliché which is the inevitable outcome of what Wordsworth implies.

Frank Sinatra's reemergence as a front-runner on
the pop scene has been at a time when he would have
to be labeled, by definition, rock 'n' roll, merely because *everything*, at this historical moment,[5] is contextualizable as rock. But, to make it tough for even
non-nominalists to refuse him as a rock superstar,
he produced his first consciously inauthentic work,
"That's Life," which produced in turn the massive
inauthentic disc jockey reaction of "sounds like Ray
Charles."

In (at least) two obvious ways this whole Frank
Sinatra rock bit relates to the Monkees' rock significance. First, Frankie can sell his songs but he can't
any longer sell himself (except as Mia Farrow's
husband-for-a-while and Nancy Sinatra's father, nice

[5] *What* historical moment? I don't know, guess.

out-of-context legitimacy), while the Monkees are selling themselves like crazy, and who even knows who their music is by?

More important, the reduction that makes Sinatra now rock 'n' roll is generally reversed to treat the Monkees not as true rock but as "television."

Just because the Monkees are "bad," rock people want to use this second (valid) reduction. But why not keep them more in context and get at the real nitty gritty by actually bothering to cope with them? Anyway, it is fitting that you have to back into the Monkees apologetically and seem senile in the process. Like, it's a valid rock critical sentiment (apology/ senility), so why not use the Monkees as a ready object for it. So:

The Monkees are great, even a merely significant pole in what's happening in rock today.

I still don't know all their names, but I promise to learn them sooner or later. This casual sooner-or-laterness fits their aggressive familiar anonymity well. As individuals with names they are like the Beatles by way of the Stones. While the first great Beatle innovation was familiarity with the names of every member of an entire (four-man) group, the Stones contributed five men, one of whom was Mick Jagger and the rest of whom also had names while being (at first) basically traditional anonymous rock guys. And the Monkees are sort of both.

And now old Micky Dolenz and David Jones stuff (hey, I know the names of two of them!) is being

released as salvaged readymades, almost like Joan
Baez's "There but for Fortune" and Ringo's "What'd
I Say" but since nobody as (geographically) far from
show business as the standard mere fan ever gets a
chance to find out who really records the Monkees'
material, these Dolenz-Jones oldies become their only
real efforts on record about which to feel (irrelevantly) certain. Once upon a time the Beatles gave
WMCA in New York a sloppy tape of "The Night
Before" which sounded like something recorded by
nobody recognizable and merely labeled, in R. Mutt
fashion, "Beatles." And anyway, Billy Mundi plays
Michael Clarke's drum work on some of the Byrds'
recordings. So the Monkees do a few extra things for
this tradition.

Beatle emulation, imitation, and plagiarism have
been interesting over the years. "Mr. Tambourine
Man" was of course by the Beatles the first few times
you heard it, but then you found out it was by the
Byrds, who sure as hell went off on their own thing
immediately. "Lies" was pretty close to a John Lennon lead vocal but then the Knickerbockers, who
actually did it, just faded away. The Who's "The Kids
Are Alright" was Lennon again in the form of old-
Beatle cliché; but since then the Who has shown its
awesome ability to fill in the Beatle tiredness gap for
a while and has ultimately done something altogether
different (except for occasional dips into new old-
style plagiaristic maneuvers without any more immediacy of plagiaristicity, like with "Armenia City in the
Sky") (and some say that Keith Moon sometimes
fills in for Ringo on recordings). But only the Monkees (ever since the McCartneyesque "Last Train

to Clarksville") have persisted as objectified "mere Beatle imitators." Great.

At the earliest temporary peak of the Beatles' success it was thought that the coincidence of success and quality at such high intensity was remarkable, and the possibility of eventual non-quality super-success by somebody or other was ignored. There was, however, pondering as to who that somebody might be: a 94-year-old dwarf on kazoo? eleven lesbians? a revitalized Mormon Tabernacle Choir? Well here we have just that expected "non-quality" success, and it's been accomplished by four standard long-haired males (just like last time, except long hair wasn't yet standard then). Just as the Byrds have utilized self-contextual mere meaning, the Monkees are now self-contextualizing mere success.

There has always been a school of mere personality-cult rock on live television (like Don and the Good-times on *Where the Action Is*), so it has been in-evitable that such rock would sooner or later reach Monkee proportions (and immediately change its TV form by becoming so regular and elaborate as to merit being *filmed* like the Beatles while still retaining the pseudo-intimate TV aura). *Hard Day's Night* was always the forced newsreel; *Help!* was the full-color newsreel of the Beatles as titans. Monkee shows are mere *Hard Day's Night* imitations, never true *Help!* imitations at least because they're not universally in color (not everybody has a color TV): and what better movie to *imitate* (or *merely imitate*). As mere TV personalities the Monkees are the standard "Mc-Luhanesque" (ha) non-personal personalities, perfect example of even (hack) McLuhan's inability to cope with the Beatle super-personality in films of them as "Beatle films."[6] The Monkee pole move has always been obviously inevitable: the overstatement of its eventual actuality is its rock grandeur. And being "quite prepared for that eventuality" has been big since *Hard Day's Night* anyway.

It's been just as inevitable that finally one particular explosion would be a rock *First Family* or *My Son, the Folk Singer*. Paul Revere and the Raiders are a minor precursor. The Monkees are *it*. Good immediately non-legitimate success. A great achievement in the annals of rock.

Fulfillment of mere *a priori* inevitability is at least okay.

Their music? I refuse to listen to it more than once (or twice), not enough for even a cursory arbitrary analysis. And not-worth-listening-to rock is a perfectly valid class. And you can certainly groove on it, too.

And "Little Bit Me, Little Bit You" is even "good," whatever that means. (Quality superimposed on perfection of obscure trends.)

And the Sinatras' "Something Stupid" is more of the same old great impotent (but now incestuous) swill. (Unity of form and content.)

---

[6] McLuhan's only move is the pop status he has inadvertently attained. And his jargon is nice as misused plagiarism.

('68) Hey Monkees even do their *own stuff* now: their own swill repetition.[7] And "Valerie" is the weakest version of Paul Anka's "You Are My Destiny," which summed up 1957 for the first and last Big Legitimate Gravity Move, which got played out like anything else. Time has thus added *a priori* inevitable mere insipidness. Or mere time has revealed stuff in general to be merely insipid after all.

And now that the Monkees perceive their own self-necessitated pit they have ease enough to admit it and consciously mindlessly grope around it with glory. Only the Monkees (although they were late at it) can digest the Zappa system, and (after all) it was almost a gift from him[8] (plus all the similar and better gifts from television itself), "they can only do it be-

---

[7] In the realm of Picasso's "retakes" on Velasquez and Delacroix paintings and the United States of America's version of the second of Charles Ives' "Three Places in New England" (in their "American Metaphysical Circus") is the Monkees' application to themselves of some other guys' version of them which used them as the media. After the original plagiarism/crud furor over the Monkees died down, there was not that much stylistic disparity between them and the total quasi-homogeneous scene-at-large. Mere historical juxtaposition of self-plagiarism-by-proxy with the irrelevance of plagiarism.

[8] He used to talk it up with them and he did a lot of offering himself to their show and forthcoming feature film. Word was that he was supposed to sneak up behind them while they're singing and interrupt with "That's a lot of," interrupted by a honk or bleep. One of the farthest reaching dissonant-worlds-of-quality moves that the Monkees (or their producers) have carried out has been their TV scene with Liberace destroying a piano with a sledge hammer before an appreciative chamber music audience.

cause they're so low it's a (less boring) mere move up for them," a worst-of-all-possible-worlds authenticity move. And they're pleasant as hell at a time when nothing else is, almost.

And now a word or two about dope. And dope is as big a totally contextualizable form/content for rock as sex ever was. In fact, Suzy Marijuana,[9] prominent cross-continental groupie, has substituted drugs for sex (or at least a bulk portion of it),[10] illustrating just a little how drugs are capable of becoming more awesomely surface-depth topical-eternal than sex for rock.

Okay, now the great big moments in drug rock are the Stones' "Nineteenth Nervous Breakdown," which makes mundane sensationally explicit mere descriptive banter about pot and acid a viable rock surface:

> You were still in school
> When you had that boo,
> It really messed your mind,
> And after that
> You turned your back
> On treating people kind;
> On our first trip
> I tried so hard
> To rearrange your mind,
> But after a while

---

[9] Susan Harwin, friend of Howard (Tripmaster) Klein.
[10] Once, in the early days of the Doors, she surprised everybody with DMT, and another time she was able to supply three Stones at once (grass) without being a conventional deviant.

I realized
You were disarrangin' mine[11]

and the Beatles' "Lucy in the Sky with Diamonds," the greatest political song of all time (initials LSD and the fact that Lennon's son thought up the title; slick dreamy opulence like "marmalade skies" and "looking-glass ties"), and in between the Byrds' "Eight Miles High," the *official* greatest Byrds song and political song and flight song of them all. And why not add Dylan's own "Mr. Tambourine Man" as well as the Byrds', since it has, with time, become official as mere blatancy (from poetry to pottery, 'cause who needs poetry landmarks anymore?)?

And then there's dope as surrender to causality. A chief representative is none other than Jimi Hendrix, who left the U. S. and r&b for England and acid[12] and would have become the Monkees but instead became the Monkees.[13] And, right, the Beach Boys' demechanization and debrutalization of the vibrations (knowing full well the easy similarity/unity of the oceanic, the automotive, the sexual, the cosmic and the acidic), the removal of unreflective arrogance, and the dis-

---

[11] Doper medicinality is more in context in rock (and dope is medicinality self-contextualized anyway) than is sexual medicinality, except to such people as Blue Cheer ("Doctor Please"), who (physiologically more than physically) are deft at both.

[12] Not as if there were a contradiction, for there ain't. In fact Pig-Pen of the Dead takes care of any apparent acid-r&b contrariety by dealing with r&b as a good acid outlet like any other.

[13] He refused to tour with the actual Monkees once.

covery of the "art" label: a minor (thus important)
form-content shift plus a minor shift of attitude toward creation, all visible beginning with *Pet Sounds*
(even in "Sloop John B.," an old chestnut but one
with "this is the worst trip I ever been on" and gram-
matical correction, "feel so *broke* up"). Also too, the
removal of reservations about saying anything (particularly about acid): the Grateful Dead and everybody else in interviews, George Harrison in monolithic
Eastern freakouts, Morrison all the time (and with
intent). But, best in the class is Moby Grape, the
Charlie Parker shoot up and drink yourself to death
move without the ultimacy of physical self-destruction, acid as frivolity rather than cosmic research.
Note the famous Skip Spence smile and the fact that
he was dumped from the Airplane for his sloppy attitude but not until after he had given them "My Best
Friend," with talk of "love streams" and later labeled
so "mamby pamby"[14] that Marty Balin dropped it
from the Airplane's stage repertoire. And he even
made the small great change from drums with the
Airplane to guitar and vocals with Moby Grape.[15]

In the tactics of the rock-doper life, the Spoonful
bust and gentle Donovan's great strong-minded lie

[14] Marty Balin, some time in spring '67.
[15] Rock by way of acid isn't much of a move since
rock's own reservation removal is much more thorough
and specific. But the alignment of rock with topical instances of frivolous acid reservation removal is a far more
viably x-like move than an acid view of rock could be
merely from within acid uncoupled with rock. Old Tim
Leary is at his best as a pop star and a businessman
using guitarist Peter Walker (*Rainy Day Raga*) in his
show. And Leary and Skip Spence (as well as Brian
Jones) have similar doper eyes.

about leaving dope are probably the biggest relevant news. Steve Boone and Zal Yanofsky of the Spoonful, in order to avoid Zal's deportation to Canada when they were busted for possession of grass, turned in a dealer, virtually ending the Spoonful's career when news leaked out to the doper audience masses. Like as if preservation of the mere members of the Spoonful wasn't most important. And as if it wasn't a great thing to do anyway, like it would've been widely cheered if Dylan ever did it and all that. Well to the question of whether being big ought to enable you to commit an indiscretion is the answer of sure man like it's rock not traditional conventional politics and the major taboo-level indiscretion would even seem preferable over all others particularly at this stage of the game. Anyway, revealed therein was the oft neglected dope-wisdom discrepancy: the audience, even if (sometimes particularly if) doped up, is going to miss the point unless it just happens to know what's going on. Dope helps and hinders just like reason: dope version of the ethical aspects of Plato's *Meno*. Meanwhile, poor wise Lovin' Spoonful (and their "Younger Generation" is the only major song to mention LSD *per se*).

And Donovan. He said he was finished with dope[16] (and all the kids oughta keep away too). He wasn't. But what's wrong with the lie qua lie? It's only one

---

[16] The subsequent Maharishi (straight freaky "religious") replacement of acid is an almost natural one for rock as far as that goes, since rock is, after all, the first great in-context/out-of-context revealed religion other than the two-person love unit, the real domain of the Spoonful ahead of all other love-rock people (ain't that spit in your eye?).

more truth-functionality stance. And honesty is no more an integral facet of the acid syndrome than of the soul scene, although honesty is chosen as a paragon of legitimacy in dialogue with a not much more shaky philosophical tradition.[17]

The Stones' arrest-jail-release occurred too late, well after the despecification of their surface contempt[18] and institutional contempt reaction they incurred, and only continued public dope topicality made it major or even possible. But the Stones' subsequent cell door noise and retoxification of love in "We Love You," and the later "Where's that joint?" on *Satanic Majesties* realign everything in the Stones' usual mundane contempt fantasy groove.

Dope-rock stamp collection specifics: Country Joe's "Bass Strings" ("pass that reefer 'round," "one more trip now, I'll never come down") and "Acid Commercial" ("Maybe ya oughta take a little bit of LSD"); Dylan, finally overt in addition to surreptitious, with "Rainy Day Women #12 & 35," the "How Dry I Am" of grass ("Everybody must get stoned") which made number one in places; and Dylan's warning about *mixing* in "Memphis Blues Again"; Keith's name sounding like kief; the Fugs' prehistoric "Comin'

---

[17] John Lennon's great statement-denunciation sequence about the Beatles' popularity exceeding that of Jesus is in the same philosophy of science mainstream as Donovan's lie. Denouncing what you've said is twice as good cause two statements is twice as many as one. And if the first was *true* (and it is, because with the Beatles, and not Christ, popularity is an *analytic* component) . . .

[18] The Stones' less famous *piss bust* is, on the other hand, their shining hour, being much more basic bustwise.

Down" (about cocaine) and "I Couldn't Get High";
Donovan's methedrine "crystal spectacles" and "elevator in the brain hotel" in "Epistle to Dippy"; Zappa's concentration on the silliest dope aspects of all,
the psychological and the technological, and his dull
assumptions about dope-rock conditioning affinities[19];
Grace Slick's "White Rabbit" Lewis Carroll readymade white knight/white light with the Airplane;
Airplane Jorma's talk of playing dominoes on a "hash-
ish trip"; Tim Buckley's acid degeneration into a
brutal performer[20]; the Stones' definitive dope ontology in "Back Street Girl" ("I don't want you to be
high, I don't want you to be down"); The Byrds'
lavish "5D"/"Eight Miles High"/"Why" fantasy and
"Mr. Spaceman/"Mind Gardens" castoff of insulation; the Beatles' "Penny Lane" ("there is a barber
showing photographs of every head he's had the pleasure to know") and "Tomorrow Never Knows" ("Turn
off your mind, relax and float downstream," "That you
may see the meaning of within, it is being") with its
borrowings from Leary's borrowings from the Tibetan
Book of the Dead; the Association's "Pandora's
Golden Heebie Jeebies," which merits quotation in
full but boils down to the ultimacy of "cry" and "die,"
which sounds indistinguishable from "cry," and is
acid-snapper Gary Alexander's virtual swan song
(sparrows are in it too) with the wholesome Association; David Roter's "I'm a Doper" ("and I'm not
ashamed"); Morrison's discussion with Owsley at
Ondine of the blood trip; Owsley's peripheral visceral

---

[19] But the great Charley Payne outdid all of Zappa
with his single comment at the Baltimore '67 Monkees
concert while on STP: it was all Pavlov! Like, sure.

[20] Buckley's the only person to drop acid every time he
played at the college dope capital, Stony Brook.

contact with rock as a manager of the Dead, a liner poet for Blue Cheer's first album,[20a] a dance dope supplier for the Group Image, and the greatest real mad scientist since Luther Burbank; super-sensitive Eric Burdon's "Girl Named Sandoz," who taught him "my mind has wings" and is the best *commercial* acid; the Velvet Underground's "Heroin," dope/death scare music; "Blues in the Bottle" (Spoonful, Holy Modal Rounders), whose "silly putty" must be a psilocybin reference.

For the audience, drugs present a readymade intensity-intimacy source. But it leads guys to look elsewhere, like 60¢ double features, to *get into* stuff, since art oughtn't ta hafta expand, you ought to expand yourself *into it*, etc. So these guys come down and say hey there's so much that's great & freaky, actually everything, wow rock guys oughta look all around, it's not rock it's everything. But alas *that's* rock so no further (apologetic) considerations on its behalf are needed. And as for branching out into other materially specific media, the Group Image is busy with parlor games and Group Image Flakes.

Another more crucial rock aspect of acid is detail proliferation and simultaneous constancy of centricity, with the centered entity of the self as a model for rock attention:[21] systematic causal insurance of con-

---

[20a] And creator of a variety of acid called Blue Cheer.

[21] And any member of the audience is, via drugs, at one with the artist himself and/or he is the (only) author of all plots for interpreting what the artist (held in esteem and/or taken to be irrelevant) has produced as raw content. As Dylan renders it for the voyeur/creator, "I'm ready for to fade into my own parade." So it's also acid

stancy for rock form/content extension/expansion.
Explosions and voids have to be everywhere.

And like what's all the dismay about ego trips qua
ego trips? Structurally they're really meaty. And the
teleology of the ego trip is separately usable according to taste. Epistemologically it represents externally
forced/self-generated confusion, and what's wrong
(or any less outrageous) with the self as a cause (of
certainty, etc.) among others. And the Beatles' "I
Am the Walrus" plays the ego transcendence trip for
all it's worth by way of the ego centricity move:

> I am he as you are he as you are me and we are
>   all together.[22]
> See how they run like pigs from a gun, see how
>   they fly, I'm crying.
> Sitting on a cornflake waiting for the van to
>   come.
> Corporation tea shirt, stupid bloody Tuesday.
> Man, you been a naughty boy, you let your face
>   grow long.
> I am the eggman, they are the eggmen, I am the
>   walrus, goo goo a' joob.

as forcing yourself on yourself, as well as the whole early
pop art abandonment of self (except in initial preferential choice of raw content) plus so much irrelevance for
all possible world centers not contained therein that self
and object both find (without even the self-*discipline* of
actual object construction) world-filling spectacle to define themselves and each other.

[22] Recalling Dylan's note on the consequences of the
transcendence-of-*other* trip (as well as those of any
excess trip): "Ain't no use in talkin' to you, just the
same as talkin' to me."

The dope-oriented concept of "change," "changes" and all that is a nice unwieldy, disruptive label for what rock is already working with. For the Grape, it sometimes becomes change rather than the tongue. Change as change can become so fat that it obliterates, and thus is change from, the initial tongue framework which already accounts for change. "Can't Be So Bad" is a perfect example of change which overshoots the tongue. Or anything by Zappa or the United States of America, who were never tongue masters anyway.

The whole drug thing generates enough content of sufficiently usable richness without even resorting to the source (the drug *experience*): a great mass commodity move. Also a nice duality about directness of contact with being—which is more "adequate," via dope or straight, via the "deep" experience of dope or the "superficial" surface acceptance of its sensory content, etc.? Which leads to a nice "scientific" justification of rock authenticity nullification along with its authenticity opacity. The emergence of the most outrageous mere exemplary content of all time: color, electricity, anything strange, horror, beauty, recollections from high school vocabulary tests, the all-of-a-sudden all: it's all dope stuff!: an identity-of-indiscernibles coalescence capable of both organic and linguistic self-elucidation. Giving us the likes of "Tapioca Tundra" by the Monkees, "Incense and Peppermints" by the Strawberry Alarm Clock, and, if actual knowledge of actual doper commitment is waived as irrelevant, "Broken Arrow" by the Buffalo Springfield. And, as a case of mere super-doper dope pitch making it only indirectly as just another easy mere exemplary content, the 13th Floor Elevators.

And the pretty pretty pretty balloon flight song, the
Fifth Dimension's "Up, Up and Away," would have
been a far afield doper whopper if it hadn't been for
Sgt. Pepper, which came out about two weeks later
and buried it in both flight and dope.

Once, not long ago, as the doper thing was busy
expanding, it seemed as if the Youngbloods were the
last of the (mere) alcoholic groups; but soon everybody (seemed to) surge back to booze, spearheaded
by acidic Jim Morrison (rumored to have developed
cirrhosis of the liver) and all of the acidic Big Brother
and the Holding Company, whose James Gurley has
called a bar a "boozeria"[23] and whose Janis Joplin
prepares for performances through the Southern Comfort causality and is legendary enough to be mentioned in the Elec-Flag's "Wine."

So the Beatles became the first concrete historical
constant(s). Since clearly only the Malebranchian
occasionalist creative divinity can stand next to Heraclitus in that neck of the woods, that's just what
they are (for a while): the Malebranchian divinity
with moments of sleep ("and after all I'm only sleeping"). And not very long after the mere line "a
funny looking dog with a big black nose"[24] presented
itself as the obvious beginning of all history and his-
toricity, slam bang what do the Beatles do? Well they

---

[23] In a car, after the Monterey Pop Festival. He also
answered a request for the name of the best California
beer by "Whattaya want, one that gets ya high or one
that tastes good?"
[24] "Snoopy vs. the Red Baron" by the Royal Guardsmen, which is even a "Hang On Sloopy" referent and
also mentions Baron von Richthofen himself.

just go ahead and sum up *geography* even more totally than history had just been worked out. Dig: geography on more than an equal footing with the history-time bit. Some day "Strawberry Fields Forever" and "Penny Lane" will be by themselves the first geography course anyone will ever be exposed to: could easily be an in-context totalitarian educational and standard traditional theoretical constant. Viewing poetic space as real physical space is about as pleasant as you can get.[25] The Stones' later "2000 Light Years from Home" is only a slightly more and much more descriptive Beatle Space. Jimi Hendrix, Jim Morrison and the Crazy World of Arthur Brown are only the most athletic navigators of this total metaphor concretion space of *Sgt. Pepper* and all the standard hack virtuoso followups by the whole real rock world have merely solidified the universe as palpably (physically) real. The exploration of Beatlesque Morrison Space is sort of the scene in "In Another Land," which even named the Stones space Bill Wyman with utterly minimal actual modification: the Morrison part is block-like increments of additive acceleration by the mere Stones without Bill. Internal spatial references. Goody.

On bitterness of public surface personality alone the Stones generated the most antagonistic phase of

---

[25] And the Beatles' "Nowhere Man," who is "sitting in his nowhere land" and "making all his nowhere plans for nobody" (and "isn't he a bit like you and me?"), demonstrates the difficulty of concretizing negative space and the abstract analogical character of all geographic notation for localization, as well as not even the impossibility of articulating any specific chaos except through the cliché-rich lack thereof.

political rock (oh it's not political) without even
trying and with a quick flip of the coin they became
the first real drug cult (then still a mere official cult)
leadership group (followed by the Byrds and Dylan,
San Francisco, the Doors, and the Beatles in that
order: the Stones actually started the eventual Beatle
aristocracy, a natural aristocracy that just needed a
Stones push). Thus the Stones are the source of the
internal rock hierarchy, *the* source, and of course it
was even more important as an inadvertent genesis,
wow the Stones have always been right there with
the ball in play, interpreting the whole strategy perfectly either inadvertently or a little late but perfectly.

Stones are seemingly more temporal than spatial
(oh nonsense) and more temporal than the Beatles.
"Time Is on My Side." "By the time you're thirty
gonna look sixty-five." "2000 Man." Well, "Goin'
Home" sure is overly temporal: the first real sudden
long-as-hell rock-proper track (11 minutes plus) and
it's only minimally spatial except by reference to letters in the mail and planes and most prominent for
the temporal ambiguity involved in its march to the
quasi-flesh grunting at the end. It's also great as tri-
partite (if ya care) structurally and inevitable and
inevitably boring (even by the accident of later juxtaposition with the Doors' "The End," which just comes
on stronger to displace "Goin' Home" as the most
famous and topical long track[26]): a non-Warholian
temporal analysis of boredom. Etc.

---

[26] But it's just like other *firsts* (Redi-Whip, Temptee
whipped cream cheese, Lestoil liquid cleaning stuff) being
temporarily (and thus generally forever) displaced in
prominence with the original awe of firstness displaced.

But, as usual, the Beatles find the gimmick to come out on top with non-non-devious cosmic moves, by doing this time the whole time-history-cosmos thing which later utterly failed in Dylan's case (also always positively).

Beatle stuff is on a different rooftop, the rooftop *beyond* the rooftop of the Drifters' "Up on the Roof" and (not) impervious to assault by John Sebastian and the Spoonful's "Darling Be Home Soon" ("Go and beat your crazy head against the sky" . . .)

And hmm Love comes in here with some sort of great trans-cosmic gimmickry to do the whole thing: how will I work that in? I forget but that's just the systematic move necessary here. Establish a whole new transplanted cosmos, cosmogony and eschatology with a whole new set of cats and with the proper amount of forgetfulness to blank out the also systematically essential pre-established *actual* eternity. Okay? And anyway, *Forever Changes* accomplishes some sort of equivalent internal move for Love, being Love's 3rd album, Love's 3rd coming etc. Possibly because their leader, Arthur Lee, learned how to encompass the entire Stones gimmick within (mere) poetry alone.

Short summation of Love moves: orchestral move (inner inadvertent wisdom of show music and other trash), you can see it in "You Set the Scene," post-doper word contraction cuteness, that's there in "¡Que Vida!," reaffirmation of Johnny Mathis, oh a lot of other moves too . . .

(The last _____ paragraphs are a lot of hogwash. Don't believe any of it, even if you can find belief predicates in it. Beatle density too high, an embarrassment of plethora, Beatle-Stone density too high, Beatle-Stone-Spoonful-Love density too high too.)

"Miss Amanda Jones" contains the very first use of "live happily ever after" as a *future* eternal possibility. "And they *lived* happily ever after" has always been jarring, calling for Leibnitz's discussion of multiple eternities and other destructively relevant crap like that. "Amanda Jones" is the Stones' first very own Chuck Berry tune, one Chuck Berry composition per record being a normal expectation after their earliest albums, even in these days of nothing but Jagger-Richard compositions. More than mere Berry influence or quotation tongue field, this song illustrates how the Stones tend to generate elusive categories. "Miss Amanda Jones" is "my favorite track on the entire album," an example of categorization which earlier would have been difficult to pin down and retain.

Rhythmically, "Penny Lane" exhibits a relentless precise awkwardness, manipulated largely by the greatest sloppy drumming and sloppiest great drumming Ringo has ever displayed; McCartney's bass is another great unsettling unifier on this level. The nervous jaggedness of the trumpet break is just the thing (although anything the Beatles could have used in the context of this song's break, even a scissors solo by George Martin, would have been just the thing to do—it's a song whose temporal break after a not-so-temporal "hourglass" reference rises to the occasion

a priori) to form the heart of the break-reentry most like that of "Baby's in Black" in recent years. Also nostalgic is the pronunciation of "customer" as "*coostomer,*" like the "mooch" ("much") of the old days.

Throughout "Strawberry Fields" a vacuum cleaner sort of momentary sucking sound is perplexing. It sounds like single guitar notes played backwards, suggesting that maybe the entire vocal (which *does* contain strange enunciation with peculiar marginal speed variations) had been recorded, played backwards, learned as backwards, recorded as performed backwards, and played backwards again to sound, ultimately, "forwards." Mere forwardness (even if just straight actual forwardness with overdubbed vacuum cleaners or backwards guitar) is a radically secure and graspable form of ambiguous apparent/actual temporal directionality, particularly when "misunderstanding all you see."

The temporally ironic "meanwhile" of "Penny Lane" is all that holds the content of the song "together" except for the rock provincial humanness scattered throughout. The unlikelihood of the simultaneity asserted by this "meanwhile," particularly in its repetition not even as a relationship at the close of the song, provides the song's most absurdly secure and out-of-context verbal pole. Other Heraclitean oppositions and quasi- and pseudo-oppositions and non-Heraclitean non-oppositional, obliquely similar groupings supply the rest of the metaphoric meat: "fireman" and "rain"; "mack" and "rain"; "blue suburban skies" and "pouring rain"; "fish" and the wetness of "rain"; "play" as imagined and real anyway; "I sit" and "banker sitting waiting for a trim";

ambiguous "there" and anywhere concrete (spatiality is as silly and unsilly as anything else here). "Very strange" functions about the way "I don't mind" and "the weather's fine" did in "Rain"; more tiredly resigned and naively understanding (and generally far-reaching) than Heraclitus' Logos, as usual. And though it seems as if everything resolves and fits and all that, it does anyway.

"When I'm Sixty-Four" generated its own antiquity in order to be utterly wasted by the time of its reappearance in "Your Mother Should Know," which is the safe relocation of the antiquity somewhere else.

Between the Buttons uses the word "yesterday" 25 times.

George Harrison's "Love You To" spews forth "Each day just goes so fast,/I turn around it's passed,/You don't get time to hang a sign on me-e-e-e-e," where personal identity is even faster than you might expect if you can't quite catch it to label it. Or maybe it's just "me" getting older right before your eyes. Or maybe it's just little "you" who can't manage a moment of temporal fixity. And the passed-past bit too.

Cream's "Passing the Time" passes the time with "passing the time."

Dylan's "My Back Pages" (and the Byrds doing it much later as a flashback to their Dylan period): "Ah but I was so much older then, I'm younger than that now." Age as years, age as growth potential; time incremental uniformity, time incremental disuniform-

ity; meaning expansion, mock meaning expansion;
yesteryear meaning of meaning, movement of mud.
And Eric Burdon, who's still young enough to have
been older and live to tell about it and want to tell
about it, reappraises his own past with the same ap-
praisal: "I was so much older then" in "When I Was
Young": appreciation of past maturity in retrospect,
he had sufficiently cumbersome maturity to miss the
point of the Byrds as they recalled his old idol Dylan.
But the Who make it well beyond this escapade with
their own, "I Can't Reach You," the real big move in
the pleasant articulation of the inability to conceptualize physical means of overcoming non-physical
gaps conceptualized through the physical spatio-
temporal metaphor nonetheless: "I'm a billion ages
past you, a million years behind you too . . ."[27]

And the Who's "I Can See for Miles" is timey, being released years after it was recorded and being
miles long as well as being no-longer-in-their-live-
repertoire-although-otherwise-current.

Steve Miller's *Children of the Future:* children
who will grow into and produce the future, children
living in the future, children given birth to by the

[27] Also worth a mention is a Richie Havens comment,
which because it is just a (extramusical) *comment* is
"timeless" and "just like any old poet guy" and "dated,"
just another okay addition to the family of "My Back
Pages" temporal afterthought redefinition, but time as
concrete poetry this time: "I feel at least 1,027 years
old. But I know that's not very old." (*New York Times,*
July 21, 1968, p. D 19.) And the kind of traditional
ageless articulate mere sincerity Eric Burdon was looking
for but couldn't reach because he had to fit it into a song
and just because.

future; rock as the form of all future art awareness. Steve Miller's "In My First Mind": further immersion in the "Sad Eyed Lady" Muzak principle: any succession of increasingly poignant-repulsive continuations of the palatable extend the range of palatability if fulfillment is expected at the end: this time there is transcendence of Dylan's fadeout, actual fulfilled ending (sounding like the Duprees) since there's a next track afterwards which is closely enough associated: this track bursts, dissipates, disappears into the next instead of fading out into just the sound and consciousness of mind and room (and it's called First *Mind* too and fades into doper oblivion track which includes peaceful reentry into normal compositional expectancy) (really center-stage normalcy for when it takes place although standardly cross-temporally freaky and corny) last track is even called "The Beauty of Time Is That It's Snowing." Rather than fading tracks out or into the standard way, Steve Miller Band fades one track out only after it has continued into the next track a little more than usual (radio station multiple-play/continuity technique: more along the *Who Sell Out* trail than the *Sgt. Pepper* trail, a little more and it's a matter of little).[27a] "Fanny Mae": multiple beginning: "you don't like that one, dig this one"; (later) "sock it to me Chicago style."

[27a] The Stones' "We Love You"/"Dandelion" encompasses both sequence and space-between with the *single* alone, using a portion of "We Love You" after the finish of "Dandelion" and an off-speed something other after the finish of "We Love You." And Bobby Freeman's monstrously archaeological "Do You Want to Dance" performs this disappearance-return move within the span of a single *song*.

Pearlman knows the following full well:

The Byrds have real formal constancy. From time
immemorial they have grounded their music in what are
—or what seem to be—obviously regular rhythmic patterns. It is out of this ground that all developments and
variations seem to rise—as it were—to the surface. This
sound is dense, but not obviously and impressively complicated. That is, it is very coherent. It works because of
its unity, not out of an accumulation of contrasting
effects such as volume changes or syncopations. Here the
contrasts inherent in any rhythmic pattern are not at all
emphasized. The changes in the basic rhythmic patterns
are not necessarily gradual but rather nondramatic. The
Byrds' music is not at all progressive. In comparison to
say the Jefferson Airplane, the Doors or the Yardbirds
it's awfully calm. It doesn't go anywhere. The resolu-
tions are not dramatic. They don't obviously end anything. Instead they are cyclical. But the cycles aren't
closed. It's clear they could quite probably go on for far
too long. It's really nice that the Byrds should stop only
when somebody decides to do it. Not when it's necessary.
The great Byrds challenge the tradition of the fadeout
by making it into a mere decision rather than a matter
of pleasure, logic or endurance. The Byrds are eclectic.
That's what the guy on the back of the second album
said. ("This album is eclectic.") But the prominence of
the form undermines our knowing anything about all
that. When the Byrds got started somebody (in *Hit
Parader*, I think) said that their first album was very
nice, but it all sounded the same. Now we are up to
taking that. It's become a virtue. What started out as a
folk-rock style on the first album has been turned, via
repetition, into a form. The formal structure of a constant rhythmic ground can overcome any material. The
rhythmic ground is so dependable that once when lying
on a cliff overlooking the Long Island Sound, not so far
from where Walt Whitman did it, I thought I heard the
earth turning beneath my head and it reminded me of—
of all things—the Byrds. That is, the Byrds' music has
that sort of dependable self-energizing kineticism. It
doesn't go anywhere. But it never comes to rest. Turn!
Turn! Turn! And that's very strange and also very sad.

He's written it eleven times.[28] From it you may gather
that the Byrds are capable of massive unknown
tongues with only the slightest manipulative change,
and "C.T.A. 102," the only space song they ever did
that matches their straight cosmic rock and their only
song anything like "P.T. 109" (except for "Draft
Morning"), sets up the all-time massive tongue expectation field with even more than fifty seconds of
space modulation (containing the moment-to-moment implicit tongue pressure field and irrelevance
tongues both by bassist Chris Hillman) followed by
not much more than the biggest rubber-band tongue
of all time.

"It's a bright sunny day when I see you run my
way, but it took me 20 years to get to you" sing the
Byrds. Took 20 yrs to get to you and took 6 tracks
to get to "Get to You" or would you say 5 tracks
cause it's the 6th itself; well with yrs if it was the
20th yr itself you'd probably call it 20 yrs, so why
the hell be more rigidly formal with track-designation
than year-designation, should *tracks* be more *universally* concrete than other non-existential public time
conventions ((is a track non-existential in its time
encapsulation, particularly when it varies in public-
time content; well the standard unitary insulated
track *is* that: but once you get to non-unitary tracks
(containing lots of distinct or disconnected stuff, or
y'know clear & distinct and separate, inside) which
are also not temporally separated from each other but
blended into the next etc. is back toward a conventional time: convention of existentiality and beyond;
what about when the non-unitarian quality is spatial,
like blend-of-differences in "Going Back," and what

---

[28] *Crawdaddy!*, August '67, among other places.

about the implications of abolition of *spatial* separation of tracks, particularly when the whole thing is circular (or spiral) and in motion when of significance; also reappearance (of horns) as means of not expected spatial tie: "Draft Morning" & "Artificial Energy")).

Repetition of dissimilarly sized tracks on albums is like proliferation of waves in the sea: "Dolphin's Smile."

In "Draft Morning," move out of central sound part is like the shaking out of the Beatles from the orchestral sound in "Got to Get You into My Life," but Byrds use Hillman's (martial) bass as intermediate move with bass in between bombs and the Byrds' mere group sound; in "Wasn't Born to Follow," they bring in the whole band together from oblivion.

"Get to You" remotely resembles the "In Another Land" move of separation.

"Artificial Energy": an original listening ambiguity thing: are Byrds now knocking dope (acid) or knocking knocking or what? Finally, it turns out to be speed ("I'm coming down off amphetamine, and I'm in jail cause I killed a queen") and so you get the ambiguity in reverse: is speed a drag (and acid still sacrosanct) or what etc. (and what about Crosby's cryptic Monterey comments about flashing) and is it just maintenance of style/style-non-maintenance through content (dope) since for the Byrds style is a *given* and is it post-dope as well as post-porno and don't the style just contextualize post-anything anyway?

Byrds go beyond Beach Boys inability-to-remastur-bate point: "Natural Harmony." *Notorious Byrd Brothers* almost a carbon copy of (of all things) second Country Joe album (political-personal split-fusion, guitar in "Change Is Now," etc.[29]) even to drum move into "Draft Morning" (like into "Eastern Jam"). "8 Miles High"-"5D"-"Why" trilogy took two albums to complete (*Fifth Dimension, Younger Than Yesterday*).

"Natural Harmony": smell of apples, smell of grapefruit, smell of bananas.

Songs like "Get to You" & "Going Back": ever-present *erased* duality of styles, as C&W + somber dense early Byrds (a hypothetical real entity)—sometimes unmixing of the blend, like at end of "Going Back," but so ticklishly peculiar in juxtaposed separation from the rest that it is both extra treat and ridiculous addition yielding strange inappropri-ateness as appropriate content which only works in the rejection-of-appropriateness framework: science-fiction paradox—why believe any ending to or resolu-tion of any sequence of challenges to credibility, in fact silliness is the most *likely* awareness-of-paradox move, hence also the most *credible*, hence the most *incredible*, hence just right: just about where Zappa attempts to get his licks in, but no co-present non-silliness, or at least not enough . . .

Re Byrds and silliness: along with the stand-ard how-do-you-explain-it-to-the-unbelieving(-after-

---

[29] Country Joe's "Magoo" sounds like the drone of D. Crosby's "Everybody's Been Burned" in spots and drone.

coming-down-from-it) you sort of gotta be silly
(maybe tie in overstatement here, the fish story,
Davy Crockett, Old West, Jumpin Jack Flash, etc.);
wowee and Byrds are even (fake facsimile) Old Western and Grand Ole Opry now, and wow there's even
a "coming down" explanation.

Term: temporal hokum. And geological hokum
(feeding in C&W twangs longitudinally).

Whole album sort of just like Kingston Trio would
have got to if they hadn't feared over-commercialism;
and because they "meant" it (in just about same
sense as Byrds "mean" it) they could never *really*
be/go bad even though it seems so: Louis Armstrong
Lethargy seen as a Byrds *move move*.

"Dolphin's Smile": continuation of transportation
dialogue with the Beatles ("Lear Jet Song" and "Yellow Submarine"), sea version of "Flying"; instrumental break with ahs: like superimposition of "C.T.A.
102" wave delineation, superimposition (masturbation) over "Flying" space.

And the whole control and position in the flow
thing that the transportation metaphor is at the heart
of (Beatles are not at the crest of waves but "beneath the waves in our yellow submarine," Stones
ponder "Who's Driving My Plane?"[30] it's not them,

---

[30] Driving rather than flying, nice combination. And
it's not driving as *sport*, as with drag stuff, just like it's
not surf wave crests the Beatles are beneath (but cur-
rents of current surface being). But the Byrds' type of
vehicular commitment is on the spiritual side of (surf/
drag/etc) sport (the "we" of "Mr. Spaceman" is a team
tip-off). And they're California guys all right, a lot like

Byrds envision the trip as other than vehicular method trip only, since it's a long-term investment for them: "Off to sea for a year" and what's important is what you see, the dolphin's smile you see in the greater trip context, "Childhood dream, have you ever seen a dolphin smile?" and it's off on a dolphin trip then, and in "Mr. Spaceman" it's "out into the universe, we don't care who's been there first" so you don't even know the vehicle[31] and you've gotta be poetic and promissory) is a big Byrds thing in general:

So you want to be a rock 'n' roll star,
Then listen now to what I say,
Just get an electric guitar
And take some time
And learn to play,
And when your hair's combed right
And your pants are tight
It's gonna be alright,
Then it's time to go downtown
Where the agent man
Won't let you down,
Sell your soul to the company,
Who are waiting there
To sell plastic ware,
Then in a week or two
If you make the charts
The girls'll tear you apart.

Words and music by Roger McGuinn and Chris Hillman. Used by permission of McHillby Music Company.

the Beach Boys but rarely frivolous except for the purpose of setting up a good story.

[31] "Artificial Energy": Byrds can even sometimes get "contemptuous" of other people's vehicles qua clichéed vehicles. "I took my ticket to ri-i-ide." Somebody else's cliché made into vehicle made into vehicular cliché and designated mechanical doper-functionality.

"Wasn't Born to Follow": what C&W hokum would
be if conventional C&W had been allowed to drift
into the conventional contemporary public freak
scene ("you may lead me to the castle where the
rivers of our vision flow into one another"): the real
John Wesley Harding move if Dylan had continued
to be aware instead of being engulfed by the Duchamp quasi-retirement move; both it and "Going
Back" are written by Goffin & King, move toward getting others to do your dirtywork (that's part of reason why Crosby, dismissed forever, was even allowed
on the album). (But maybe Country Joe's "Janis"
beats this all out by being a sea chanty or something;
Country Joe: a parallel sometimes-even-better version of the Byrds: anybody, even the Blues Magoos,
even Boston's Unicorn's house band C. C. & the
Chasers, can do the Byrds.)

And getting rid of Crosby frees them from subservience to politics so they can do whatever they want
including being political (like keeping Crosby's great
"Lady Friend" off the album): but it especially opens
the door to poetics of mere speculation etc. (since Joe
Tex's humor move is almost the same sort of science-
fiction as the Byrds', it is his own stylistic-political
subservience which shackles his own speculative
leap[32]) (also they've caught up to Gene Clark, who
couldn't stay a Byrd twice because he wouldn't fly in
planes, compositionally).

But if it also seems that the Byrds have out-muscled
the Beatles it is only because they have shortened
the ball park so that home runs would be bigger and

---

[32] As Arthur Lee says (in "You Set the Scene"), "The
things that I must do consist of more than style."

frequenter: an implicit reniggerization, the stylistic jumble anyway. Soul guys can *produce* more viable readymades—but Byrds can use English readymades and be spade-like in their conception of musical primarity anyway.

When Byrds musically outdo the Beatles it's in Morrison athletic fashion but too late (?) (in Morrison's case it's much later but passage of time/timing is irrelevant in that case) and it requires straight tongue pressure anyway, helping them catch up to *Yesterday . . . and Today* while everybody else is fumbling his way through *Sgt. Pepper*; "5D": "And I will remember the time that is now that has ended before the beginning" (pre-temporal eternal fixity: nice). Byrd improvements are not stepwise.

Deciding that his first name was just something some guys who didn't know him had stuck him with, Jim McGuinn wrote away to some Subud guru for a new one which would this time at least be selected by someone Jimmie knew. The guy told him to pick ten names beginning with "R," one of which he (guru) would encircle. So Jim became Roger.

Transcendence of Crosby's official ego put-down of ego trips: athleticism as a natural outcome. And of course, "We don't care who's been there first." Record-breaking non-record-breaking-oriented athleticism.

Another possibility is that they saved part of what they had originally too long, they saved it too long. Anyway, discomfort with totalities, but always just one step away from comfort in discomfort and too bad cause isn't stepwise. Intersection of comfort-discomfort with harmony-disharmony.

Easily usable spatio-temporal self-alienation (that is, out of step with themselves in terms of capability of stepwise realization and/or total realization). "Renaissance Fair" (vs.) "Tribal Gathering."

Hmm... "Dolphin's Smile" is a Crosby song, so good things (dismissal of Crosby interpretation) aren't that simple.

Ringo type drum move at end of "Going Back."

"Taps" at end of "Draft Morning": remember "Reveille Rock"?

Someone else's case of expanded logical form, in "Cherish" by the Association: "Cherish is a word that more than implies/All the hope in my heart each time I realize..." *More than* implies, okay. One convenient way of constructing anti-intelligible formalizations is to string together elements more or less artificially with conventionally undefined chains of connectives, yet to interpret from the conventional well-formed-formula context (use regularity to interpret regulated aberrated regularity). And if you put music back with formalism (the way it started, with Pythagoras), you wind up with the Byrds' pseudo-counterfactual conditional, "If You're Gone"[33] by Gene Clark:

> If I need you then to me you're everything
> If I have you if I love you just the same
> If you're here the night is rightly gone before
> If you're gone I'll see the daylight and that's all

---

[33] One of the three occasions in American rock for the reiterated meta-tongue fadeout. Other two: Spoonful's "Summer in the City" and Doors' "Alabama Song."

If I stand on understanding what is now
If I ever need someone to show me how
If the daylight can be hidden by the sun
If you're gone then I know I will need someone

If I love you if I know how much I care
If I find the things you want in anywhere
If I know you I may never know your name
If you're gone then there is nothing that remains

Words and music by Gene Clark. Used by permission of McHillby Music Company.

This ambiguous ambivalent string of if-then connections is either readily understandable despite and because of misleading sign-design or it is meaningless
gibberish. But to use intentionally manipulated structured meaning toward this latter end is leading to a
"higher order" (in a convenient hierarchy of cognitive
frustration) meaninglessness more than the use of
Dada construction techniques which might never hint
at conscious order. The Beatles' fadeout to "Rain" is
a segment of Lennon's vocal played backwards; the
intergalactic foreigner babble in "C.T.A. 102" is who
knows what played backwards.

By taking material or content as prior, or content-
form relationship as prior, a new focus is possible
which allows for content shifts to constitute instant
innovation (with extent of innovation clarified by
raunch epistemological criteria). Rather than seeking
a law of nature form to fit a natural content, the goal
becomes the search for a content to fit a form. Dylan
has utilized the tautology with interesting material.
In "Visions of Johanna," "highway blues," now a familiar Dylan referent, is a collapsed metaphor for that
which Mona Lisa's smile evokes). Bob Lind, father
of mere-poetry rock, plays mere-metaphoric content

for all it is worth: ". . . 'cross my dreams with nets of wonder I chase the bright elusive butterfly of love." The Beatles utilize tautology with almost interesting content, plus additional information, as, for example, in "It's Only Love":

> It's only love and that is all;
> Why should I feel the way I do?
> It's only love and that is all,
> But it's so hard loving you.

Incidentally, with content taken in priority over form, the identity of indiscernibles becomes (again) no more than a convenient principle of irrelevant super-imposition.[34] In the Byrds' "The World Turns All Around Her," the content is merely enough neutral matter to insure a rock-tautology with sufficient revision for it to be a sloppy tautology (switches from second to first person; "wish" in addition to "think") which still fulfills all rock quasi-empirical expectations:

> Well if you think she's everything you could want,
> And if you think she's everything that could be,
> Well I still think the world turns all around her,
> And I still wish that she belonged to me.

And in rock: fitting the tautology mold *by choice, allowing* yourself to be something *by necessity*. And

---

[34] Or keep the form of content priority prior and you get the Beatles' "All You Need Is Love" sermon style: "There's nothing you can do that can't be done, nothing you can sing that can't be sung." Sermon certainty based on not only itself but additional external attainment ("It's easy, all you need is love"): total contextual understanding of the Sermon on the Mount.

it's all out of a priority by designation and the Byrds
are so formally strict (musically) that *you* have to do
the designating and then it's easy and you even have
the Byrds' music backing you up.

"Natural Harmony" is dissonant. A system which
allows for dissonance may thus have procedures for
systematically or sub-systematically reinforcing dissonance. Empirically, it just happens to be the case
that there is no universal context for scientific en-
deavor (just as it merely happens to be the case that
from certain standpoints Newtonian gravitation may
be represented by $F=Y(Mm)/r^2$), and thus an all-
embracing system (whatever that may be) *must* contain the anti-systematic. So now then there's that
passage in "Fifth Dimension":

> And I opened my heart to the whole universe
> And I found it was loving,
> And I saw the great blunder my teachers had
>   made,
> Scientific delirium madness . . .

Words and music by Roger McGuinn. Used by permission of McHillby Music
Company.

So there's "anti-scientific" McGuinn just to round
(systematic) things off officially, and since it's early
McGuinn (and late early McGuinn) it's just more
icing on the cake in favor of (Hegel's historical Geist-
reduction of inconsistency) too constructively positive a view of inconsistency, since Crosby was caught
in the ramifications of negative inconsistency with his
Monterey refusal to do early Byrds stuff with a
"Times They Are A-Changin'" brushoff quotation
from earlier Dylan-Byrds. So Byrds type celestial
harmony may be found in the entire Byrds cosmos,

(particularly) sometimes because there isn't even a trace of it.

Because there's so articulate an indication to assume/discover it. And the big *Notorious Byrd Brothers* pillar of explicit teleology, "Space Odyssey," is a mere drag—good. As Carl Kordig has set up the subject, discovery may be field-opening or non-field-opening. Reappraised, its forms are instead larger-field-opening and non-larger-field-opening. A discovery revealing no wider field than itself, such as the discovery of a nest of termites in a closet, is still a discovery of termites in a closet. Any such discovery could *still* be interpreted in terms of smaller and at least nominally larger fields. Termites in a closet are both "those whitish bugs rotting the wood" and members of an ecological community of insects. To open an even wider field in the discovery by realizing, "Hey, I can generalize this to all closet-bound insect communities (if I really want to bother)," this *can* make field-openingness a matter of magnitude more than qualitative differentiation if the discoverer so chooses such an approach. On the other hand an established larger-field-opening discovery can be berated since any discovery is not in the largest possible frame, as yet unknowable, always as a potentiality. Discovery in its standard use denotes both finding and understanding, but both these facets are contextualizable. One can find inadvertently an Einsteinian formalized law statement, $E=mc^2$, by stumbling upon it on a dirty piece of paper in the street or on a 1956 commemorative postage stamp depicting Einstein or on a page of an elementary physics textbook and claim to be its discoverer. Of course he is not the

first discoverer of the equation and could thus be
called a crude plagiarist, but on what merely scientific
ground does this moral (aesthetic) disrepute rest?
He may come to understand it by further physics-
book reference or he may come to understand it by
his own brute effort, using it in its final form as a suggestion, or he may come to understand it by tedious
Platonic memory into his immortal soul or he may
refuse to bother to cope with it entirely, knowing that
he could if he ever really were to bother (or being
stupid and out of the picture). And thus he would
combine finding and understanding in a perhaps more
random manner than merely together in one act.
Other distinctions are worth introducing, that between private and public discovery and that of Reich-
enbach between discovery and justification. First
there is no real universally public discovery; even the
object of discovery holds varying import to contextually separated individuals, even if they all, broadly,
"understand" it. Justification reduces to the establishment of less transitory credentials for the "acceptance" of discovery than mere "Eureka" context
of discovery presents. Such a convention is oriented
toward public revelation and/or private memory reinforcement, and in both cases loss of the raw data
and ultimate structure of the object discovered are
preventable, although the loss may be preferable.
Descartes' discovery of the Cogito is a case of an object of discovery alien in the context of out-of-context
justification. Justification as proof that one has actually discovered the object he claims to have discovered can also be viewed negatively by a teleology
similar to that of the field-opening orientation; a complete justification of a scientist's discovery may leave

him with nothing new to accomplish, thus closing his private field of operation. With all this in mind, it's quite satisfactory that "Space Odyssey" is too much of a drag to be even decisively non-larger-field-opening in the face of the album's return of the Byrds to public inspection. And the first discovery by or involving the Byrds was that the group singing "Mr. Tambourine Man," sounding like the Beatles or the Beatles with Dylan and Joan Baez, was indeed a new group called the Byrds.

(Not a) funny thing is the Byrds' public image (and public appearance quality level) does kind of stutter, in contrast with their Mr. Consistency style of styles, and it's always likely that the "Artificial Energy" line "I've got a strange feeling I'm going to die before my time" will work out well for them.

Just as automotive rock is great over the car radio with car sounds all around, the Byrds are a good follow-up to listening to the indoor hi-fi system warming up from indoor silence, a good inside-your-physical-head content for stereo headphones, and a dandy accompaniment for sensing the erotics of the physical hi-fi and detecting the seasons of the outside public physical world by means of humidity and crackle.

The Byrds (McGuinn the guitarist) didn't beat Cream (Clapton the guitarist) to alienated virtuosity because the Byrds never misused virtuosity (it misused them) except at live performances, making it subserviently occasional and subserviently merely electronically contingent for audibility. And the great McGuinn solo in his second version (album version) of "Why" is all squeezed into a corner and the squeeze is (of course) part of its greatness and the final seven-note ending is nice and there to be counted, one-two-three four-five-six-sev'n, or, if you want, one-two three-four-five six-sev'n-eight-nine (the nine-note ending).

On a massive *scientific* level, a field of science fairly new as sciences go, that of rock statistics, makes use of the application of a new content, rock record purchasing, to an older form, statistical generalization. The top 40 survey is thus the first obvious contextualization of the originally out-of-context form-content relationship of statistics to such fields as quantum mechanics and genetics. It has superimposed upon an art which is absurdly statistically oriented (costs of Donovan album packages, total time of the longest Rolling Stones track, etc.) but somewhat masked (under the thrill of the sound, the flash of the cover, etc.) an absurd statistical grid ordered into a surface which has transformed mere statistics into ratings on a boisterous top 40. The geographical limitation of any rock rating, as to the United States, or New York City, or West Islip, New York, or Excelsior, West Virginia, allows for raunch epistemological vulnerability (from the rock content in origin) in terms of geographical contingency at the level of scientific law statement. And the *so what* response is (scientifically) legitimate at any time.

The top 100 survey of hit songs for 1966 on WABC in New York featured Sgt. Barry Sadler's "Ballad of the Green Berets" as its top-rated song of the year. Anyone familiar with the year's recordings would realize that Frank Sinatra's "Strangers in the Night" was a bigger hit; but if WABC declares otherwise, so be it. Barry Sadler is number one and at least number one even if not in any other way the biggest. There is something quite valid about accepting the law decree of WABC simply because it is "official" and "on the books." Out of the rock context comes a new scientific criterion, instant self-fulfilling awe, an awe at awe itself. There is a degree of *ad hominem* involved in all scientific law acceptance of any particular item. The acceptance of *this* particular law claim, under *this* universal schematism, taken in light of the possible absurdity of any particular concrete *this* must rest on awe which is mere awe or objectified awe.

With the rock systematization of finite description and the non-systematic universal, the official public world is of particular relevance as an avowed spurious universal which lays claim to all other universals. Dylan comes in here with one of his initial rock moves, the public world art summation move: the most ridiculous move of all is to "move" the "public world" (or any other world cliché) in the most ridiculously real/symbolic manner. And with the demise of conventional AM radio control over this original great sham universality of official exposure and success and retreat into the world of albums (and FM), the move becomes continuance of *total* exposure and success via the merchandisable single, because album/live-concert/FM exposure isn't quite total enough: extension to the more-universal/pseudo-universal, maintenance of a *now* nullified-in-relevance public standing, easy near-senseless masochism oriented making sure of things for the hell of hit. The Beatles, knowing they can always have another hit single, do stuff like "Lady

Madonna" backed by the nth George Harrison freakout, "The Inner Light," which is saleable hit-material-
anyway. The big hit not coming as easily to the
Stones anymore, they've gotta do "Jumpin' Jack
Flash," success by way of Blue Cheer, the nth instantiation of ancient Stones influence patterns, and
repetition of early Stones somehow infallible big-beat
hit prerequisites.

Johnny Mathis, Mick, Donovan, McGuinn, Lennon: an unbroken burlap arrow blazing with the flame
of after-the-fact-*ad-hominem*-transcendence-anyway
on the one obvious (Lennon) end and with feathers
on Johnny M's anus and Johnny M singing his
Johnny Mathis song(s) on the other, with Arthur
Lee laughing in the form of a circular vinyl arrow
someplace in North America. And transcendence of
one's own *ad hominem* pressure is a valuable thing.
Here's an illustration how.

Well the standard rock short track is a hard vehicle
for generating boredom and repulsion. Unless you
play it a lot. And it's short so you and all the radio
stations can play it a lot. Richard Harris' "MacArthur
Park," the first nationally prominent 7-minute hit
(Dylan's 6-minute "Like a Rolling Stone" was cut
into halves for air play), despite the temporal ordeal
that it is, doesn't carry with it in air play the quack-
quack-quack tedium generation of something like
"Stoned Soul Picnic" by the Fifth Dimension, a
shorter and smaller hit played more often because it
is shorter. Okay. And to be repulsive and conducive
to future avoidance on an early hearing a short track
must be *really repulsive*, it's gotta be that bad. After
all, it's too long to be a bee sting and far too short to

be a when-will-it-end ordeal. Which brings everything around to a use of *ad hominem* transcendence power:[34a] given the short track, how do you institute a true *change* in its repulsiveness level so that you can get into the full gamut of repulsiveness/acceptability *within* the single track (which we see to be pretty solid) (so you don't have to resort to sequence on an album and so you already contain the key to album expansion anyway)?

First, why would it actually be so difficult, and isn't it largely the case in general? Sure, it's easy and it's typical. But. But it isn't quite so easy for the *good* rock guys to handle it. Tommy James and the Shondells were once capable of myriads of repulsiveness level changes but that's all gone now and "Mony Mony," with so much meaty repulsive digression, is only a good song now and only nostalgia (or unfamiliarity) will allow for the audience interpretive move on behalf of short track multi-leveled grandeur; the first note sets the pace for the evaluation of the whole thing. Early Tommy James, lacking even a modicum of *ad hominem* grandeur/repulsiveness sedimentation except again by the way of nostalgia (back to the days of early early-rock), is in the same boat; Tommy James' multifaceted repulsiveness move is always out of step with its presentness.

Maybe you could start a track going with quality and by quality and then ruin it. The Stones try it on "She's a Rainbow," they try the violin bummer. It

---

[34a] *Ad hominem* transcendence power: not power to transcend x stemming from *ad hominem* pressure, but *mere* power to transcend being in *ad hominem* control at all.

doesn't work, it's still a Stones bummer emergence and that's change, to be sure, but a far cry from actual repulsiveness level manipulation qua really repulsive.

Hmm, well how about *ad hominem* limbo? That oughta work, and it does if you can find true representatives of this scene. Eric Burdon, a real trouper in this regard, shows you how with "Good Times." Nothing interferes with anything else and, consequently, you can be enraptured and/or repulsed with any individual part of it, from Eric's own "When I think of all the good times that I've wasted having good times" to some other guy coming in with "Yes we are all having a good time" and rinky-dink piano.

But maybe the real key is the other guy. Not only is *ad hominem* pressure a matter of a big-time guy being never capable of the true true bummer, but it is, more crucially, concerned with any one guy in any one song. Change the personnel and you almost automatically alter the repulsiveness level, unless of course you're stuck with everybody as big-time, the way the Beatles are with Ringo and everybody else in "A Little Help from My Friends," which calls for co-requisite hypothetical repulsiveness fragmentation in order to be experienced as true level change; otherwise it's either great all the way through or a repulsive mere traditional Ringo mockery all the way, with Ringo-Lennon and the boys being just question-and-answer structural balance.

So who that's "good" really uses the other-guy formula successfully? Not the United States of America with "California Good Time Music," for with them *ad hominem* pressure is itself merely hypothetical (not in limbo) and change is too structurally relevant and evident. True, you can come in at any part and preferentially groove on it over all others in total neglect of any sort of unitary explicit beginning-end setup. But the warrant for it is the audience's, not Joe Byrd's. Which is the same situation with any song by Bobby Vinton. And hey, you know Bobby Vinton's "My Girl/Hey Girl" (along with the Lettermen's "Can't Take My Eyes Off You/Goin' Out of My Head") handles at least bipartite repulsiveness level change by mere reference to two divergent previous levels of two other sets of guys (Temptations, Freddy Scott) who both get the same hack translation job; neat structural package but referential and not totally self-contained (a criterion just for the hell of it).

Further evidence of the problem is Moby Grape's (and everybody's) virtually shortest track ever, "Naked If I Want To." It ends all their albums (two so far) and it's paradigmatically so short that no durational cuts, repulsiveness-oriented or otherwise, would be able to convert it into such a work as we are now seeking. So what Moby Grape does is to make it more repulsive in its second appearance in its totality.

And Arthur Lee, across the board and virtually preference-free, manages only once and in similar circumstances, in "Revelation" (18:57), which is paradigmatically *long* enough to be his father.

Zappa. He's the man who can do it. A self-belittled *ad hominem* pressure for himself and the whole anonymous/familiar crew and the whole show, and lots of guys with amorphous *ad hominem* setups of their own. And even on cursory listening with the fact of

orchestration of *ad hoc* repulsiveness level changes as
the big interest harbinger of the moment, some nice
vocal moves, mostly by Mother Ray, are nice enough
(and some parody collapses of the so-familiar-that-
specific-history-is-irrelevant are bad enough) to make
it what we're after. Stuff like "Brown Shoes Don't
Make It"/"America Drinks & Goes Home" (10:09)
contains some durations even shorter than "Naked
If I Want To," so it goes pretty fast altogether and
hints that Zappa could do the true short track with
as much cumbersome facility. And the fact of excessive fragmentation allows for all fragments, in this
case the entire 2:43 "America Drinks & Goes Home"
(*Absolutely Free*'s terminal cut) to be felt as essentially short and, if not, extendedly short. And the
density of gimmicks utilized to make you aware of
the fact-of-recordedness limitation-qua-repulsiveness-
in-general (artistic outrage, actually), stuff like the
sound of rapidly slowing down the turntable to a stop
and all those inaudible details in their simultaneity
just 'cause technology isn't yet up to twelve-track
stereo at home, might just force you to understand
the magnitude of formal potentiality.[35]

And Dylan's "Sad Eyed Lady of the Lowlands" is
appropriate tomfoolery for a long-track navigator like
Dylan. Only a little over 11 minutes long, it takes up
an entire album side, giving the impression of being
at least 13 or 23 minutes in duration. And while being
the most prolific of all long-track men, Dylan has never
been a true long-track man because of the actual as-

---

[35] And the cover notation on both *We're Only in It for
the Money* ("Is this phase one of Lumpy Gravy?") and
Lumpy Gravy ("Is this phase two of We're Only In It
For The Money?") present the necessary formal twin
set membership interchangeability.

sorted relevance his actual long tracks take on in their actual appearances. "Desolation Row" was sure long long before any other rock guys were into that, but its appearance was dwarfed (on *Highway 61 Revisited*) by a shorter long muffin, "Like a Rolling Stone," and of course he was just in the process of getting officially official about being a rock guy anyway, so length was partially a carryover rather than a rock consequence.[36] And length is often alienated from its own proper topicality by juxtaposition with more length, as on *Blonde on Blonde* where everything is long, so the noticeable length move is the great spurious visual length implication of "Sad Eyed Lady" in its separateness, the double-albumhood of the whole album unit, and the full two-cover cover photo of Dylan at length.[37] And what about the length of post-

---

[36] Inside rock, the approach to the long track by way of the short one came about (why not) through Beatles' "You Won't See Me" carrying out Stones' "Last Time" theme reiteration, Stones' "Nineteenth Nervous Breakdown" picking up on it and carrying further (sudden confrontation with length possibilities, then why-not note past blues-stuff length scenes, etc.), presto Stones' "Goin' Home." Then Dylan in mainstream and by influence, and jazz, instrumental (old hat Yardbirds rave-up back again), Doors-Who and all that and zero to five minutes plus became *short* track length: "Something Happened to Me Yesterday" and "Within You Without You" were short tracks; "A Day in the Life" (because of all the arbitrary-cut-off-option moves it made available, and because it's cut into sections, and) became the first definitive *long-short* track at (officially listed) 5:03.

[37] *Playboy* centerfolds are three-piece, but two of them are smaller than the third and the fold is different (at least half the Dylan photo is visible from the outside when the album is closed, so there's no hiding and he's not nude anyway).

accident seclusion? And Dylan's novel, *Tarantula*, in its never-to-be-publishedness and use of awesomely lengthy forgettable imagistic grocery lists with only occasional delight-type relief is a sign that this man can't stand public exposure of mere superlength from the (now distant) past. Or that *hiding* it as long as possible is the super-Sad Eyed Lady move.

Duchamp's total retirement move[38] was not enough to devalue all the mere objects he gave significance pressure to, but Dylan's short-term vacation has been enough to do just that for his own objects, and not even in the Duchampian sense of nearly instant antique,[39] just the way Elvis Presley's army hitch set up the same situation for him. Duchamp's position is too *a priori* loud with longevity without the necessary labeling of *him* as just another flash in the pan, a too appropriate artist-object art-non-art readymade solution. Temporal gaps are important in rock, with gap control as a chief device in the manipulation of *ad hominem* pressure and dissemination. The Beatles have more than once faked a layoff or retirement, only to counter with *Revolver* and *Sgt. Pepper*. But Dylan has never paid non-metaphoric time no mind, so it's not directly controllable havoc upon his system and its contents can't be anything more than a breath of fresh air, particularly when you can use any of his album covers as fans to assuage actual heat, seasonal or otherwise. And the flexible English cover of the

---

[38] In 1966 Duchamp "redid" some of his old readymades (affixed signature and date) because they had been stolen, and that's about all he did except play chess for a long time.

[39] 30 years was the time interval Duchamp proposed as the major increment of initial aging.

Zombies' *Odyssey and Oracle* ought to work even better in emphasis of *their* geographically reinforced even longer absence from the American rock scene.

Lou Christie did some returning too. And his "Lightning Strikes," a masterpiece of latter-day double-standard rock ("When I settle down I want one baby on my mind . . . but till then, when I see lipstick to be kissed, I can't stop, no I can't stop" and stuff about a guy wants a girl he can trust), is also an archetypal work in the archaeology of the present (appeared during the advent of folk-rock, resembled it, appeared during, resembled that too, appeared, that also, and, yes again). Archaeology is the shameless imposition of the present on the past. This is great and appropriate for rock, just as respect for original context, cause this is in original—(trash) context—double standard move form. And with short-term archaeology evincing forgetting qua freedom, Lou Christie's return as a present-day archaeologist via double-standard rock is involved with just all sorts of this sort of stuff, particularly since he never forgot (his old stuff) and his archeological focus was shorter than short. Etc. (Jim Morrison: "learn to forget" even the shorter-than-short interval.)

Them. Van Morrison. *Van* Morrison, author of "Gloria" and maybe that's a reason for Jim to use it. Van Morrison one of the greatest archaeologists of the century, and at least the greatest we know about. "Here Comes the Night." *Night* as super-meaningful just because an eruption of new metaphor level for *night*, rest of song in step with night as in "Tonite-Tonite" (Mello-Kings): opposite of Beatles' "In My Life" ending (nostalgic recurrence of early rock high-note outburst made even more telling by the opulent facade of elderliness). "I can see right out my window walkin down the street my gir-irl with another guy-yuy. His arm around her like it used to be with me oh it makes me want to die-ie-yie." And the "Rain-drops" (Dee Clark) big-fat ominous line throughout and *arm* not *arms* that's just "like it used to be" ("with me" in reserve for now). Then: pow: "Yea yea yea well here it comes": "Here comes the night, here comes the night, oh oh oh oh yeah." So it's 1. Bobby Vee (when he was raunchy by definition and respect and he *was*) by way of Dante Mario Giarrusso and then: 2. Mick. Which means 1. taking in all the unvoiced meta of old, all the unmanifest even-then-there horror, and 2. (Mick ground into the dusty bursting bubbles of r & b history) at the same time real brute metaphor (pre-whatever-that-means) forced back to its merely frivolously gratuitous roots (pre-wherever-they-are). More: back for some me-stuff, reconstruction of the whole non-inevitable inter-section with the inevitable night, reconstruction from the direction of the *subject*. "There they go it's funny how they look so good together wonder what is wrong with me-e. Why can't I accept the fact she's chosen him and simply let them be." Not only subj recon-struction but perfect fitting of ancient-content subj-obj given. So, reconciliation of the lack of (given) geometry between sectors of a dual past (night as unambiguously meaningful, dates and all that, irrel-evant for pain except at a broken date; night as scene and metaphor for pain and its dark character and all) which bear geometric relationship to a single present, without recourse to polarization geometry reeruption jargon except when pertinent to an outpost in the past. Hence, interruption of noncyclic night with one big hell of a night and/or cycle of pain maybe starting tonight or this afternoon. Coupled with etc.

"Mystic Eyes" (Them). The tracing of death (not life or the steps leading to death or the history of deaths or any of that) the tracing of death back to Zacherle. And Mick forced back to Gary U.S. Bonds. And it's an "*old* graveyard." And all. A different type of autosalvage, one with a strong consistency of membership and a different reclamation problem. And not just reclamation but the reclamation of the reclamation metaphor and expected side effects and affinities. "Sunday morning" and "mystic eyes" together over the old graveyard. So simultaneous history/phenomenology/psychoanalyticity of the death/fear/religion bit, and the revival of *that* whole impenetrably dead scene too, all at your friendly neighborhood graveyard. That's why the Mummy movies took on a different (mere monster movie) character once the scene shifted from Kharis' tomb to the U.S. without subsequent *localized* tomb-terror revivals/discoveries (and they, the mummy movies, disappeared except for *Abbot and Costello Meet the Mummy*, while *werewolf* movies, in which the whole werewolf bite thing must be shared locally, went on, and yeah they had the additional advantage over vampire movies of allowing for the guy to walk around all day and be seen in mirrors and change hairy once in a while, and mummy movies lost out on that after the switch from the normal unwrapped look of Boris Karloff in the original version of *The Mummy* to the wrapped-up look of the later series).

And a real archæological leap: Them as people not ants.

"T.B. Sheets" (Van without Them). Presumably tuberculosis. Presumably death or sickness and recovery therefore. And tuberculosis hasn't been known as "T.B." since it became obscure and Christmas Seals expanded their area of charitable pertinence. And hmm "T.B." couldn't have been in vogue very long (it used to be *consumption*) and the HEAF tests they give you in school these days are for *tuberculosis*. But the ring of T.B. still lingers, so when "Julie baby" comes down with one of those ever rarer cases of it Van says about it, "I can almost smell your T.B. sheets."

Archaeological news: old days of rock 'n' roll—fewer things endlessly proliferated, summing up many (but simpler) cosmic stances, but in different temporal orders and hierarchies—moves were cruder and less obvious because contained too much (not yet definitive/definable enough to be referential) bulk.

Everly Brothers as the first Moby Grape,[40] next to Buddy Holly as link between Elvis' not yet usable influence chain and rock at large (spade stuff, on the other hand, was always available). In those days, singing loud and fast was guarantee of charisma, or at least if you sounded like Elvis or etc—interchange of charisma was easy (Sal Mineo made the move into rock proper from movies just by singing, just by singing anything, and he sang "Start Movin' " and "You Shouldn't Do That"; Tommy Sands, Nancy Sinatra's

---

[40] Moby Grape isn't a fully analogical counterpart of the Everlys because no Everly principle/function exists (or is possible) anymore; but the Everlys exhibited, in their time, a Grape function.

initial husband, made the move by releasing "Teenage Crush," the theme he had sung in a TV fictionalization of the Elvis star-fan freakout)—virtuosity was easy—& virtuosity assured charisma. Buddy Holly: introduction of subtlety to charisma, holding something back in all the noise. Buddy Holly as the first McGuinn-Dylan-Jagger-Van Morrison. (What about J. Morrison: "Heartbreak Hotel," Elvis himself.) (Was there no Ray Davies or John Lennon vocal back then?: look to presumed paleontologism of "Alley Oop" (Hollywood Argyles?)? hence Buck Owens and depaleontologized Carl Perkins with an English accent? maybe just English rock guys cause Lennon used to *look* like Hank B. Marvin of the Shadows? Davies as Dion? Who's "Rael" as "Little Star" while Roger Daltrey as Gino of Gino & Gina? Janis Joplin as JoAnn Campbell rather than Bessie Smith? Mojo Men as Poni-Tails?)

(Question-Mark and the Mysterians, also known as ? and the Mysterians: post?-smut, post?-vulgar.)

"Babalu's Wedding Day" by the Eternals. Stand-at-attention tongues in baseball park and wedding. Nice location for such a tongue. Nice juxtaposition of events.

"So Tough" by the Original Casuals. "I really love you too," (then) "I really love you so" (the expected first line). "I love her and she likes me" (in a class with the Turtles' "Happy Together": "The only one for me is you, and you for me"). "We're gonna stay together just wait and see, call it love babe yessiree" (the days when love was respected for its frivolousness and spuriousness).

"Peek-a-Boo" (Cadillacs). Omnipresence of laugh-able horror: "Look in the dark, you see my face (ahh!!), don't try to hide, I'm everyplace." Prehistoric soul play/word play: "When you dance the sole right off your shoes, peek-a-boo, I'm watching you."

"Stood Up" (Ricky Nelson). Jargon (stood up) even for the minimally disastrous, and easy immedi-ate jargonal prediction of the additional further dras-tic: "I've been waiting ever since eight, guess my baby's got another date." "Raindrops" (Dee Clark). Evasion of jargonal/topically universal and its impli-cations by means of minor substitutions: "There must be a cloud in my head, rain keeps falling from my eye-eye, oh no it can't be tears cause a man ain't supposed to cry." "Be Bop Baby" (Ricky Nelson). Snappy jargon to designate merely snappiness.

Animal sadism, only pervy by view as a composite, in "Battle of New Orleans" (late Johnny Horton):

> ... barrel melted down
> so we grabbed an alligator and we fought
>   another round
> we filled his head with cannonballs and powdered
>   his behind
> and when we set the powder off the gator lost his
>   mind

And masochism in excess of animal masochism:

> ... ran through the briers and they ran through
>   the brambles
> and they ran through the bushes where a rabbit
>   wouldn't go,
> they ran so fast that the hounds couldn't catch
>   'em ...

And "*nigh* as many" must have been a grammatic upheaval move of sorts (Phi Beta Kappa Pat Boone's "if she *don't* love me" in "Too Soon to Know" came earlier).

"Younger Generation" (Lovin' Spoonful). Contains the only major rock mention of LSD *per se*. After all.

"Whole Lot of Shakin' Going On" (Jerry Lee Lewis). Orchestration of the movement move, all the way down to the enunciation of criteria for the minimal (same as suggestion for the minimal): "All you gotta do honey is kind of stand in one spot and wiggle round just a little bit, that's all you gotta do, yeah." Interpersonal concretion of infinitesimal unit within a plethora (and the certification of the unit convention): "You can shake it one time for me."

"Session Man" (Kinks). Comment on minimally successful maximum use of minimality of membership.

Bonzo Dogs' "Sound of Music"—destruction of biggest pop(ular) metaphor for universal music (and plot of wholesome conversion from rock idol).

Patti LaBelle & the Blue Belles' version of "You'll Never Walk Alone": popularization of gospelization of pop, plus God is cool.

"The Way You Do the Things You Do" (Temptations). Multiplicity of available roles for man ("You got a smile so bright, you know you could have been a candle; I'm holding you so tight, you know you could have been a handle; the way you swept me off my feet, you know you could have been a broom; the way you smell so sweet, you know you could have been some perfume," written by Smokey Robinson). And the Temptations' usual multiplicity of voices is spread least thick here because it is formally appropriate to this particular song and because it is actually spread less thick than usual.

Bill Haley and the Comets' "Thirteen Women" ("Last night while I was dreaming, I dreamed about the H-bomb") is a portent of Dylan's "Talking World War III Blues": both are serio-comic, but with reversals: Dylan's (functionally) serious about the bomb and (functionally) comic about the rest of the stuff, whereas Haley's (functionally) comic about the bomb and (functionally) serious about the rest ("There were thirteen women and me the only man in town").

"Do the Mouse" (Soupy Sales). Not only a very early sign of the indistinguishability of novelty from mainstream, but also indistinguishability of external parody-of-rock novelty from mainstream.

Commercials (Jan & Dean, Ray Charles, Four Tops, everybody else for Coke or Pepsi; Jefferson Airplane for Levis; Who, Blues Magoos, Yardbirds for Great Shakes): rock for the purposes of furthering external commerciality, rock outside the domain of its own additional competitive commerciality, etc. Grapefruit: group with the endorsement of the Beatles. (Apple.)

Insectival stuff. "Butterfly" (Charlie Gracie): several similarities to "Dandelion" (Stones), plus masterslave ("I'm clipping your wings, your flying is

through, cause I'm crazy about you, you butterfly").
"Honeycomb" (Jimmy Rodgers), use of the bee in
avoidance of birds-and-bees suggestiveness and in
(nice) avoidance of birds-and-bees corn (get only
storybook corn). "Birds and the Bees" (Jewel Akins):
birds-bees overlap with nature, love interjection could
overlap either but more just an interjection. "Green
Mosquito" (Tune Rockers), an instrumental, mos-
quitoes are good instrumentalists, okay.

"Turn Down Day" (Cyrkle). "It's a turn down
day, and I dig it." Can you dig it (the presumably
unable-to-avoid-being-corny-or-two-to-three-years-
out-of-it use of "dig")? How could you dig anything
else?

"My Guy" (Mary Wells) & "You Got What It
Takes" (Marv Johnson): don't-look-like-and-don't-
have-to-be-a-movie-star rock. Gracious for a star to
feel that way. Irrelevantly graciously heaven-rock in-
dulgent for an audience to let a guy who feels that
way to become a star.

"My Guy": "Like birds of a feather we stick together": Ben Franklin type maxim as *a priori* or provisional *a priori* (Arthur Pap). "Tell Me What You
See" (Beatles): "If you let me take your heart, I
will prove to you we will never be apart if I'm part
of you": proof-oriented establishment of the provi-
sionally non-provisional *a priori*.

"Susan" (Buckinghams) (album version): use of
the "Day in the Life" finale readymade as attachable
anywhere (as at the end of "Susan"). *The Loves of
Ondine* (Warhol film) (male nudie dump-the-food-

and-garbage scene): use of the post-finale (included-in-the-finale) silence as fill-in space for anything, including the earlier and that which precedes ("Day in the Life" quietly played in the background followed by calm followed by "When I'm 64"/"Lovely Rita").

"Uptight" (Stevie Wonder). "No one is better than I, I know I'm just an average guy." And where else could superiority conceivably be located?

Cheap Thrills (Big Brother & the Holding Company). Second album, an apparent move to say good-bye to that (officially) abominable first one. But, better still, they demonstrated this time around that they can even get around the obstacle of decent recording equipment and engineers and a non-hostile company: instrumental inadequacy even when you can hear it, mere solidity when it's there. Thus, great, and better than could have been expected.

"Ding Dong, the Witch Is Dead" by the Fifth Estate, the third instantiation of the Tokens (second was the Happenings, produced by the Tokens themselves). The most wildly affirmative of death songs, both then ('39) and now.

Now here's the long haul necessary for listing Canned Heat as other than another short mere listing (or, in this case, a geographical footnote to Spyder Turner: your baby's cheatin, you gotta get a gun, where do you go, well if you're in NY you go to —, if it's SF you go to —, but I'm from LA so I go down to —: plus no accent imitation attempt). Duchamp: precise planning = canned chance. Canned Heat: canned group name may even be something else canned already, with canned admission of other canned affinities: "A house without Canned Heat is merely a home." (On the list of) non-list moves (and non-moves).

Beatles: permitted on a miscellany? (Persistent-yet-) dust-gathering (significance-absorbing) rather than self-destroying or etc? (Beatles' "Revolution"): exothermic significance absorption resistance: because of endothermic significance comfort internally taking up all ——.

DeKooning as assertion pressure in lieu of form/ content of either Van Gogh or Vlaminck (proficient youthful come-lately with total form given vs the non-proficient disruptive freakout). And of course Sly & the Family Stone as the better and more irrel-evant DeKooning. And of course R. Crumb as the best of both and more irrelevantly assertive than either. And if you really want to get technical, Beatles as the prior/later DeK/VG/V/S&FS/RC/ //

"Hurt Yourself" (Frankie Valli without any other Four Seasons guys). Meta-tongues of exothalmic rel-evance galore.

"Norman" (Sue Thompson).

"Must to Avoid" (Herman's Hermits, writ by P. F. Sloan). Herman's Contradiction via the logical clarity of what the words aren't: "She's a muscular boy, a complete impossibility."

"Porpoise Mouth" (Country Joe). Big awesome proliferation of mere more-than-mere exoticism: open-ing not unlike that of "5D"; ducks & astronomy; non-fish/mammalian; mouth/orifice; "my organs play a circus tune"; :zoo/circus; list of physiognomy (knees, feet) and organ relevance of lists.

"Let's Do It Again" (Beach Boys). Call it actual recapture of what lingers as crystallized mere memory, clearly more easy than pre-rock Dylan envisioned for just a handful of crystals in that old song (I forget the name) (but you can look it up) (it's on his *Free-wheelin'* album) about thinking about all his friends on a train going west, with the chances against recapture being "a million to one."

"Valentine Melody" (Tim Buckley). George Brecht's rearrangeable calendar plus awesome specific relevance-subservience givens for labeled time.

Arachnoid rock: "Boris the Spider" (Who): "Creepy crawlycreepy creepycrawlycreepy crawly-crawly" (formal foreshadowing of "I'd love to tur-ur-ur-ur-ur-ur-urn you-ou-ou-ou-ou-ou-ou o-o-o-o-o-o-on" in "Day in the Life"). "Spider and the Fly" (Stones). The cobwebs of "Cobwebs and Strange" (Who).

Birds. Lots of real or artificial birds in sound all the way up to "End of the Season" (Kinks). But "Rock-in Robin" (Bobby Day) is the only song about a specific bird ("He outbopped the buzzard and the oriole"). And oh yeah, "Bluebirds over the Mountain" (Ersel Hickey), which was the shortest hit single ever. Etc.

Another underwater masterpiece: "You" by the Aquatones.

In "(A) Day in the Life," negatively concrete space as delicious as asphalt:

> I read the news today, oh boy,
> Four thousand holes in Blackburn,
> Lancashire
> And though the holes were rather small
> They had to count them all
> Now they know how many holes it takes to fill
> the Albert Hall.
> I'd love to turn you on.

Language move addendum: "Getting Better" (Beatles): "Me used to be angry young man, me hiding me head in the sand."

"One of Us Must Know (Sooner or Later)" (Dylan): the most blatant title-manifest tautology of all time. The most blatant hidden tautology too, and "I couldn't see what you could show me, your scarf it kept your mouth well hid." Even non-tautology and non-resignation to the unpredicted contained within wider tautological structure and even "I didn't know that you were sayin good-bye for good." Proto-retrospective vision of all the gears and all the metaphoric functional gears never capable of concretion. Woowee! Surely Dylan's greatest, bar none.

The Vox Poppers (bet you don't remember them) once appeared on Dick Clark's Saturday night TV thing lip-synching their "Wishing for Your Love" (never a hit): they were all wearing different suits! In their time that was no move, that was sloppy planning or poverty, they weren't even gaudy. These days four guys dressed the same is regarded as over-uniformedness, the only guys who go in for it are Beatles, Chambers Brothers, Union Gap, that sort. The Monkees used to, they gave it up and adopted the uniform of multifaceted costumedness. Etc.

The lipsynch move. What a move. You can't say enough about it. So why say anything?

"Jelly Jungle" (Lemon Pipers). Hint of the locale of the jungle itself shows its face through "Marma-lay-lay-lade."

"Mecca" (Gene Pitney). Before the introduction of new instrumentation and raga rock, the mere content Eastern freakout.

More clothing: "No Chemise, Please" (Gerry Granahan). Environmental recalcitrance (toward environmentality alteration moves). Specific formal spatial assertion vs. mere space. (Shape of the tit): "Bring the sweater back."

"Coca-Cola Douche" (Fugs). Unsolicited ad with sales expansion potential beyond that of mere introduction of any new context of drinking. Yet, get some ice cream and "Come on down for an ice cream soda."

"Yummy Yummy Yummy" ("I've got love in my tummy") (Ohio Express). Same scene without the convenience of taste.

"Kind of a Drag" (Buckinghams). A drag even before it was enough of a hit to be that kind of drag, but not an immediate drag.

"Goin' Fishin'" (Spoonful) is the mean proportional between "Surfin' Surfari" (Beach Boys) and "Boobs a Lot" (Fugs).

Wonder of non-diminished intensity throughout repetition module. More obvious when transformed into the mere attempt at non-diminished intensity: "Sister Ray" (Velvet Underground), "Hey Jude" (Beatles) (or attempt at non-non-diminished intensity etc). Others.

"Strawberry Fields" continues the Beatles' fadeout supremacy with a double fadeout. The first fadeout could be called a justification fadeout or affirmation fadeout, as opposed to a *re*affirmation fadeout (to be found in works like "It's All Over Now" and "And Your Bird Can Sing"). In it George plucks around excitingly but so sketchily that the listener might just feel like hearing more. So he does, and what comprises this second fadeout (or fadeout to a fadeout) is reportedly this first one played backwards (a possible lie), not quite in the same vein, but *more* something and therefore okay. Nice tension between awesome moreness and not-just-quite-what-you-want-but-okayness.

"If You Want" (Smokey, Miracles). The phenomenology of need.

Brenda Lee. First pushed as a thirteen-year-old kid remarkable enough to have the voice of a thirty-four-year-old. Then the wrinkles started to show in photos. Then she was older but since she was older anyway it was a matter of older or older.

Fats Domino. Vocal influence of Leadbelly in the
actual rock mainstream. "Blueberry Hill": fantasy
geographicalization of fantasy raunch.

"7-L" (the Three Graces). Rock concretion being
an obvious easily accessible early move, great merely
crude concrete poetry was an early inevitable outcome, hence the geometricity of jargon: "You draw
a 7 in the air, you add an L, whattaya got, you've got
a square." "That's my baby, he's a square." "But I
love him and I don't care." Further formalism: "He
thinks he's Elvis when he sings a song, he plays a
guitar but the chords are always wrong."

"Poison Ivy" (Coasters): "She'll really do you in,
if you let her get under your skin." Further penetration and acceptance thereof as challenge in "Tell
Him" (Exciters): "If that guy gets into your blood,
go out and get him." Minimal penetration, minimal
elapsed time, and its immediate positive move in
"Hey Jude" (Beatles): "The minute you let her
under your skin, then you begin to make it better."
Not only that but "So let it out and let it in," both
ways, and the first time they sing it it's hidden in the
background then they let it out. If you don't let it in
you don't let it out either, you keep it out, and keep
it in, but you don't keep it out and keep it in. Just
wait for the big OSMOTIC TONGUE PRESSURE MOVE.

"Little Darlin'" (Diamonds). "I Want to Hold
Your Hand" (in actual proto-"I Wanna Hold Your
Hand" form) plus "The Word" (in actual pre-univer-
sal "Word" form) plus "Lovely Rita" or "Rael" (as
dominance of sound and dominance over sound). ". . .
to hold in mine your little hand, I'll know too soon

that all is so grand, *please* hold my hand." Plus cha-cha-cha, not to be verbalized (again) until "Let's Spend the Night Together."

"Endless Sleep" (Jody Reynolds). Late persistance of the early Elvis vocal and he saved his baby from the sea.

> I looked at the sea and it seemed to say,
> 'You took your baby from me away,'
> My heart cried out she's mine to keep,
> I saved my baby from an endless sleep.

Words and music by Jody Reynolds and Dolores Nance. Used by permission of Beechwood Music Corporation.

Morrison to be sure, but "breathe underwater till the end" as prior to "let's swim to the moon, uh-huh, let's climb through the tide" but not very prior.

Capital letter moves: Dylan's *Blonde on Blonde* on-record title listings:

2. MEMPHIS BLUES AGAIN
3. Leopard-skin Pill-box Hat
4. JUST LIKE A WOMAN

3. VISIONS OF JOHANNA
4. ONE OF US MUST KNOW (Sooner Or Later)

That facets of primary experience and the secondary (?) reflection thereon cannot be fully separated, even for the purposes of analysis, as some have attempted, is best shown by the parenthetical bracketing of many rock 'n' roll titles: "(I Can't Get No) Satisfaction," "When I Grow Up (To Be a Man)," "Remember (Walking in the Sand)," "Sometimes (When I'm All Alone)." Satisfaction, growth, memory, occasionality are taken as universal states, while deprivation, awareness of maturity, physical movement, anxiety of alienation are instances of primary experience which may induce the reflection necessary for the inductive foundation of these universals. "Sorry (I Ran All the Way Home)" encounters opposition in its bracketing, with the sorrow and the spatial movement necessary to report it not even being able together to form a single connected phrase. But this title points out the actual source of bracketing, the temporal separation of the two word groupings as voiced in the song itself. "Sorry (I Ran All the Way Home)" is sung as "Sorry, sorry, oh so sorry . . . uh-oh . . . I ran all the way home." "(I Can't Get No) Satisfaction" is sung as "I can't get no . . . sa-tis-fac-shun." Hence, phrasings not fully sustainable together, and not any mere alignments into experiential distinctions, produce bracketing. Raw pleasure-principle experience and the self-directed reflection of Aristotle's unmoved Mover are to rock part of the same hairy phenomenon. And the two parts of "The Beauty of Time Is That It's Snowing (Psychedelic B.B.)" are component non-parts of the same song.

That such bracketing might indicate at least a concern for logical set differentiation is demonstrated to be utterly false by Gene Chandler's "Duke of Earl." Or perhaps, obviously, logical categories and chaos categories, when aligned, are quite resolvable. But this is idle chatter in the face of his "Dukedom, . . . Dukedom of Earl," a fantasy which could lead to "Baron of Count" or "Dodgers of Giants" and has already led to the Yardbirds' "Heart Full of Soul."

Just as factors other than original essence of content have contributed to the exact method of designating titles, factors other than relative finality of content have affected methods of ending songs. Most songs by the Rolling Stones end with fadeouts, gradual reductions of volume and clarity, suggesting that the chaotic content of songs like "Empty Heart, Empty Life," "It's All Over Now" and "The Last Time" may be mirrored in the unresolved nature of the songs' conclusions. Their "Not Fade Away" strongly expresses a fear of the inevitable failure of resolution. On the other hand, the tragic finality of "She's Not There" is seen in its overwhelmingly sudden ending. A complete ending shuts out the chance of revision of destiny, while the fadeout can never have a destiny. But the situation is not so bleak, for often fadeouts are merely the results of recording engineers' judgment simply to end recordings for any of a variety of acoustical reasons, even in the middle of an extended recording. The Beatles seem to be playing upon the prior prejudice concerning resolution through ending in the elaborate Ringo drum whatchamacallit ending "What You're Doing," while they take full advantage of the engineer's reduction of volume by *barking* at the last audible moment of "I Feel Fine." And McCartney's interjection just before the final fully audible "da-da da da . . ." of the enormous fadeout of the 7:11 "Hey Jude" is a slightly-louder-than-the-rest "Well then-a . . ."

(The string thing at the close of the Stones' "Something Happened to Me Yesterday" is taken from Paul Jones' "High Time," not even a far cry from what the Stones might themselves do, played as if in a manner they'd keep a safe distance from, etc.)

(The Hollies' "Look Through Any Window" hands you the focal point for viewing the totality of perverted normalcy, all the way down to "little ladies in their gowns," and the voyeur bit only heightens it all.)

Acid chemist William Stone has suggested that the proper perspective for observing a rock 'n' roll phenomenon is with the objective of paralleling the existence of geologic matter. A rock has the principle of inertia in its stasis, and yet it can become kinetic and roll. The Rolling Stones likewise contain both principles, and their movement eventually terminates in the Eastern consciousness of a stone scene. The Clay People of the *Flash Gordon on Mars* serial are the archetypal men of rock 'n' roll, proclaiming

all the unity but absurdity of the cosmos.
all the unity but absurdity of the cosmos.
all the unity but absurdity of the cosmos.
all the absurdity but unity of the cosmos.
all the all the all the.

Rainer Maria Rilke has written perhaps the best description possible for the preceding pictures by noting the inadequacy of any language in dealing with things in themselves. After all what does anything say about anything else, especially rock 'n' roll and rock 'n' roll analysis? Here is what the inadequacy of Rilke's language has to say:

Ich fürchte mich so vor der Menschen Wort.
Sie sprechen alles so deutlich aus:
und dieses heisst Hund und jenes heisst Haus,
und hier ist Beginn und das Ende ist dort.

Mich bangt auch ihr Sinn, ihr Spiel mit dem Spott,
sie wissen alles, was wird und war;
kein Berg ist ihnen mehr wunderbar;
ihr Garten und Gut grenzt grade an Gott.

Ich will immer warnen und wehren: Bleibt fern.
Die Dinge singen hör ich so gern.
Ihr rührt sie an: sie sind starr und stumm.
Ihr bringt mir alle die Dinge um.

The trend cited by Rilke has gone so far that, in Big Dee Irwin's "Swinging on a Star," celestial phenomena are not only named "moonbeams," but they are objectified and counted, "One moonbeam, two moonbeams."

On a televised Murray the K show during early summer, 1965, Martha and the Vandellas sang the "tragic" "Nowhere to Run, Nowhere to Hide" while riding in a new Ford Mustang. The sheer materiality of their vehicle is solace for their torment, and they smile happily. To Berdyaev, the creative act is the act which will bring about the end of the world. The commerciality which rock 'n' roll wallows in has so affected the systems of meaning and meaningfulness that rock 'n' roll may be bringing about the
end of the world . . . .
end of the world . . . .
end of the world . . . .
end of the world . . . .
end of the world . . . .
end of the world . . . .
end of the world . . . .
end of the world . . . .

INDEX

339

Index

341

Made in the USA
Lexington, KY
17 April 2012